More Praise for *The Mosaic Principle*

"A powerful case that the jack-of-all-trades can be a master of many. Nick Lovegrove highlights the rising costs of specialization, encouraging us all to unleash our curiosity and go broad."
   —Adam Grant, Wharton professor and *New York Times* bestselling
   author of *Originals* and *Give and Take*

"*The Mosaic Principle* underscores why critical issues like national security and economic advancement cannot be adequately addressed by people with one-dimensional skills and experience. We need many more people who can cross between different walks of life, sharing their expertise and perspectives—not just in fiction, but in real life. Nick Lovegrove's book is a must-read that offers us a practical and compelling guide to meeting this challenge."
   —Daniel Silva, #1 *New York Times* bestselling author of the
   Gabriel Allon novels, most recently *The Black Widow*

"In a society where even elementary schools kids are told to pick one sport, Nick Lovegrove's conclusion that the best life path features wide-ranging experiences, even those we aren't good at, should be a breath of fresh air."
   —Peter Cappelli, George W. Taylor Professor of Management,
   The Wharton School

"A thoughtful plea for breadth of experience and learning over intense specialization. . . . All readers looking to break out of an intellectual box of their own making will find a refreshing new viewpoint on their personal and professional lives in this convincing manifesto."
   —*Publishers Weekly*

"We pay a high price—both individually and as a society—for our obsession with narrow specialization and the trap of being a 'one-trick pony.' Nick Lovegrove's pragmatic guidelines—such as a developed moral compass, a prepared mind, and a robust intellectual thread—provide the road map for a more fulfilling life and an extraordinary career in an ever-changing, complex, multi-dimensional world."
   —Erin Meyer, professor, INSEAD, and author of *The Culture Map*

"Nick Lovegrove's book compellingly makes the case for why the world needs more 'tri-sector athletes'—to build a more long-term, inclusive capitalism will require just the kind of breadth of experience and perspective these leaders possess."
   —Dominic Barton, global managing partner, McKinsey & Company

"*The Mosaic Principle* persuasively draws upon great historical figures like Winston Churchill and Theodore Roosevelt, as well as numerous more contemporary examples, to show that a broad-minded and eclectic approach to life is much more likely to yield inspirational leadership than that of narrow specialism. Lovegrove argues passionately that we need to reverse the pernicious trend towards over-dependence on career specialists, which is leading us astray in so many arenas of modern life. Intelligent, witty and well-written, this book is a call to arms."

—Andrew Roberts, best-selling historian and biographer

"Lovegrove compellingly draws on examples from his own careers to illustrate the benefits and pitfalls of each skill area, and he bolsters his narrative with anecdotes about other successful people in a variety of disciplines. Lovegrove balances his book neatly between the nuts-and-bolts approach to being successful and the more philosophical sense of understanding yourself first before seeking to change the world for others."

—Kirkus Reviews

"A perfect balance of the practicalities of achieving success and the philosophy of what it means to change your life. This is a compelling argument and handy guide in one, a call to arms to resist the forces of specialisation that keep us separate and blind us to the power of different possibilities in the world around us."

—Carolyn Fairbairn, Director-General, CBI

"A very readable paean to the virtues of living a diverse life, not getting stuck in ruts, however well-rewarded and high status, and to becoming more 'T shaped', broad as well as deep. It's wonderful to have deep knowledge of a particular field, but far less wonderful if that comes at the cost of any peripheral vision."

—Geoff Mulgan, Chief Executive of Nesta, the UK's National
Endowment for Science Technology and the Arts

"Nick Lovegrove's book argues passionately that we will do better in tackling the challenges of our time if we live broader lives, draw upon a richer array of traditions and perspectives, and push against the constraints of specialist orthodoxy. It is a persuasive call-to-arms to those who are designing their lives and careers, and to those who are educating them to be citizen leaders."

—Ngaire Woods, Dean, Blavatnik School of Government, Oxford
University

THE

MOSAIC
PRINCIPLE

THE
MOSAIC
PRINCIPLE

THE SIX DIMENSIONS
OF A SUCCESSFUL
LIFE & CAREER

NICK LOVEGROVE

P

PROFILE BOOKS

First published in Great Britain in 2017 by
PROFILE BOOKS LTD
3 Holford Yard
Bevin Way
London
WC1X 9HD
www.profilebooks.com

First published in the United States of America in 2016 by
Public Affairs, an imprint of Perseus Books, LLC,
a subsidiary of Hachette Book Group, Inc

10 9 8 7 6 5 4 3 2 1

Printed and bound in Great Britain by Clays, St Ives plc

A CIP catalogue record for this book is available from the British Library.

ISBN 978 1 78125 651 0
eISBN 978 1 78283 256 0

For Alyssa

CONTENTS

PROLOGUE:
WHAT IS THE MOSAIC PRINCIPLE?

IN 1953 SIR WINSTON CHURCHILL won the Nobel Prize. This seemed like a fitting tribute to the esteemed British prime minister who had led the successful fight against Nazi Germany in World War II, and who had then helped restore peace across a shattered Europe.

But Churchill didn't win the Nobel Peace Prize—he won the Nobel Prize in Literature. As author of the four-volume *History of the English-Speaking Peoples* and the six-volume *The Second World War*—as well as many other published books and hundreds of speeches—Churchill was heralded "for his mastery of historical and biographical description as well as for brilliant oratory in defending exalted human values." He was celebrated for the captivating splendor of his words—but perhaps even more than that, for the inspiring example he set as a broad, multidimensional human being, committed to living a very full life.

———

OF COURSE, NONE OF us can match Winston Churchill. Yet in shaping our lives, each of us does have a choice: greater breadth or greater depth. In today's world, there are intensifying pressures on us to choose depth, because the world is increasingly obsessed with the power of narrow specialist expertise. But if we always shape our

1

lives that way, then we all too easily become "one-trick ponies," defined and directed by the limited parameters of our one trick—and perhaps we lose something of what makes us special and distinctive as individuals. If all of us make that same choice, then we find ourselves living in a "one-trick pony world"—and in a society much less equipped to tackle the complex, multidimensional challenges that now confront us. More of us are experts, but few of us have the coping skills to succeed in our ever-changing, more complex, and diverse society.

If, instead, we resist the siren call of ever greater specialization, if at least sometimes we move in the direction of breadth, diversity, and life outside the comfort zone, then we open up all sorts of possibilities. People who take this broader approach to their life and career—and there are more than a few of them—are following what I call the *Mosaic Principle*.

The word "mosaic" derives originally from the Greek word *mouseios*, "belonging to the Muses"—hence its artistic application. Most mosaics are composed of small, flat, roughly square pieces of stone or glass of different colors, known as tesserae; but some, especially floor mosaics, can be composed of rounded pieces of stone and are called "pebble mosaics." In truth, any collection of small, textured, or colorful items will produce an image of eclectic breadth and diversity—but when one steps back, the visual impression is of a multifaceted unity.

As an art form, the mosaic has a long history, going back to Mesopotamia in the third millennium BC. As a metaphorical concept, the mosaic has an almost equally durable heritage—as the defining image for a multicultural society: ethnic groups, languages, and cultures that can coexist without losing or abandoning their own individual character.

This book defines the mosaic as an organizing concept not just for society but for each of us as individuals. The essence of the Mosaic Principle is that we can each build a remarkable life and career of eclectic breadth and diversity—rather like assembling small pieces of material and placing them together to create a unified whole. When we follow this principle, we too can experience the pleasure and fulfilment of a full, well-rounded adaptable life.

When we follow the Mosaic Principle, we have more options in our career and more choices in our life. We see things through a wider lens and are better able to understand the big picture, the forest as well as the trees. We are also better equipped to adapt and apply whatever specialist skills we may have accumulated to be a more effective expert in our field, wherever that may be. When we choose this path, we are more likely to become truly *broad-minded*—tolerant, empathetic, and understanding of differences in perspective and points of view.

This is partly a matter of personality type—each of us may have an intrinsic propensity for greater breadth or depth. But mostly it's a matter of personal choice—each of us determines, by the choices we make, whether to shape our life in the direction of greater breadth or greater depth—whether to follow the Mosaic Principle and to what degree. Over the course of our lives, we can decide just to swim in our lane or to use the whole pool; to do more of the same or to change things up from time to time; to define ourselves narrowly or to bring our whole self to our life and work.

Because we have considerable discretion over how deep or how broad we become, it is important to consider why this matters and what to do about it. That's what this book is about.

So whom is this book for? Well, as they say at the start of a circus performance, it is "for children of all ages." Whatever your current stage of life, you have important choices to make about how you build (or in some cases, rebuild) your life and career.

If you're in the early stages—at school or college or just starting your professional career—then you have an almost unlimited set of choices, at least in theory. But the temptation to focus on a narrow specialism will already be there—reinforced by well-intentioned counsel from mentors and peers. That early path toward a deep but narrow life may already seem difficult to reverse, lest you lose your foot on the ladder. This book will give you both the courage and capability to build the foundations for a broader life—and at minimum, to go broad before you go too deep.

If you're in the middle of your life and career, you may feel that your path is now set and your destination determined—you may already feel imprisoned in the golden cage of your accumulated experience and expertise. But if you are looking for something more and different, I hope you will find here both the tools and inspiration to broaden your life and career, through steps small and large.

If you're at the peak of your career, perhaps with others looking to you for leadership and direction, this book will suggest how you can get the most out of yourself and those around you—how you can retain and nurture a broad-minded approach to leadership, rich with nuance and perspective.

And if your formal career is over or soon will be, I hope you will draw from these pages a sense of further opportunity to broaden your life, capturing in every sense the scope and potential offered by "active retirement"—and proving that with time "we do get better at living."

Indeed, each of us has the opportunity to build a broader life, whatever stage we have reached—but the task of doing so is up to us. This book shows why it matters—to each of us as individuals and to our society. And it explores, in practical, real-life terms, how to do it—by applying a set of skills that will enable personal and professional fulfillment. If you apply the Mosaic Principle, you too can have a remarkable life and career.

PART 1

WHY BUILD A BROADER LIFE
AND CAREER?

1

THE SAINT AND THE SINNER
The Six Dimensions of the Mosaic Principle

> Our age reveres the specialist, but humans are natural poly-
> maths at our best when we turn our minds to many things. We
> can't all be geniuses. But we can and still do all indulge in poly-
> mathic activity. Life itself is various—you may need many skills
> to live it.
>
> —Robert Twigger, "Master of Many Trades"

Toussaint Louverture Airport, Port-au-Prince, Haiti—July 12, 2010
Once you get past the jury-rigged check-in desks and the security
screens that seem to be held together by chewing gum and string,
this could be any regional airport in the United States or Europe.
The departures terminal is in fairly good condition—and the sight
of a couple of American Airlines 757s waiting to be boarded adds to
the impression of familiar normality. Several times a month I travel
through airports much like this one in various places around the
world.

The passengers, waiting patiently for their flights, also look quite
normal—although there seems to be an especially high proportion
of travelers very obviously in organized groups, wearing the same
customized and colorful T-shirts that announce their affiliation with
the South Western Louisiana Volunteers or St. Thomas' Episcopal
Church, Tampa. The agonizingly slow late-afternoon journey to the

airport, through streets crammed with rush-hour traffic and bustling pedestrians, was also tediously familiar—the kind of physical and emotional endurance test you have to put up with in most major cities these days.

It's only when you look out beyond the departures terminal that you see this airport is very different. The tarmac on the airport apron has large gaping cracks and craters, around which arriving and departing planes are forced to navigate. Although the departures terminal is in fairly good shape, the arrivals terminal certainly is not. Indeed the building where passengers used to disembark is now reduced to a barely organized heap of rubble. In its place, arriving passengers are shepherded into a makeshift warehouse on the outer edges of the airport. There—in the absence of any meaningful ventilation—they endure one-hundred-degree heat and 90 percent humidity as they wait to be processed through slow-moving immigration lines and to reclaim their luggage from barely functional conveyor belts. Then, already bathed in sweat and gasping for fresh air, they are funneled out through a narrow walkway and into the clamoring hordes of awaiting family members, cab drivers, and insistent hustlers.

I have been traveling to this airport—the main entry point to the island nation of Haiti—with a few of my colleagues every week or so since February. The conditions have perceptibly improved on each visit—but it is still very evident that this is a major disaster zone. Exactly six months ago, on January 12, 2010, Haiti suffered one of the most catastrophic earthquakes in history—7.0 on the Richter scale, with an epicenter near the town of Leogane, approximately sixteen miles west of the capital, Port-au-Prince. Nobody knows the exact death toll—but estimates range between 150,000 and 250,000. Everywhere you go in Port-au-Prince, you see piles of rubble and wholly or partially destroyed buildings—including the National Assembly building, the National Cathedral, and the UN Mission. This morning I attended the six-month anniversary ceremony on the grounds of the Presidential Palace, which looks like a pulverized wedding cake, quickly becoming the iconic visual image of the 2010 earthquake all around the world.

I am making slow progress walking through the departures lounge—and the reason is the person with whom I am walking. Dressed in an unremarkable jacket, black jeans, and black T-shirt, he nevertheless seems to be instantly recognizable to all the Haitian citizens packed into the airport buildings. Every few steps he stops to greet somebody he knows, sometimes modestly to accept their gratitude, sometimes to respond to a request or suggestion. One person wants him to take a letter with him to the United States; another has just seen his own doctor and wants a second opinion; yet another wants to discuss how to transform this ailing nation's infrastructure and social services. Each of them wants the attention of the man they call "Dokte Paul." He listens to each of them patiently and cheerfully, and then heads quietly toward our plane.

Dokte Paul's full name is Dr. Paul Farmer—and he is the primary reason I am in Haiti, along with the earthquake and former president Bill Clinton. Officially, Farmer is Clinton's deputy as UN special envoy to Haiti; informally he is Haiti's de facto surgeon general, as he has been for much of the past twenty-five years. Clinton and Farmer are the pro bono clients who have engaged my colleagues and me on a program of institutional reconstruction and recovery, as Haiti seeks haltingly to deal with yet another catastrophe in its two-hundred-year history of social, political, and economic strife—interspersed with unpredictable natural disasters. It is one of the most challenging and exhausting professional experiences of my career—and also quite nerve-wracking, because the seismic aftershocks have only just begun to fade, and our team is required to travel everywhere with armed security, because Port-au-Prince is still essentially lawless. But somehow none of this matters when you're working with Paul Farmer.

Farmer is one of those people who has made broad and imaginative choices about how he wants to live his life and affect those of others—choices that have taken him well beyond the conventional tramlines of his chosen profession. By doing so, he has built a remarkable life and career—a broad life, fully lived; a life of meaning, consequence, and profound fulfilment.

He started along this path of breadth and diversity in college when he chose to study both medicine and anthropology. He is now a professor of both disciplines at Harvard Medical School, as well as an attending physician at Brigham & Women's Hospital in Boston. But that is what he does for only half the year. The rest he spends with the nonprofit organization Partners in Health (PIH), which he and some friends founded in 1987 when he graduated from medical school; and he spends a high proportion of that time here in Haiti.

When he was accepted by the Brigham & Women's Hospital, he learned that a Brigham resident could get permission to pursue another interest. So he split his residency with a colleague, so that he could spend half his time in Boston and half his time in Haiti. And throughout his increasingly distinctive career, he has continued this practice of splitting his time across a broad and complex portfolio of interests.

PIH has enabled him to pursue the obsession he has had with Haiti since his undergraduate days at Duke University, where he started working with Haitian immigrants in the North Carolina tobacco plantations. That was also when he began studying liberation theology, whose foundational concept is "the preferential option for the poor"—choosing to focus his medical studies on epidemic diseases because as he later observed, "any serious examination of epidemic diseases has always shown that microbes also make a preferential option for the poor." PIH has focused on creating community-focused health-care programs—first in Haiti, and then in eleven other countries including Peru, Rwanda, and Russia. It is now a substantial social enterprise, which, with the backing of the Clinton Foundation and other philanthropists, employs more than 13,000 people and caters to many more patients.

Farmer and his team started PIH with a simple objective: "Let's see what we can do in one little place." As they got started in that one little place—the rural enclave of Cange in Haiti—Paul told his colleagues, "We have to think of public health in the broadest terms possible." The single health-care clinic—called Zanmi Lasante—that Paul and his friends started in Cange more than twenty years ago now plays a much broader role in its community. It is a free-standing system of public health and social services that sends more than 9,000 students to school each year, employs more than 3,000 Haitians, and feeds many thousands of people every day.

That is a lot of work for a community organization to do—but it's not all that Zanmi Lasante has done. It has also built hundreds of houses for the poorest patients, cleaned up water supplies, and installed water filters in some people's homes. And PIH's influence now spreads well beyond Haiti. It has played an influential role in how AIDS is treated in sub-Saharan Africa. Its recommended approach to the treatment of multidrug-resistant tuberculosis, based upon practical experience in the field, has now been adopted by more than one hundred countries. These and other public health crises have taken PIH—and specifically Paul Farmer—all over the world, accumulating millions of miles on planes like the one he will fly in this evening.

You would think that all of this would require Paul Farmer to spread himself quite thin—to make numerous trade-offs and sacrifices—and there's certainly some truth to that. But he learned early on that there were at least as many benefits as costs to taking such a broad and imaginative approach to his life and career. As a student, for instance, he learned that Haiti was a much better site than Boston for his graduate work in anthropology, given the practical insights he could gain there. He had very high grades in medical school, in part because he also worked for large portions of each year as a rural doctor in Cange, dealing with more varieties of illnesses than most American physicians see in a lifetime. And in Haiti he also learned firsthand how to design a clinic and a public health system, building them from scratch in the most difficult of circumstances.

As Tracy Kidder observes in his extraordinary book *Mountains Beyond Mountains: The Quest of Paul Farmer, a Man Who Would Cure the World*, "It was impossible to spend any time with Farmer and not wonder how he happened to choose this life." When he is asked, Farmer responds that many things coalesced into a vision of his life's work. But "this happened in stages, not all at once. For me, it was a process, not an event. A slow awakening, as opposed to an epiphany."

One commentator has described Farmer as "the world's most well-known doctor who advocates for the poor." But in all honesty, he is far from a household name—and here in Haiti he mostly seems like just an unheralded rural doctor tending to his patients one at a time. The contrast is striking and evokes a complex set of emotions— one of them being moral envy. As Tracy Kidder notes about readers' reaction to his own book, "Some people have read *Mountains Beyond Mountains* and said, in effect, 'Damn, I wasted my life. I should have done what Paul Farmer's done.'"

But Farmer himself never conveys a sense of moral superiority— indeed he is always generous about the work of others, including our own. When it comes to our mission, which is focused on setting up the government's recovery administration with a clear set of management goals, processes, and procedures, he thinks that he has as much to learn from us as we do from him about Haiti, public health, and social welfare. Kidder eventually concludes, "I think of him simply as a friend. I don't idolize him, but I'm grateful that he is living on this planet."

As we approach the gate, there is no interruption in the flow of people who want to speak to him—a former patient reporting on his recovery, an aid worker who wants his advice on her restoration project in a nearby village, and two or three people who just want to say hello. Only once on board can he settle back in his seat and become just another passenger on American Airlines flight 201, which will take less than two hours to cover the six hundred miles to Miami, the first stop on his journey back home to Boston.

Hotel Arts, Barcelona—October 11, 2000
"If you don't get it, then I am sorry—that's too bad. I can tell you with certainty that this is the way business will be conducted in the future."

The speaker holds his audience in rapt attention. He goes on: "We are on the brink of a broadband revolution—unleashing the power of the Internet and digital technology to transform the business world.

Every kind of business is going to be disrupted—not just traditional media and bricks-and-mortar retailing, but also so-called utilities like gas, electricity, water and transportation. This will enable us to break up outdated industry structures, and minimize the burden of redundant assets sitting on our balance sheets."

This is a great time to be an attacker in business. The monolithic and bureaucratic companies of the past are just sitting ducks. Using the custom-designed modeling algorithms we have developed and the digital trading capability we have built, we can already capture much of the premium value in our businesses—and we are just getting started. Our asset-light business model is perfectly suited to today's world.

To make all of this happen, we are focusing most of our attention on human capital—on creating the most powerful talent machine in the business world. We are hiring the best-of-breed technical specialists in every category—the top business modelers and analysts, MIT and Stanford PhDs, the ultimate quant jocks, who can develop the most powerful algorithms for our businesses. We want people with deep, specialist expertise and obsessive focus. Some of them are pretty crazy people—the kind of people who think they can model anything. But that's OK—that's what we want. It's up to people like me to integrate all that talent and convert it into a powerful business. And that's what I'm doing. I invite you to come along for the ride.

When he finishes, the charismatic speaker gets a prolonged standing ovation from his enraptured audience, punctuated with enthusiastic whoops and hollers. On his way out of the room, he is high-fived by audience members, many of whom know him personally and view him as a much-admired friend. And as the audience filters out into the surrounding coffee stations and bars, all the talk is of how this is indeed the way of the future, and the most frequently asked question is, how can we be part of it?

The speaker is Jeff Skilling, the highly respected chief executive officer of the Enron Corporation, and the audience comprises the senior partners of McKinsey & Company from around the world. I am one of them, sitting in this audience along with 250 of my most distinguished colleagues. We have gathered here at the Hotel Arts in Barcelona for our annual senior partners' conference to celebrate our achievements over the past year and set the direction for our firm in the year ahead.

In recent years, it has become our custom and practice to invite high-profile external speakers—either important clients or conspicuously successful alumni of our firm. Jeff Skilling meets both criteria—only a few years ago he was sitting among this same group as a senior partner of McKinsey, where he spent thirteen years of his career; and since he joined Enron, he has continued to employ the firm on a series of strategic and organizational engagements. Among the proudest people in the audience for Skilling's speech are the current partners who lead the firm's relationship with Enron. When Rajat Gupta, the firm's worldwide managing director, speaks later in the day, he calls them out for special acclaim, and they too are applauded.

At the end of a memorable day, we gather for a celebratory gala dinner, and reflect upon how fortunate we are to have such clients, alumni, and colleagues. Not a few of us are probably thinking that one day we'd like to be invited back as senior executives and clients, having completed a similarly successful transition to the highest bastions of corporate leadership.

———

LESS THAN A YEAR LATER, Jeff Skilling's career was crashing around him—and within a few years he was on his way to jail. On August 14, 2001—just ten months after his appearance at our partners' conference—he unexpectedly resigned as CEO, citing "personal reasons," and sold a large volume of shares in the company. Then-chair Kenneth Lay, who had previously led the company for fifteen years—and been advised by Skilling during his time as a McKinsey consultant—returned as CEO. Shortly afterward, in December 2001, the company declared bankruptcy. It had taken just fourteen months from the moment when Skilling declared Enron "the future of the business world" to corporate bankruptcy with the loss of 20,000 jobs—and as collateral damage, the collapse of Arthur Andersen, Enron's auditors and at the time one of the world's leading accountancy firms.

That was just the beginning of Skilling's troubles. Early in 2004 he was indicted on thirty-five counts of fraud, insider trading, and other crimes relating to what was now routinely referred to as "the Enron scandal." On May 25, 2006, he was convicted of all but the insider trading charges; and on October 23, 2006, he was sentenced to twenty-four years in prison and fined $45 million. Despite several appeals—including a case that went all the way to the Supreme Court of the United States in 2010—he remains in prison. According to the Bureau of Prisons, he is currently incarcerated in Federal Prison Camp Montgomery and is now eligible for release on February 21, 2019.

A story like this has many of the elements of a Shakespearean tragedy. Indeed some time later the British playwright Lucy Prebble did put the story on the stage—albeit in the form of a tragicomic musical entitled *ENRON*. The opening scene is set in Skilling's office on January 30, 1992, as he and his colleagues hold a rambunctious party to celebrate the Securities and Exchange Commission's approval of Enron's very distinctive form of accounting for gas contracts. By Act 3 Skilling has become chief executive of the company and is being acknowledged as one of the most admired business leaders in America. In Act 5 he is sentenced to twenty-four years in jail.

SAINT AND SINNER—OR BROAD AND DEEP?

Paul Farmer and Jeff Skilling have quite a lot in common. They both went to elite universities in roughly the same era, distinguished themselves academically, worked extremely hard, applied their considerable natural talents, and reached the loftiest heights of their chosen professions—garnering along the way devoted followers and widespread acclaim. Until Skilling's spectacular fall from grace, they were both widely viewed as role models of successful leadership in their respective fields. People wanted to be just like them, if only they could figure out how.

But given the differences in their respective fates since 2001, it seems more instructive to view them as a study in contrasts. The most obvious and straightforward of those contrasts is between good and bad—"saint" and "sinner."

Paul Farmer has devoted his life to tending to the poor and downtrodden—often in the most hazardous and challenging of circumstances. He has forgone considerable opportunities for fame and fortune to do so—indeed, the first impression that he evokes in those who know and observe him is that of personal self-sacrifice. Jeff Skilling, in contrast, has focused his talents on generating enormous personal wealth for himself and a few people around him; abused the trust placed in him by shareholders and staff; led a large corporation into oblivion, wrecking the careers and pensions of thousands of employees; and broken the law of the land multiple times. His continued presence in a federal penitentiary tells its own story.

And yet the "saint and sinner" interpretation of these stories seems too simplistic—too morally neat and tidy. Paul Farmer is undoubtedly a very good man, but as his closest friends (and he himself) will attest, he is not perfect. Meanwhile, Jeff Skilling's friends (including some of my former colleagues) still struggle to think of him as simply a "bad guy." Clayton Christensen, the highly respected Harvard Business School professor, was a classmate of Skilling's thirty years ago. He says of him, "The Jeffrey Skilling I knew from our years at HBS was a good man. He was smart, he loved his family . . . and yet when his career unraveled with his conviction on multiple federal felony charges relating to Enron's financial collapse, it not only shocked me that he had gone wrong, but how spectacularly he had done so. Something had clearly set him off in the wrong direction."

What was the "something" that had set him off in the wrong direction? What was the underlying reason for such a spectacular professional and personal collapse? The answer may lie in a different and potentially more revealing contrast between Skilling and Farmer. That is the contrast between breadth and depth—and it is the dominant theme throughout this book.

In his early years, there was no reason to think of Jeff Skilling as an intrinsically deep or narrow person. He had every reason and opportunity to live a broad life, given his education and eclectic early experiences—including his thirteen years as my colleague at McKinsey. But, when he joined the senior management of Enron, he chose to focus his leadership approach on a model of extreme specialization—in common with many in the modern era of financial and technological sophistication. In his Barcelona speech to the McKinsey partners, he boasted that Enron was "cornering the market in MIT and CalTech PhDs with sophisticated algorithms and mathematical models." He made it clear that he expected these technical specialists—these "quant jocks"—to revolutionize, and to a large extent automate, the company so that it could transform the world of business. Indeed, Enron under Skilling's leadership exemplified the increasingly pervasive belief that highly talented people, working in narrowly defined specialist silos, can achieve miracles.

But when Skilling resigned and when soon afterward the company he had led unraveled so quickly, it became apparent that he and his board colleagues had been sucked in by the mythical virtues of deep specialization—and that that approach had led the company down the road to self-destruction. The Powers Commission, set up to investigate the causes of the Enron collapse, concluded that the management and board of Enron—and especially Jeff Skilling—completely failed to understand the operational risks of the company's mark-to-market business model. They did so because they lacked (or had lost) the breadth of perspective to see how it could go so badly wrong—and how to react when it started to do so. The consequence of this false confidence in the benefits of deep specialization was catastrophic for Enron and its employees and shareholders, not to mention those of Arthur Andersen.

Paul Farmer has shaped his life in a very different way; he has consciously and explicitly chosen breadth and diversity at every stage. At college, he chose to study both medicine and anthropology; as a medical resident he chose to divide his time between a renowned Boston hospital and a rural clinic in Haiti; while continuing to practice as a physician in multiple locations, he chose to create a nonprofit enterprise to further his model of community medicine; he chose to expand the reach of this nonprofit to more than a dozen countries; he chose to become a prolific writer so that he could spread his ideas about Haiti, medicine, and even theology; and he chose to help formulate public policy through the United Nations and his association with Bill Clinton.

As a consequence of his intrinsic personality, but especially as a consequence of the choices he made, today Paul Farmer is a physician–anthropologist–professor–social entrepreneur–author–activist–philosopher–policy adviser—and probably a few things beyond. If you ask him why, he says simply, "I needed to operate on a broader canvass. I didn't want to be bounded by a single specialty."

Farmer does in fact have a distinct specialty—the treatment of epidemic infectious diseases—which he has developed, honed, and applied to treat patients and influence policy choices all over the world. But he has not let that specialty exclusively define or constrain him, nor has he allowed himself to go so deep into that specialty that it has obscured his vision of everything else. Rather, he has shaped his life around the belief that his specialist knowledge will be more useful, more likely to do good than harm, if he takes as many opportunities as possible to broaden and extend his experience and perspective.

The pressure on each of us to specialize and focus reflects the marketplace at work, operating as we do in a modern economy that is dominated by human and technological services. As citizens and consumers, we all want to receive the services we need from fully credentialed experts—especially when technical expertise and experience are evidently required. When we get on a plane, we want to hear that our pilot has flown thousands of hours and learned how to deal with any manner of possible in-flight emergencies. When we decide to build a house, we want to be assured that our architect has designed lots of beautiful and safe buildings and that our contractor has built them so that they will withstand the elements for decades to come. And, of course, when we go to the hospital, we want to hear that our surgeon has performed hundreds of surgical procedures similar to the one we need, with most patients returning to good health.

It's just human nature and common sense to want somebody with that kind of specific experience and expertise to provide us with such critical services. We want to put our fate in the hands of qualified specialists, because we know that they have invested their careers and their lives in deep knowledge and specialist proficiency, and that matters to us. We all depend upon that level of expertise in the marketplace for professional and technical services. Indeed, we have come to expect deep levels of specialist excellence in all walks of life—even when they are just for our entertainment, such as in musical orchestras or sports teams. Think of specialist punters in football, and closing pitchers in baseball.

When it comes to this kind of deep technical expertise, it is hard to dispute the premise that practice makes perfect—or the "10,000 hour rule" originally defined by the neurologist Daniel Levitin, which captured the popular imagination through the writing of Malcolm Gladwell. This concept states simply that "performing a complex task requires a minimum level of practice," and more specifically that "ten thousand hours is required to achieve the level of mastery associated with being a world-class expert." It is indeed hard to imagine how world-class expertise in any significant field could be achieved with less commitment of time and energy—even if you happen to be born with the intrinsic gifts of Wolfgang Amadeus Mozart or Tiger Woods, two of the extraordinarily talented people whom Gladwell cites as proof of the 10,000 hour concept!

But in today's world, we have gone too far in our increasingly pervasive obsession with technical expertise. We now live in a world sold on depth; indeed, some believe that we have entered the era of super-specialists. In our globalizing, technology-driven, ever-more-complex world, we have become convinced that the route to excellence lies in narrow specialization—in deeper and deeper levels of focus and concentration. The surgeon and writer Atul Gawande notes of the medical profession in which he practices, "Surgeons are so absurdly ultra-specialized that when we joke about right-ear surgeons and left-ear surgeons, we have to check to be sure they don't exist."

In medicine, as in so many other fields, we have ceded authority to superspecialists who have focused their time and talents on practicing one narrow thing until they can do it better than anyone else. In doing so, we have taken to new extremes Frederick Winslow Taylor's concept of scientific management—that as individuals we should concentrate on doing one thing very well within an orchestrated system. Over a hundred years ago, Taylor presciently wrote, "In the past the man has been first; in the future the system will be first." But even Taylor didn't envisage the kind of superspecialization that we have today.

The roots of this obsession with specialization lie in our education system, and they go quite a way back. In 1963 my own father, Bill Lovegrove, who went on to a distinguished career as a teacher and high school principal, wrote a dissertation on this very topic. He noted, "Many have for long had serious misgivings about the high school curriculum which, in order to meet the needs of university entrance, is geared to intensive work in specialist subjects. Few object to a degree of specialization, but many are horrified by the limited horizons of the specialist who never ventures out of his field." My father's dissertation includes a quote from A. D. C. Peterson, then head of Oxford University's Department of Education, who said of the curriculum that "it compels too early a choice between arts and science. It provides no real general education. It starves either the moral and aesthetic or the logical and empirical development of our ablest adolescents, and no valid justification has been found."

In the intervening sixty years, specialist and vocational education has continued to advance at the expense of broad-spectrum liberal education. The foreign-policy commentator Fareed Zakaria, who grew up in the highly specialized Indian education system (then a legacy of British imperial rule), warns, "Those that would seek to reorient U.S. higher education into something more focused and technical should keep in mind that they would be abandoning what has been historically distinctive, even unique, in the American approach to higher education."

Starting with our education system, the emphasis on specialization has now become the central premise for how we organize our society. We are prioritizing depth in our most significant institutions—governments, large companies, universities, hospitals, and schools. In each of these institutional settings, we have built a system that prizes and indeed requires deep specialization, often with only a thin layer of broader perspective. Increasingly, we have experts on top, rather than on tap.

We are starting to pay a heavy price for this obsession—individually and as a society. More and more people with a broad range of intrinsic capabilities and interests are living relatively narrow lives—because that is what they think, and what they are told, it will take them to achieve professional success and personal fulfillment. And more and more aspects of our society are being undermined and damaged by this narrow and limiting focus, by the adverse consequences of an overreliance on deep specialists.

For instance, our financial system is built around the preeminence of technical specialists. But in 2008 those specialists almost brought the world economy to its knees, and we had to turn belatedly to people with more breadth of experience and perspective to understand what was happening and how to fix it. The political systems in many countries are now built around specialist career politicians who have limited experience of doing anything else and who struggle to connect or empathize with their constituents in their everyday lives or to legislate and govern in adversity. And in so many professions—medicine, law, accounting, and my own field of management consulting—we are seeing the inexorable rise of superspecialists, a trend that is putting us all at ever-increasing risk.

This is the wrong way for us to go, and it is based upon some false assumptions. There is a growing body of evidence that challenges the preference for depth. First, the evidence shows that we have consistently overestimated the value of specialist expertise and underestimated the significance of broad experience. Numerous studies have now confirmed that specialist experts are no better at anticipating and resolving difficult issues—and that often they are worse. When we put ourselves exclusively in the hands of specialist experts, bad things often happen—like the Enron collapse, the global financial crisis, the Deepwater Horizon oil disaster, and various national intelligence breakdowns around the world. Our specialist model has often proved unfit for purpose; it has frequently exacerbated—and sometimes caused—some of our most profound problems, from failed companies to failed industries to failed states.

Second, the evidence shows that the complex, multidimensional challenges that we face in modern society are much better tackled with a broadly gauged approach—that narrow and deep specialization will be insufficient to the task. Challenges like war and peace, terrorism, poverty, income inequality, climate change, education, health care, and policing in minority communities cannot be solved by narrow technical specialists, all swimming in their own lanes. And more and more advances in science, the humanities, and public policy require a broad interdisciplinary approach. To meet these challenges, specialist expertise is often necessary but certainly not sufficient. It needs to be combined with a broader view of the world gained through diverse experience and exposure.

As a society, we urgently need to restore the lost emphasis on breadth of education, training, professional development, and personal experience—and that will require adjustment in how we organize and steer each of those activities. The economist John Kay argues that "the benefits of liberal education do not go out of date." Indeed, he notes that in the digital age, running businesses, managing assets, and advising clients on professional issues are all activities whose primary demands are synthesis. Modern technology has made a great deal of specialist knowledge essentially a commodity— and it's a mistake to focus exclusively on specialist skills that a changing world will render redundant in a few years. Instead, we should aim for rewarding employment and fulfilling lives in a future world the defining characteristics of which we can neither assume nor predict. As Kay observes, "The only thing we know about that future world is that the capacities to think critically, judge numbers, compose prose and observe carefully will be as useful then as they are today."

Harvard University president Drew Faust agrees—noting that more than half of political leaders around the world hold humanities and social science degrees; and 75 percent of business leaders say that the most important skills in their work are the ability to analyze, communicate, and write, "the skills at the heart of the humanities." "And yet," she adds, "the liberal arts education that imparts these skills is under assault. Legislators dismiss anthropology, art history, and English degrees as impractical. They call for 'more welders and fewer philosophers,' as did Senator Marco Rubio in the 2016 Republican primary campaign, while cuts in funding threaten humanities departments at colleges and universities across the country."

Third, the evidence shows that most of us would personally prefer to shape our lives in the direction of breadth, if given the option. The concept of a broad, well-rounded life is intuitively attractive to most of us—it is what we would naturally do if we weren't schooled to specialize so exclusively. Most of us are instinctively interested in a lot of things. Few of us really want to focus only on one thing to the exclusion of all others—to be a one-trick pony. It's much more fun to follow our interests and passions and to see where they take us. As the poet Robert Twigger says, we are instinctively and naturally broad, at our best when we turn our minds to many things. We embrace the unusual and the unexpected; we seek new experiences; we revel in things that we have not seen before; we celebrate the surprising discoveries enabled by serendipity.

So the argument of this book is that breadth is often better—for individuals, for institutions, and for society—and that it is a viable route to professional success and personal fulfillment. As a society, we should place greater emphasis on fostering breadth of intellectual and professional development, so that we can tackle our most profound challenges. We should remove the psychic handcuffs that have constrained so many intrinsically broad and capable people from achieving their aspirations for personal impact and fulfilment. And as individuals, we should make more of our choices in the direction of breadth, because if we embrace diversity of education and experience, we can each have a remarkable life and career.

HOW TO BE BROAD

To paraphrase President John F. Kennedy's 1963 declaration of America's commitment to go to the moon within a decade, we choose a life of breadth not because it is easy but because it is hard. In today's world, it's not at all easy to be broad and effective—there are all sorts of challenges and pitfalls along the way. When you shape your life in the direction of breadth, you have to confront more complex trade-offs, to resolve more difficult moral and ethical conflicts, to master more subjects and disciplines—at least to a functional level of understanding—to develop and apply more skills, to meet and know more people so that you can build mutually supportive networks, to understand and adapt to more contexts, and to prepare your mind for more variety and complexity.

As a McKinsey consultant and partner for more than three decades—first in the United Kingdom and more recently in the United States—I have observed many of my clients, colleagues, and friends wrestling with these challenges; and I have grappled with them myself. In addition to my life in the business world, I have worked in and around government, academia, and the nonprofit sectors, and I have seen at close hand the challenges they face and the kinds of people they need to address them. I have come to realize how profound is the dilemma that many people feel between the need for depth and the desire for breadth. So in my research for this book, I have interviewed more than two hundred people, many of whom have found at least partial solutions to this apparent dilemma. They have shaped their life in the direction of breadth, without unduly sacrificing the very evident benefits of depth.

This book sets out not only to make the argument for a broader life but also to help you achieve it. It describes what my research suggests are the six skills that will enable you to lead a remarkable life and career—the six dimensions of the Mosaic Principle.

Moral Compass

A broader life typically requires you to operate in multiple different domains—often they may seem to be in conflict with each other, and sometimes they may actually be so. A good example is the challenge that will arise if you want to move among the government, business, and nonprofit sectors during the course of your career. You may want to do this for the very best of reasons—to broaden your impact on society and enhance your personal development. But others may challenge why you are moving among these very different arenas; they may even impugn your motives for doing so.

How will you reconcile the different motivations in your life, and how will you reconcile the apparent conflicts of interest and the ethical dilemmas that you are likely to meet? You will find this much easier to do if you have a strong moral compass—an ethical direction finder that enables you to choose the most beneficial course at any one time. This moral compass—which must come from within you—will enable you to adapt to different circumstances and value systems but to avoid the risk of becoming a completely different person when you switch between different walks of life. It will also help you to understand, evaluate, and reconcile your own motivations—to chart and then to navigate your "motivation map."

Your map may reveal a desire to create social benefit and to advocate for causes you care about, to have power and influence over important issues, to make a difference, to generate wealth for yourself and your family, and to do interesting work with compatible colleagues. You will need a strong and durable moral compass, because navigating this motivation map will be the task of a lifetime, not just of a moment—especially because the relative weight of these motivations will inevitably change over time. When I was young, I cared not at all about making money—but later I did!

Intellectual Thread

The biggest risk of a broad life is that you will come to be seen as a jack-of-all-trades, master of none. If that happens, the phone may stop ringing at work, because you will no longer be the go-to person for anything in particular. So how do you ensure that you have relevant knowledge and skills within the context of a broader life?

The evidence shows that you are more likely to be successful if your broader experience is underpinned and even enabled by a robust intellectual thread—a knowledge or skill that you can carry between different walks of life. Adopting what is called a "T-Shaped Approach" will ensure you avoid the risk of a random walk through life. The essence of this approach is that you should develop an area of real subject-matter expertise (the vertical bar of the T) and apply it across a broad range of contexts (the horizontal bar of the T). You should also apply the lessons from your broader experience (the horizontal bar) to your area of specialty (the vertical bar).

To illustrate this concept, you will read in this book of David Hayes, Carol Browner, and Roger Sant—three people who have developed an intellectual thread in energy and environmental issues. In different ways and at different times, they have each applied this expertise in government, where they set and implemented policy solutions; in business, where they helped build substantial enterprises; and in the nonprofit sector, where they built purposeful institutions and advocated strongly for environmental protection causes. If you take this kind of T-Shaped Approach, then you too can capture the benefits of breadth, while ensuring that there is a sustained focus and consistency in your approach. You will concentrate your firepower and avoid becoming a dilettante.

Transferrable Skills

It is one thing to develop a set of skills that work in one specific setting—such as the skills involved in running a successful business or in developing policy solutions for social and economic problems. It is another and more difficult thing to develop a set of skills that works in multiple settings. And yet that is the breadth requirement that you will need to meet—to develop skills that can be transferred between different contexts.

In this book you will read about the most significant transferrable skills that will enable you to be successful in a variety of settings. These include "what" skills—tools, techniques, and methodologies to define an institutional direction and solve tangible problems along the way; "how" skills—different ways to drive institutional change, no matter the setting; and "who" skills—ways to connect with and inspire people and lead teams within and across different environments. The most important skill I define as "leading yourself," because to shape your life in the direction of breadth you will need to chart a personal and professional journey, identify options, and make choices.

You will also read about people who have successfully transferred an integrated set of these skills from one arena to another—for instance, from military leadership to business and vice versa, from business to the management of government institutions and vice versa, from the voluntary sector to business, even from a religious order to government. And you will explore why the transfer of business skills to the political world seems empirically to be the most challenging of all.

Extended Networks

A deep specialist is likely to focus his or her primary resources on building contacts and relationships within a single walk of life. As a consequence, many people actually have quite narrow networks, constrained by the limits of their experience and reach. Unless you take determined steps to broaden your networks, you will likely remain a prisoner of those deep but narrow networks and struggle to break out.

I suggest three ways to build and apply extended networks. First, you can build networks that enable you to solve problems in a broader and more collaborative way, drawing upon diverse sources of insight and perspective. Second, you can build broad and diverse teams from across your networks, rather than simply trying to find people who look, think, and sound like you—you can, for instance, adopt the team-of-rivals approach that some US presidents such as Abraham Lincoln, Theodore Roosevelt, and Barack Obama have taken to constructing their cabinets. And third, you can build networks that enable you to make broad career choices, because a high proportion of professional appointments are made within pre-existing networks.

Contextual Intelligence

As you build a broader life, you will need to adapt effectively to different professional and personal environments—to quickly assess a new and unfamiliar situation, adjust your approach and even your use of language, and find a methodology that works in that specific context. The ability to adapt to new contexts is hardwired into our DNA—indeed, it has been a critical factor in our biological and social evolution. It is what makes breadth such a natural aspiration, as long as we don't allow our innate attribute of contextual intelligence to atrophy—our fate when we settle exclusively for what we already know.

Contextual intelligence enables us to adapt quickly and helpfully to new situations and challenges. Ronald Heifetz, a Harvard University professor, observes, "In our world, in our politics and business, we face adaptive challenges all the time—and each time we face the need to learn new ways." In this book, I describe how you can learn new ways to meet the needs of different contexts—how you can successfully address adaptive challenges.

Prepared Mind

Finally, one of the biggest benefits of a broad life is *optionality*. You will have a wider range of opportunities, you will be less constrained by whatever you have done before, and you will be less dependent on others to make career and life choices for you. The flip side of that, however, is that you will have a broader and more complex set of choices and trade-offs to make—including some that invite you to take the road less traveled.

You are more likely to capture the benefits—and avoid the risks—of a broad life if you take inspiration and guidance from Louis Pasteur's famous observation that "chance favors only the prepared mind." Very few of the successful people I have met and interviewed admit to having developed a career plan or a life plan for breadth—they usually protest that "things just happened," that their broader lives materialized almost by accident.

But it usually becomes apparent that they had actually prepared themselves to make some important choices—for instance, to accept a period of relative financial sacrifice to go into government, or to step away from the public spotlight to recharge their intellectual batteries in academia, or to make some money for their families while putting other, more public-spirited aspirations on hold. Some had decision rules—like "go into government when my political party is in power"—and others determined to make a change every few years in order to refresh, renew, and broaden themselves. In other words, their mind was prepared emotionally, intellectually, and financially for the challenge and opportunities of a broader life.

ARE YOU BROAD OR DEEP?

How does all of this affect you? How should you approach the question of whether to be broad or deep—or at least more of one and less of the other? Why should you care? Well, to start with it's helpful to know where you currently fall on the breadth-depth spectrum. What is your *baseline*? Are you naturally more broad, or do you instinctively veer toward depth?

Although there is no scientifically proven way of knowing this, a rough-and-ready self-assessment can help you gauge your intrinsic orientation, mind-set, and attitude. So take a look at the following statements, and answer "true" or "false" to each one, choosing the answer that applies most accurately to you:

1. _____ I prefer to know a little about a lot of things, rather than a lot about a few things.

2. _____ I am reasonably good at a number of things, rather than distinctively good at just one thing.

3. _____ In the course of my formal education, I liked to study seemingly unrelated subjects and disciplines.

4. _____ I am interested in playing different kinds of roles in my career.

5. _____ I want to work in different walks of life professionally.

6. _____ I pursue a lot of personal interests outside of work.

7. _____ I like to read widely on a range of topics.

8. _____ I seek out new personal experiences whenever I have the opportunity.

9. _____ I think of myself as a natural risk taker—both professionally and personally.

10. _____ I have friends with all sorts of different backgrounds and experiences.

11. _____ I get energy from things that are new and unfamiliar to me.

12. _____ I am not bothered if I appear relatively ignorant about an unfamiliar topic.

13. _____ I want to make an impact on a range of issues.

14. _____ I do my best work when I am outside my comfort zone.

15. _____ I naturally fit into new environments, even when they are unfamiliar.

16. _____ I like visiting new countries and understanding new cultures.

17. _____ I like to make significant changes in my life from time to time.

18. _____ I like conversations that range widely, even when I don't know much about the subject being discussed.

19. _____ I learn quickly when I am dealing with an unfamiliar topic.

20. _____ I get easily bored if I focus on one thing for too long.

Again, this is far from a scientific study. But the more often you answered "true," the more naturally broad you probably are. Left to your own devices, you are likely to skew toward the broad end of the spectrum—and to feel happiest and most fulfilled when you are doing things that broaden rather than narrow your range of experience. (In the interest of full disclosure, I answered "true" to most of the questions, especially the ones about getting easily bored and not worrying about being ignorant!)

Breadth is not quite an inbred personality type, in the same way as being an introvert or an extrovert—and it certainly hasn't had the same degree of psychological study applied to it. Starting with Carl Jung in the 1920s, numerous research approaches and tools have been developed to assess with greater and greater levels of assurance whether you are naturally an introvert or an extrovert, or where you are on the introvert-extrovert spectrum. As Susan Cain observes in *Quiet*, there is even a hybrid term—*ambivert*—for people who are halfway between the two extremes on that spectrum. The assumption that underlies this science is that you are born somewhere on the spectrum between introvert and extrovert—and that you can make modest incremental adjustments along that spectrum. But it is quite rare to find "natural introverts" becoming full-scale extroverts, or the other way round.

The breadth-depth spectrum is different. The psychological evidence is that most of us are born as naturally broad people. If you don't believe me, just watch babies or toddlers at play—they are interested in everything, especially the unfamiliar, but they rarely stay interested for very long. Their dominant characteristic is intense curiosity, often combined with a daredevil approach to the unfamiliar. That is why we clutch hold of our young children's hands when we are out and about with them—we're terrified that they'll scamper off in search of some new adventure, the riskier the better. Over time, however, most of us evolve and make choices in favor of a greater degree of familiar specialization—at school, in college, in our choice of careers, in changing jobs, in our personal interests, in the way we relate to our families.

The question is, How far should we go on that journey? If we remain as eclectic and diverse in our interests as a baby or toddler, we will probably become dysfunctional and miserable. After all, our range of possible areas of interest increases exponentially as we get older and smarter—and if we don't make choices, we'll go crazy. But if we make all those choices in favor of greater and greater special-ization, then one day we will wake up and realize that we are now prisoners of our own depth—that our options have become more limited, our range of vision has narrowed, our capacity to change and adapt according to circumstance has diminished.

DECLARING A PREFERENCE FOR BREADTH

The six dimensions of the Mosaic Principle are all within your reach, because they build upon innate aspects of your capacity and charac-ter. They may well reflect your better instincts—the kind of person you would like to be. Making them your defining qualities will be the foundation for building a remarkable life and career. My purpose in this book is to help you do just that.

You currently live your life somewhere on the spectrum between being a broad generalist and a deep specialist. At any time in your life—but especially early on—you will have the choice to move one way or the other along that spectrum. That rarely requires you to move to one or the other extreme—but rather to find the hybrid solution that works best for you at the time.

Later in the book, I will help you to identify your *breadth sweet spot*—the ideal point for you on the spectrum between being ex-treme breadth and extreme depth. I will show that even intrinsically deep specialists can take quite a broad approach in particular cir-cumstances, especially in pursuit of objectives they really care about. I will also help you to identify your *breadth frontier*—the point at which your desire for breadth will have reached its natural limit, at which your reach exceeds your grasp. Beyond this point, you cer-tainly will risk becoming a dilettante—of knowing only enough to be dangerous. Beyond this frontier, you will lack the intellectual thread to be effective; your transferrable skills will no longer be, well, trans-ferrable; and your extended networks will no longer be helpful.

The desire for a broad life means thinking about big, potentially transformative choices—life-changing career decisions; building an extended portfolio of activities and interests; moving periodically and frequently into different, even alien, environments; transforming your own life and those of people around you. For instance, in 2006 my wife and I decided to move from London to Washington, so that I could take up an attractive leadership opportunity within my firm and we could broaden our life as a family. By making that decision, we transformed not just our own lives but those of our four children forever.

But it's not always about such big choices. Meeting your aspiration for breadth also involves many small steps that you take every day, week, and month—steps that broaden your experience and perspective in the moment and just for the sake of it. For instance, you might volunteer for a nonprofit enterprise, decide to learn a new language or skill, play a musical instrument, or paint—or choose numerous other ways to participate in a different walk of life. The cumulative effect of numerous such small steps is to create a path to a broader and more remarkable life and career—to extend your hinterland and expand the definition of who you are.

IN HIS PULITZER PRIZE–WINNING history of the Renaissance entitled *The Swerve,* Stephen Greenblatt explores "how the world became modern," and specifically how the pioneers of the Renaissance created "humanism in our sense, the quest for meaning in our pleasures." The centerpiece of his narrative is Lucretius's 2,000-year-old poem *On the Nature of Things* (*De rerum natura*), which argues that "what human beings can and should do . . . is to conquer their fears, accept the fact that they themselves and all the things they encounter are transitory, and embrace the beauty and pleasure of the world."

The rediscovery of this poem in the fourteenth century contributed to what Greenblatt calls a "swerve"—an unexpected, unpredictable movement of matter. The embrace of beauty and pleasure as a legitimate and worthy pursuit underpinned the extraordinary achievements of a host of Renaissance polymaths—Leonardo da Vinci's scientific and technological inventions, Galileo's astronomical revelations, Francis Bacon's research, Richard Hooker's theology, and even Machiavelli's inquiry into the dark arts of political strategy. Above all, it enabled the artistic output of the Renaissance—painting, sculpture, music, architecture, and literature—the supreme manifestations of beauty. Because of this swerve, Greenblatt observes, "it became possible—never easy, but possible—in the poet Auden's phrase to find the mortal world enough. It became possible to prize a person for some ineffable individuality or for many-sidedness or for intense curiosity."

The Renaissance was a wonderful and inspirational period of our history. But it had one rather unfortunate and enduring effect. It initiated our use of the term "Renaissance men and women," which since that time has increasingly been applied to describe a species of extraordinary people who alone can lead a broad and eclectic life of meaning and impact. Nowadays this term is all too often taken to distinguish such remarkable people from mere ordinary mortals, as if they are a breed apart—and implicitly to persuade the rest of us to get back in our box.

But what if it was the other way around? What if such people were exceptional because they principally chose to lead such broad and eclectic lives—if their willingness to undertake such a wide array of interests enabled them to build extraordinary capabilities across a wide spectrum? What if cause and effect were reversed—if a declared preference for breadth came first, followed by the remarkable life and career that it enabled?

People like Paul Farmer—whom we might be tempted to call a Renaissance man—exemplify what the psychologist Carol S. Dweck defines as a *growth mind-set*. This is a set of beliefs about yourself that profoundly affects the way you lead your life—a belief that your intrinsic qualities can be cultivated, developed, and materially altered, and that as a consequence your life can go in a different direction than that which might otherwise have seemed preordained. This stands in contrast to a *fixed mind-set*, which assumes that you are who you are, and there's not much you can do about it.

As Dweck observes, this difference in mind-set determines much about how you live your life. "A belief that your qualities are carved in stone leads to a host of thoughts and actions, and . . . a belief that your qualities can be cultivated leads to a host of different thoughts and actions, taking you down an entirely different road." And she adds, "Although people may differ in every which way—in their talents and aptitudes, interests, or temperaments—everyone can change through application and experience."

In fact, people like Farmer really exemplify a *breadth mind-set*—a passion for stretching themselves into unfamiliar, sometimes unrelated arenas. They illustrate the premise of this book—that a broader life is not something that happens to you but something you make happen. You make it happen through a series of choices—some large, some small—that together enable you over time to build a remarkable life and career. And this is not something confined to a few exceptional people—the so-called Renaissance men and women. It is open to any of us who declare a preference for breadth.

So as each of us seeks to build our life in the still early years of the twenty-first century, we need another pronounced swerve toward individuality, many-sidedness, intense curiosity—toward the diverse gifts of breadth. Otherwise, we will be unduly and unnecessarily exposed to the perils of depth.

THE PERILS OF DEPTH, THE GIFTS OF BREADTH
Doing What the Specialists Can't Do

I should dearly love that the world should be ever so little better for my presence. Even on this small stage we have our two sides, and something might be done by throwing all one's weight on the scale of breadth, tolerance, charity, temperance, peace and kindliness to man and beast. We can't all strike very big blows, but even the little ones count for something.

—Sir Arthur Conan Doyle, *The Stark Munro Letters*

THE PERILS OF DEPTH—BEZZLE AND FEBEZZLE

I first got an inkling of the impending global financial crisis in the summer of 2005—three years before it would nearly destroy the world's economic system. I was having a casual conversation with a colleague who specialized in advising financial institutions. He started telling me about the amazing work our firm was doing in the "subprime mortgage lending space"—the first time I would hear a phrase that would later be seared into our consciousness. "It's amazing," he said. "The economic and statistical algorithms are now so sophisticated that mortgage providers can lend to borrowers who have hardly anything in terms of collateral, or even much in the way of income. It's really going to drive growth and profitability in the finance industry for years to come."

I remember at the time thinking that this sounded a little odd and surprising, but to be honest I didn't give it much thought. I figured that there were a lot of very smart people working in the finance industry—not to mention my unquestionably clever and experienced colleagues in our financial institutions practice—and that they must know what they were doing. If the specialist experts thought that subprime mortgage lending—and all the financial instruments that underpinned it—was okay, then that was enough for me. After all, they spent all day, every day working on this stuff. It was their specialty, not mine. What did I know?

Of course, I was not alone. Pretty much every smart person—and a few who were not so smart—had bought into the seemingly "upward only" momentum of the financial services industry in the early part of this century. Chuck Prince, then-CEO of Citigroup, was only echoing the prevailing consensus when he uttered on July 8, 2007, the iconic words: "When the music stops, things will get complicated. But as long as the music is still playing, you've got to get up and dance. We're still dancing."

By the summer of 2008, the first stage of the financial crisis was well and truly underway—although its proportions were not yet fully understood. Between March and September 2008, eight major US financial institutions failed—first Bear Stearns, and then IndyMac, Fannie Mae, Freddie Mac, perhaps most crucially Lehman Brothers, AIG, Washington Mutual, and Wachovia. As we now know so well, the financial contagion would spread around the world—the equivalent of what Bob Steel, then–number two at the US Treasury, would describe as "financial mad cow disease." More than twenty European banks across ten countries had to be rescued from July 2007 through February 2009—usually by a large injection of government money or more often than not by partial or complete government ownership. For a few years at least, the boundaries between the public and private sectors in finance effectively disappeared.

In his study of the financial crisis, *Other People's Money,* the British economist John Kay draws upon the preceding Enron scandal to explain what happened—why we were so duped by the specialist experts. "Like finance," he says, "and for similar reasons, accounting became cleverer, and worse." Having seemingly learned little from Enron's collapse—and other comparable financial meltdowns in the interceding years—the specialist professions retained an abiding affection for presumed future earnings, and a determination to put them in the books, even when there was no certainty that those earnings would ever materialize. But, as he points out, the prevailing philosophy was "who cares? I'll be gone, you'll be gone. We're investment bankers. We don't care what happens in five years."

This partial view of the future, allied with sophisticated tools and systems created by technical specialists, enabled the creation of so-called *psychic wealth.* And it was powered by the twin evils of *bezzle* and *febezzle.* In his definitive analysis of the preceding 1929 Wall Street crash, J. K. Galbraith explained the distinctive feature of embezzlement—"weeks, months or years elapse between the commission of the crime and its discovery. This is the period, incidentally, when the embezzler has his gain and the man who has been embezzled feels no loss. There is a net increase in psychic wealth."

After the 2008 crash, Warren Buffett's business partner Charlie Munger pointed out that there does not actually need to be any illegality in the creation of this psychic wealth: mistake or self-delusion is enough. He coined the term "febezzle," or "functionally equivalent bezzle," to describe the wealth that exists between the creation and destruction of the illusion. And as John Kay summarizes, "Valuations of future claims based on beliefs about the future give opportunities for bezzle and febezzle, and the greater the volume of such tradable claims, the greater the likely volume of bezzle and febezzle." This is what was happening in the run-up to the financial crash—we were being febezzled—and the people who were doing it were the technical experts.

Like the Enron accounting scandal, the global financial crisis that spiked in 2008 and 2009 was a direct consequence of a world sold on depth. It was a man-made disaster, created by human beings who got completely carried away by specialist expertise—their own and that of others. It demonstrated why as individuals and as society we need more breadth and to be wary of placing all our trust in depth. And it revealed the four most toxic perils of depth—*hubris, blinkered vision, unmerited credibility,* and *lack of foresight.*

First, *hubris.* Like Jeff Skilling and his Enron staff, the highly skilled specialists who powered the leading global financial institutions were paid a great deal of money for their supposed expertise and were supremely confident in their own abilities. They typically spoke in a language that few of us could understand—using words and acronyms known only to each other, although we have all had to learn more about them since, such as credit default swaps and collateralized debt obligations. Buoyed by their apparent success in generating supernormal profits, they applied their expertise and technology to develop more and more sophisticated, complex, and opaque financial products; and the gap between what they did and the rest of us understood inexorably widened.

In *After the Music Stopped,* the Princeton economist Alan Blinder argues that it was this mixture of complexity and opacity that precipitated the crisis: "In the cases of the most complex and opaque securities, nobody really knew what they contained or what they were worth—which is a surefire cause for panic when doubts creep in. One day, some ingenious Wall Street rocket scientist looked at all the junior tranches [of capital] and said to himself 'Eureka!' [More likely it was an expletive]. I can turn lead into gold."

This "complexity run amok," says Blinder, was the opposite of the KISS principle—"Keep it Simple, Stupid"—which is the best guarantor of safe and secure markets. "Here's the basic problem," he says. "Those who make and dominate markets—Wall Streeters for short—love complexity and opacity as long as the party continues. It helps them make their millions—or billions. But once the music stops, their great but fair-weather friends, complexity and opacity, can become their worst enemies. As prices fall, investors start realizing that they don't really understand what they own, or what is being offered to them—not to mention 'what those damn things are worth.'"

The financial writer Michael Lewis foreshadowed some of this in his best-selling book *Liar's Poker,* first published in 1989. He assumed then that sooner rather than later would come a "Great Reckoning . . . when Wall Street would wake up and hundreds, if not thousands, of young people like [him], who had no business making huge bets with other people's money or persuading other people to make those bets, would be expelled from finance." He also expected people to be shocked that "once upon a time" on Wall Street, the CEOs of large financial institutions had only the vaguest idea of the complicated risks their bond traders were running.

But instead, the mortgage bond market invented on the Salomon Brothers trading floor—where Lewis had started his career in finance—would lead to the "most purely financial economic disaster in history." The complex derivatives of the mortgage bond market had seemed a good idea at the time of their invention, but Lewis is clear about why the consequences were ultimately so disastrous: "Wall Street had grown so complicated that it was virtually impossible for an outsider to understand it without help"—and there was nobody who could be trusted to help. That was in 1989, nearly twenty years before the 2008 meltdown. Just imagine how much more complex and opaque things had become in the intervening two decades.

This hubristic approach to complexity and opacity is compounded by the second peril of a system dominated by specialists: *blinkered vision.* Technical specialists know only what they see and see only what they know. The 2010 *Report of the Financial Crisis Inquiry Commission* began with the eerily simple statement: "This financial crisis was avoidable." You bet it was—but only if there was somebody, anybody in a position of authority, who could see what was going on and act upon what he or she saw.

Instead, the leaders of these giant financial institutions were in thrall to the deep specialists who lacked the breadth of experience and perspective to address even the most basic questions about the financial system—like what will happen when lots of people have taken out mortgages they can't afford and when you package these mortgages in derivatives that nobody understands and when loss of financial confidence spreads to countries that are already massively exposed by their own financial profligacy and indiscipline?

At a time like this, we needed people with the breadth to understand the interlocking roles that home buyers, selling agents, investment banks, financial literacy educators, credit unions, credit agencies, pension funds, legislators, regulators, central banks, and other actors play in the mortgage system—globally, nationally, and locally. We needed people with the breadth of intellectual discipline to assess the economics, mathematics, finance, sociology, and psychology of mortgage lending and financial planning. And we needed people with the breadth of historical perspective to understand past experience with overinflated asset bubbles and economic busts, to observe how the US current account deficit was fueling the problem of excess lending, and to raise the alarm as consumers sought to purchase more than they could afford in pursuit of the American dream.

This brings us to the third peril: *unmerited credibility.* The distinguishing feature of the financial crisis was that we all believed the specialists were right up to the point that it became unavoidably evident that they were completely wrong. Before that, hardly anybody spoke up, no doubt because they were persuaded—or perhaps intimidated—by the certainty and assurance of the specialists. As a society, we didn't want to hear from the naysayers, because we believed in the power of specialist expertise—and we liked what the specialists were telling us. And just like Jeff Skilling, the financial specialists made it pretty clear that if we didn't get it, then it was our fault.

Two of the seven causes that Alan Blinder ascribes to the financial crisis speak directly to this peril of unmerited credibility. He asks, "Where were the regulators?" and he chastises "the over-rated ratings agencies" such as Moody's and Standard and Poor's. The regulators relied too much on the ratings agencies, which were caught in a classic conflict of interest. As a consequence, "they acquired a degree of oracular authority—a working monopoly on alleged wisdom—that they were never meant to have and certainly did not merit."

That they didn't merit this authority is evident from their failure to predict or do anything to prevent the crisis. This fully exemplified the fourth peril of depth—*lack of foresight*. We should not have been surprised because there is a great deal of academic evidence that specialists and so-called experts are very poor predictors of the future—even, indeed especially, in their area of deep expertise. Dan Gardner captures this observation in the self-explanatory title of his book: *Future Babble: Why Expert Predictions Are Next to Worthless, and You Can Do Better.*

Beginning in the 1980s, University of Pennsylvania professor Philip Tetlock sought to analyze the accuracy of forecasts by both subject-matter experts and nonexperts. For his study he picked an area that, similar to the financial markets, was rife with uncertainty: geopolitical outcomes. Tetlock tracked more than 80,000 predictions made by 284 professional forecasters in various complex political scenarios both within and outside of their areas of expertise and he found that nonexperts actually made the most accurate predictions.

According to Tetlock, specialist experts—those who are identified as knowing one big thing really well—display traits detrimental to the process of making accurate predictions in the volatile, uncertain, complex, and ambiguous situations that tend to predominate in today's world. They typically underestimate the complexity of the world, are less open to opinions after their own mind is made up, dislike questions that could reasonably be answered in several ways, make decisions quickly and with great confidence, are less able to understand how an opposing view can be justified, and prefer to interact with people whose opinions are not substantively dissimilar to their own.

Professor Tetlock suggests that if we want realistic odds on what will happen next, we are better off turning to "those who 'know many little things': individuals who draw from an eclectic array of traditions and accept ambiguity and contradictions as inevitable features of life. They are more likely to be prescient than those who 'know one big thing': people who toil devotedly with one tradition, and reach for formulaic solutions to ill-defined problems." This contrast between those who know many little things and those who know one big thing is the theme of Isaiah Berlin's iconic essay *The Hedgehog and the Fox,* which I discuss in a later chapter.

There are all sorts of sociopsychological explanations why specialist experts tend to be poor predictors of the future. They are especially prone to a *herding instinct,* which makes people want to conform to the behaviors or perceptions of those in their own or adjacent "communities"—especially when they operate in organizational silos with like-minded colleagues. This is often compounded by a tendency to assume a *false consensus* or to assume that others share their perception and experience, even if they don't. And then there is the subconscious tendency of specialists to overconfidence in their own prescience, and the inability to estimate accurately the pleasure or pain generated by a significant change in the underlying conditions, which psychologists refer to as *hedonic adaptation.* In other words, it is all too often the technical specialists who don't get it.

The financial specialists allowed their decision making to be governed by any number of subconscious tendencies, from overconfidence to status quo bias. They were also reluctant to engage in meaningful *probabilistic thinking,* retaining instead their preference for *binary thinking,* which reduces too many complex issues to simplistic yes/no or good/bad questions. Changing the assumptions—changing the rules of the conversation—and assigning probabilities can produce amazingly creative and innovative ideas, but only if you allow that to happen. Otherwise, you become beholden to a single, contentious, but not fundamentally challenged, view of future outcomes.

Of course, the media often prefers to feature specialist experts, place them on television panels, and call upon them to predict the future with an implied precision that they are ill equipped to provide. As I write, the 2016 presidential election in the United States is illustrating exactly this phenomenon, following a series of twists and turns that hardly any of the "experts" have accurately predicted.

In the same vein, the British parliamentary election on May 7, 2015, was an especially humbling night for the specialist experts. The consensus of the pre-election polls and commentators was that the result would be a so-called hung Parliament—which means no overall control for a single political party. Then the early exit polls on election night showed that a very different result was now more likely—a decisive stand-alone victory for the Conservative Party, which had previously had to govern as part of an uneasy coalition with the Liberal Democrats. The political experts determinedly stuck to their guns throughout the evening, arguing that the exit polls must be wrong—one (Paddy Ashdown) even promising to "eat my hat" if the exit polls turned out to be correct. When the final result was indeed a clear Conservative victory—as presaged by the exit polls of actual voters but as foreseen by hardly any of the experts—there was a lot of hat eating going on!

Why does this kind of thing happen so frequently—and not just in political elections? It's because specialists are so dedicated to their beliefs and express them so authoritatively. Their predictions, though likely to be less accurate than those of generalists, have thus come to dominate the public discourse and the search for policy solutions. That was certainly the case in the run-up to the financial crisis. As former secretary of the treasury Tim Geithner observes, "Our crisis, after all, was a failure of imagination. Every crisis is."

Every financial and accounting crisis can be attributed to an over-reliance on specialists and to the accompanying toxic mix of hubris, blinkered vision, unmerited credibility, and lack of foresight—enabling illusory short-term gains for a few at the expense of long-term losses for the many. Once the severity of the 2008–2009 financial crisis became apparent, a group of people did in fact emerge with the broad experience and perspective to address the challenge.

Tim Geithner was president of the New York Federal Reserve and then–US treasury secretary. He recalls that "by the time I went to college, I had lived in Africa, India and Thailand—through wars and coups." And by the time he became President Obama's treasury secretary, he had also lived through multiple economic crises around the world, during a previous stint at the Treasury, a spell at the International Monetary Fund, and as president of the New York Federal Reserve.

His predecessor as treasury secretary, Hank Paulson, also came with broad and relevant experience, as the former cochair of Goldman Sachs. His stature and authority were such that he was able to override the inbuilt reticence of his former Wall Street counterparts. As Bethany McLean and Joe Nocera describe in their account of the crisis, "On October 13, 2008, his $700 billion in hand from TARP, Paulson met the CEOs of the eight largest banks in a Treasury conference room. He told them they would all be taking money from the government, like it or not. Although several came to regret it, none had the nerve to say no to Hank Paulson."

Paulson and Geithner worked successfully with Ben Bernanke—a soft-spoken former professor of economics from Stanford and Princeton, who grew up in small-town South Carolina, played alto saxophone in the marching band, and wrote an unpublished novel. He graduated from Harvard summa cum laude and earned a PhD in economics at MIT. He—along with Christine Romer, a fellow professor who served as chair of the Council of Economic Advisors—had extensively studied the Great Depression.

There were similar coalitions of central bankers and regulators in other countries—such as the UK. In the midst of the crisis, Paul Tucker, then the deputy governor of the Bank of England, argued that what big institutions really need are "cultural translators," people who are able to move between specialist silos and explain to those sitting inside one department what is happening elsewhere. "Any large organization needs to have somebody, or some people, who can play that translation role because they are literate in a number of specialisms." That helps create a culture that enables everyone to interpret information—and to let different, even conflicting, interpretations be heard.

A fortuitous application of broad experience and perspective ultimately saved the US, UK, and global economy—and redressed some of the damage caused by an overreliance on depth. But that battle is far from over. In the midst of the financial crisis, I spoke with another of my colleagues who specialized in financial institutions. Because he knew I lived and worked in Washington, he went off on a tirade against the "meddling federal government, which was trampling all over the financial sector." I just walked away, shaking my head.

By the way, there's one more worrying aspect of an overreliance on specialist depth—and it is illustrated by a medical example. A while ago I was talking with my gastroenterologist about one of the medical rituals of advancing age—a colonoscopy. He told me about the procedure and then asked where I would like to have it done. "On Mondays and Wednesdays, I work at Sibley Hospital; on Tuesdays and Thursdays at Suburban Hospital; and on Fridays in a clinic nearby." Because these medical facilities are only a short distance from each other—each of them within easy reach of the same patient population—I asked why he works out of different locations.

He then reeled off a series of statistics: "I have been doing colonoscopies for thirty years; I work forty-five weeks a year, and each week I do at least fifteen procedures like this. If I didn't have different working environments to do them in, I think I would go mad." And then it dawned on me; there is a fifth peril of depth—*boredom*. I definitely wanted the doctor doing my colonoscopy to have a lot of specialist experience—but it gave me pause that he needed frequent changes of scenery to avoid becoming dysfunctionally bored. It's easy to understand why this is an issue, when you hear my specialist doctor explain: "It can be quite a disappointing profession—and sometimes quite boring. The intellectual attributes you need to qualify far exceed those you need actually to do the job on a day-to-day basis." And he adds, "It's when you get bored, that's when mistakes happen."

Despite the damage caused by an overreliance on specialists; despite the accounting scandals, the financial crash, and the ensuing economic meltdown; despite the recurrent nightmares occasioned by the four perils of depth—hubris, blinkered vision, unmerited credibility, and lack of foresight; despite all this, we continue to place our faith in deep specialists.

THE GIFTS OF BREADTH

To understand why a broader approach works better, let's take a look at the story of somebody who successfully tackled one of the characteristically complex challenges of our time—the problem of water security.

In the middle of a quietly effective government career, Jeff Seabright went over to the "dark side"—joining the forces of evil and infamy. At least that's what his friends told him he had done when they heard he was going into the private sector. At the time, Seabright's friends were mostly like him—self-defined "government types." With a degree in international politics, he had spent the first fifteen years of his career in the federal government, focusing on nuclear disarmament and arms control issues in the later stages of the Cold War era.

In the early 1990s, he started to concentrate on climate change and renewable energy as foreign policy issues. He moved from the State Department to the US Agency for International Development where he worked on clean energy development in emerging markets like Brazil, Indonesia, and South Africa. His on-the-ground experience drew the attention of the Clinton White House, which appointed him to lead the Task Force for Climate Change—with a particular focus on the Kyoto Protocol negotiations.

Ironically, it was his expertise on climate change that attracted the attention of the private sector—and specifically of Texaco, which asked him to join its public policy team. At first this seemed implausible—on top of his lack of commercial experience, Seabright had come to think of the oil majors like Texaco as the climate change deniers. After all, Texaco was a founding member of the Global Climate Coalition—a lobbying group opposed to government regulation on climate change issues.

Jeff Seabright set a condition—he would join Texaco only if it would agree to leave the Global Climate Coalition—which it did. "I took a lot of crap from my government friends," he recalls, "but pretty soon I was putting real money into efficient infrastructure to address energy challenges. Did I really sell out, as my friends were suggesting? Or was I moving up, so that I could have a bigger impact? I certainly felt good about what I was doing—although it felt a little weird to be in such a commercial environment after all those years in government."

Before too long, Seabright found another private-sector company that wanted him even more—Coca-Cola, the global beverages company that in 2001 was facing an intensifying environmental crisis. A regional government in south India and several nongovernmental organizations (NGOs) had launched a campaign against the company's excess water consumption in an area that suffered from extreme water shortage and periodic droughts. They were planning to ban it from soft-drink production in the region, and other governments in Asia and Africa were planning to follow suit.

Coca-Cola was not on strong ground—technically or morally. It was undeniably a heavy user of water—not just in the drink itself but also in the manufacturing process. At the time, making a liter of Coke consumed three liters of water. And as Seabright recalls, "It wasn't just India, there were many other areas with water issues too. And it wasn't just a PR issue. The whole area of environmental sustainability was gaining prominence." According to the Water Resources Group, a joint venture between the World Bank and a business consortium, "By 2030 over a third of the world's population will be living in river basins that will have to cope with significant water stress, including many of the countries and regions that drive economic growth."

In tackling this water scarcity issue, Seabright drew upon his experience in government—specifically in his environmental work for the Clinton administration. He commissioned a geographical information systems map—an analytical tool familiar to environmental agencies. It showed that 39 percent of Coca-Cola's production was located in the world's most water-stressed areas. He framed the issue as a risk to revenue growth and profit margins.

He then pushed further down into the organization, developing a water-risk assessment for each of Coca-Cola's twenty-three business units. He characterized the conclusions not as his own analysis but as business units speaking to other business units about what needed to be done. "This is what your plant operators are telling you about the water challenges." Using this data, Seabright developed specific water-risk models for each unit, which aggregated into a company-wide global risk model complete with watershed management, community engagement, and other recommendations to reduce the company's risk exposure.

This was the first time that Coca-Cola's business leaders had seen such a thorough and disciplined piece of work on the "nonfinancial aspects of the business" such as natural resources consumption. It persuaded them to give Seabright a budget for additional environmental initiatives. For instance, he had inherited an especially hostile relationship with Greenpeace, which had launched a high-profile campaign against Coca-Cola's use of hydrofluorocarbons in its refrigeration process at the 2000 Sydney Olympics. On his advice, Chair Neville Isdell agreed to get out of this form of refrigeration, even though they didn't have an easily available alternative. Greenpeace and Coca-Cola achieved an uneasy mutual understanding—as Seabright recalls, "They told us they would dance with Coke on this issue, and dance on top of Coke on other issues."

Today the company uses only two liters of water to produce a liter of Coke. It is more than halfway to its 2020 target for water neutrality and is regarded among NGOs as an industry leader on this issue. Seabright himself moved to Unilever in 2014 as chief sustainability officer—charged with embedding sustainability into all core business functions, such as strategic planning, human resources, governance, marketing, and consumer engagement. Although Seabright has now been in the private sector for more than a decade, he feels more engaged with government and NGOs than ever. He feels that he is "putting the objective before the business, rather than the business before the objective"—helping his company to meet both its financial and social goals, to serve the interests of its shareholders and other stakeholders, to do well by doing good.

———

JEFF SEABRIGHT IS A GREAT example of a *trisector athlete*. He is somebody with the capacity to engage and collaborate across the three sectors of our society—business, government, and nonprofit—and to achieve objectives that are important to all three. There's not much doubt that to solve the most vexing problems in our society, we need people like Seabright who can move easily among these spheres of activity—people who are as motivated by public value as by shareholder value.

Two things struck me when I learned about Seabright's experience. First, it was apparent that issues like water scarcity for industrial and domestic consumption are exactly the kinds of problems and challenges we face in today's world—complex, multidisciplinary problems with different stakeholders who hold contrasting views on cause and effect and who have even greater disagreements about alternative solutions. It's genuinely hard to imagine how problems of this scale and complexity can be solved just by government, business, or nonprofit organizations and the people who lead them acting alone.

It's not possible or even desirable to eliminate all cultural and structural barriers between the three sectors of our society. Businesses do need to prioritize revenues and profits; NGOs rightly value mission over efficiency; and governments must function through policy formulation, persuasion, and sometimes through legal sanction. Not every leader who crosses sector boundaries will make a successful transition and create value by doing so. But as a society we need to find ways for more of our most passionate, committed, and creative individuals to bridge gaps between sectors and facilitate a more cohesive approach to our most difficult problems. And the evidence suggests that the people who do so enhance their own lives and careers.

The second thing that struck me about Jeff Seabright's experience is that issues like water security require much more than a tri-sector mind-set and approach that bridge the gaps among business, government, and the nonprofit sector. They require breadth of experience and perspective across multiple dimensions. And it is this observation that has inspired me to ask, "What is it that people of breadth can do that narrow and deep specialists can't?"

The answer is that they can understand and address the broad complexity of today's problems. There are many dimensions to those problems, but there are five that typically matter the most—sector, industry and issue, intellectual discipline, culture, and function. Let's explore in more detail, using the Seabright/Coca-Cola case to illustrate each.

Trisector Breadth

Was the Coca-Cola crisis a business problem or a government problem or a social problem? The answer, of course, is all of the above. It was a full-scale, acute, multialarm, trisector problem. It directly engaged business and government leaders, and required them to deal with powerful and professionally run nonprofit organizations. It demanded a proven trisector athlete like Jeff Seabright who could understand what was going on in the heads and hearts of government and nonprofit leaders. His experience of working in government at the State Department and White House enabled him to do that, reinforced by his experience of partnering with nonprofit organizations such as the World Wildlife Fund (WWF) and Greenpeace.

This is such a common feature of today's world—the need to collaborate among business, government, and the nonprofit world. Muhtar Kent, chief executive of Coca-Cola, has a term for this kind of collaboration among government, business, and civil society to provide lasting, sustainable solutions. He calls it the *Golden Triangle* at work. Citing NetsforLife, a partnership dedicated to battling malaria in sub-Saharan Africa, and other Golden Triangle partnerships to combat AIDS and increase access to vital medicines in Tanzania, Kent argues that companies like Coca-Cola can and should unleash the "vast, largely untapped potential of businesses, governments and NGOs to collaborate creatively together."

In their book *Everybody's Business,* Jon Miller and Lucy Parker tell what they call "the unlikely story of how big business can fix the world." They suggest that "some of the angriest fault lines in the relationship between business and society have become fertile ground for collaboration." They argue that working in partnership across the sectors is "the new front-line of doing business"—although they also observe that some of the companies and corporate leaders who most exemplify this trend have had "their own dark nights of the soul: today's heroes are sometimes yesterday's villains."

Whatever their motivation, it's clear that this kind of collaboration will be commonplace only when there are a whole lot more trisector athletes. People who are able to work across sector boundaries are typically more creative, they foster empathy and openness, and they encourage people to go beyond traditional ways of thinking within a single sector. Although there is no substitute for direct employment in each of the sectors, being a trisector athlete is a mind-set, not just a resume feature. It comes as much from broadening how you think and whom you know as from changing your place of employment.

As it happens, Coca-Cola's direct competitor, PepsiCo, has taken a similarly strategic approach to issues like water security and obesity—concerned perhaps by headlines like the one that appeared in *Forbes* magazine: "Are Coke and Pepsi the New Big Tobacco?" CEO Indra Nooyi specifically sought to reorient PepsiCo toward what she called "good for you" products. And she also led a recruiting campaign to find trisector athletes (although she didn't use that term)—people like Derek Yach, formerly executive director of the World Health Organization, head of global health at the Rockefeller Foundation, and professor of global health at Yale University.

Like Jeff Seabright, Yach was sometimes branded as a "traitor to the cause." But as global head of health and agriculture policy for PepsiCo, he saw an opportunity to make a difference on the issues on which he had previously been working—in his case, issues of public health. "I never thought I'd join a private food company. But when I saw the seriousness of the planning and investments that were going to come in R&D and innovation, it seemed a great opportunity."

Industry and Issue Breadth

Was Coca-Cola's water security crisis primarily a concern for the beverages industry, and was it primarily an issue of environmental protection? On the face of it, the answer is yes to both—but it soon became apparent that it was much more than that, when local Indian farmers were unable to produce their crops because of water shortages.

What Seabright was discovering the hard way was what is now often called the "energy-water-food nexus," which is fast becoming a fundamental issue for governments, NGOs, and businesses. More than 70 percent of water use around the world is for agricultural production. The production of energy also requires a huge amount of water, and the operation of water infrastructure requires large amounts of energy. The world's growing population and increasing prosperity are pushing up global demand for energy, food, and water supplies—and are now a critical factor in determining the sustainable rate of economic growth. And this—combined with the effects of climate change—can initiate significant geopolitical events like the Arab Spring and the fall of governments in North Africa.

It no longer makes sense to view one industry as isolated from any other. In the twenty-first century, the lines between the banking industry and the housing industry, or between the technology industry and the retail industry, for example, are rapidly blurring. Companies like Amazon drove a wedge through those kinds of industry boundaries. When Jeff Bezos translated his experience as a highly quantitative financial analyst and trader at the New York hedge fund D. E. Shaw into the original concept for Amazon, his initial focus was on disrupting the book publishing and retail industries. But these days Amazon sells just about everything imaginable.

Brad Stone's book about "the Age of Amazon" has the title *The Everything Store*. But in fact, as Stone himself observes, Bezos wanted Amazon to be an "unstore"—not bound by traditional rules of retail. "It had limitless shelf space and personalized itself for every customer. It allowed negative reviews in addition to positive ones, and it placed used products next to new ones so that customers could make informed choices." And when it launched the transformational Amazon Web Services—which facilitated the launch of thousands of Internet start-ups—Stone says, "Finally, after years of setbacks and internal rancor, Amazon was unquestionably a technology company, what Jeff Bezos had always wanted it to be."

Amazon's talent strategy has consistently reflected this disruptive approach to traditional industry boundaries. For instance, when Amazon selected toys and electronics as two of the company's primary new merchandise categories, Jeff Bezos chose Harrison Miller to run the business, even though he had no prior experience in either sector. Stone observes that "in a pattern that would recur over and over, Bezos didn't care. He was looking for versatile managers—he did indeed call them 'athletes'—who could move fast and get big things done."

This elimination of industry boundaries is not just confined to business. Governments are rethinking the scope and scale of services they provide under pressure from budget deficits, technology, and changing citizen expectations. And nonprofits are continually adjusting to altered social needs and funding motivations to enhance their own effectiveness. Alertness and agility to these changing boundaries have become a key to professional success.

Intellectual Breadth

Was the water security issue that confronted Jeff Seabright an issue of biology or chemistry, or of social science or environmental policy, or of business management and operations, or even of ethics or moral philosophy? Again, the answer is all of the above. Seabright couldn't possibly educate himself in all of these intellectual disciplines—although he had been studying international relations and environmental sciences throughout his career.

Water security is one of the many issues in our society that requires the integration of discrete and specialized intellectual disciplines. The scientific philosopher Edward O. Wilson says that this is not unusual: "Most of the issues that vex humanity daily—ethnic conflict, arms escalation, overpopulation, abortion, environment, endemic poverty—cannot be solved without integrating knowledge from the natural sciences with that of the social sciences." But it is not just a matter of solving vexing problems; it is also a matter of conquering new intellectual frontiers—what Nietzsche called in *Human, All Too Human* "the rainbow colors around the edges of knowledge and imagination." Wilson argues that the consequence of a broader and more eclectic approach to intellectual discovery is "the capacity to imagine possible futures, and to plan and choose among them."

The most challenging issues and intellectual opportunities require what Wilson calls *consilience*—the principle that evidence from several independent, unrelated sources can converge to a stronger conclusion than any one intellectual domain might enable. William Whewell, in his 1840 thesis *The Philosophy of Inductive Sciences,* was the first to speak of consilience, literally a "jumping together" of knowledge by the linking of facts and fact-based theory across disciplines to create a common groundwork of explanation. A more contemporary figure, the cognitive neuroscientist Joshua Greene, uses a different term—*supervenience,* a general framework for thinking about how everything relates to everything else.

Water security is the kind of issue that cries out for consilience or supervenience—for an integrated approach to intellectual breadth. On environmental issues like this, Edward O. Wilson imagines four quadrants of intellectual activity—environmental policy, ethics, biology, and social science. "We already think of these four domains as closely connected, so that rational inquiry in one informs reasoning in the other three. Yet undeniably each stands apart in the contemporary academic mind. Each has its own practitioners, language, modes of analysis, and standards of validation." The result, Wilson warns, is frequently confusion—the kind of confusion that Francis Bacon warned four centuries ago "occurs whenever argument or inference passes from one world of experience to another."

The solution lies in what Wilson calls "the new age of synthesis, when the testing of consilience is the greatest of all intellectual challenges. Disciplinary boundaries within the natural sciences are disappearing, to be replaced by *shifting hybrid domains* in which consilience is implicit." And this synthesis goes further. Given that human action comprises events of physical causation, why should the social sciences and humanities be impervious to consilience with the natural sciences? He concludes, "There has never been a better time for collaboration between scientists and philosophers, especially where they meet in the borderlands between biology, the social sciences, and the humanities."

Cultural Breadth

Was Coca-Cola—one of the most global of companies—culturally well equipped to deal with problems in south India? You would think so—but every day we see companies and their leaders struggling to adapt to local norms a long way from their home base. Situations like this call for the nuanced understanding of cultural norms, expectations, and sometimes even language. But this kind of cultural breadth is rare, because as Erin Meyer observes in her book *The Culture Map*, "The sad truth is that the vast majority of managers who conduct business internationally have little understanding about how culture is impacting their work."

The problem is that if you go into every interaction assuming that culture doesn't matter, your default mechanism will be to view others through your own inherited cultural lens and to judge or misjudge them accordingly. Meyer cites the example of performance feedback, contrasting the French and American approaches. In a French setting, positive feedback is often given implicitly, while negative feedback is given more directly. In the United States, it's just the opposite. So if you use the popular American method of three positives for every negative with a French employee, she will leave the meeting with the praise ringing delightfully in her ears, while the negative feedback will have sounded very minor indeed. One reason for the difference in cultural expectations is that there are seven times more words in English than in French (500,000 versus 70,000), so that French relies on contextual clues to resolve semantic ambiguities to a greater extent than English.

Erin Meyer is a professor at INSEAD, the European business school in Fontainebleau, just south of Paris. I studied at INSEAD for my own MBA in the 1980s. Although the school's setting is very French—located as it is only a few hundred yards from a spectacular royal chateau in the heart of a beautiful and historic municipality—the faculty and student body are much more culturally eclectic. Meyer estimates that only 7 percent of the students today are French and that with so many nationalities represented "everyone is a cultural minority." This is especially relevant among the large number of midcareer executive students who have lived and worked all over the world, many having spent their careers moving from one region to another.

Jeff Seabright did not study at INSEAD, but he had just this kind of broad-based cultural background—and consequently was more prepared for the challenge he faced than the average American business executive would be. He had worked on foreign policy issues in India, as well as Brazil, Indonesia, and South Africa; he had worked in postapartheid South Africa for USAID through much of the 1990s; and he had a working relationship with the World Wildlife Fund's India Office. Seabright's experience across borders and cultures is a model that many leading institutions try to replicate today. Large multinational firms like Nestlé, Unilever, and GE especially aim to prepare their future leaders for a multicultural world by rotating them across geographies, affording them access to different cultural perspectives on how to do business—so essential in a globalizing world.

And there is good reason for that. Think of the challenge that BP's British CEO Tony Hayward had in dealing with the aftermath of the April 2010 Deepwater Horizon explosion in the Gulf of Mexico. Hayward's failure to communicate effectively with his key American stakeholders ultimately cost him his job and exacerbated an already existential crisis for BP. If a highly experienced and well-traveled chief executive like Hayward can't handle a communications problem in the United States, speaking his own language, think about how much more difficult it is to operate effectively in a country where you don't speak the language or intuitively understand the cultural norms and expectations.

A recent *Harvard Business Review* article states the recommendation of the authors very clearly in the title: "Be a Better Manager: Live Abroad." Its authors observe that "people who have international experience or identify with more than one nationality are better problem solvers and display more creativity." And to make it even more specific—people with this kind of cultural breadth are "more likely to create new businesses and products and be promoted."

Adam Grant, the Wharton professor and author, cites research on very creative people, which shows that they had typically moved to new geographies in their childhoods, ensuring they were exposed to different cultures and attitudes. Frederic Godart, a strategy professor, and his team of researchers demonstrated the most creative fashion collections came from houses where the directors had spent considerable time living and working abroad—the more different the cultures the better.

As Erin Meyer observes, "cultural relativity" is the key thing to understand: "If an executive wants to build and manage global teams that can work together successfully, he needs to understand not just how people from his own culture experience people from various international cultures, but also how those international cultures perceive *one another*."

Functional Breadth

Was the problem facing Jeff Seabright and Coca-Cola in south India a government relations problem? If so, he would have been extremely well equipped to tackle it, given his lengthy professional experience in the public sector. But pretty soon, it became much more than a government relations problem—it became an issue of marketing and branding, and the ultimate solution required a substantial re-engineering of Coca-Cola's whole production operation. At that point, Seabright was dealing with engineers, plant designers, production flow experts, and operational technologists.

Clearly, Seabright himself was not an expert in all of these disciplines—that would be impossible for any single individual. But he did have a sufficient breadth of functional knowledge and understanding to be an effective interlocutor with his colleagues and counterparts.

The most critical issues that face large institutions are typically cross-functional in nature. In business, they straddle finance, operations, marketing, technology, and human resources; in government, they often involve a mix of policy formation, regulatory law, operational management, and political calculation; and in the nonprofit world, there is an added dimension of fund-raising and impact measurement. The evidence shows that you are much more likely to predict accurately, analyze insightfully, and react productively to the most critical issues facing your organization if you have a significant measure of cross-functional experience.

WHY BROAD PEOPLE MAKE SUCCESSFUL LEADERS

Leaders have to be equipped to tackle all of these dimensions of today's world. We might think of them defensively as silos within which to operate, domains to protect, challenges to confront, or even enemies to overcome. But we would be better advised to think of them as new worlds to explore, lenses through which to look, capabilities to develop and apply.

Lucy Parker and Jon Miller argue that today's corporate leaders should nurture not just the conventional elements of business management—products, services, marketing messages, operational and financial tools. They should also develop and communicate a *point of view* about the big issues of the moment, and especially about how they might contribute to the productive resolution of those issues. They refer to "*the Eleven Conversations*—a way of giving shape to the big debates in the public information space." Business, government, and nonprofit leaders are drawn into these eleven big conversations—enduring themes in the global debate such as energy and climate change, education and skills, health and human rights—because they're concerned about the challenges facing the world and want to help craft solutions.

As individuals we are much more likely to be successful leaders if we can positively and confidently address these issues and challenges. As a society, we all benefit when we have leaders who can operate effectively along several of these domains. Indeed, if we had more multidimensional people like Jeff Seabright, we would be collectively much better equipped to tackle the kind of broad, complex issues that continually vex our society. There would be greater shared empathy among government, nonprofits, and business; more of a common language of opportunity creation; a less adversarial approach to policy-making and regulation; a shared commitment to innovation; and a more sustainable model of inclusive capitalism.

Even the most technical and specialized of institutions tend to have people of breadth in senior leadership roles. After all, it's in the nature of what we typically call *general management* that you need to know at least a little about a lot. Much like a sports team, almost all organizations have 4 or 5 individuals who are at the top; people who can 'do it all.' A 2016 study of recently graduated MBA students showed that generalists got better offers than specialists. Experienced hiring managers said they preferred people who had a diverse range of skills.

The evidence indeed shows that people like Seabright develop a kind of *inner diversity*—enabled by the range of their personal experiences and networks. Although they may act alone, they intrinsically exhibit the *wisdom of crowds*—they are programmed to be *collectively smart*. They also develop a kind of professional ambidexterity—greater capacity, flexibility, and adaptability. They are inherently less constrained by or captive of a single type of experience—precisely because their experience is so much broader. They are much less likely than the average person to exemplify the old maxim "If all you have is a hammer, everything looks like a nail"!

Indeed scientists would suggest that people with broad experience have unknowingly increased the *plasticity* of their brains. Although the brain was once seen as a rather static organ, recent neuroscience studies have shown that the organization of brain circuitry is constantly changing as a function of experience. Psychologists have long assumed that the nervous system is especially sensitive to experience during development, but only recently have they begun to appreciate the potential extent of plastic changes in the adult brain.

It is these features of inner diversity, of collective wisdom, and of mental plasticity that make breadth such a necessary characteristic of leadership. Leaders with broad experience have the capacity to cope with complexity and ambiguity—both in the issues they have to tackle and in the development of their own careers. Successful leaders are typically advocates for change and experimentation, rather than seeking to preserve the status quo—indeed, that is often cited as the distinction between leaders and managers. Those leaders who are able to draw upon an eclectic array of interests and experiences can advocate for the biggest changes and the freshest approaches.

So breadth is a profound basis for successful leadership; but by its very nature it typically takes time and varied experience to accumulate it. And sometimes it arises in unusual ways. Reading the biographies and life stories of successful leaders, I am often struck by two common themes.

First is the counterintuitive but empirical observation that the most direct route doesn't take you all the way to the top—that remarkable lives and careers are frequently nonlinear, often rather complicated, sometimes even a bit messy. More than a few of the most heralded political and business leaders have spent lengthy periods in the wilderness, suffered seemingly disastrous career setbacks, or taken a circuitous route to the top—and some have endured all three. Their personal narratives—the way they tell their stories—often include an explanation of why they chose an unusual career path, rejected advice based upon conventional wisdom, or found a way to recover after a significant career misstep or fall from grace. If history is any guide, if you want to get all the way to the top, don't take the most direct route, and don't succeed at everything you do.

For instance, in his sixty years of life Theodore Roosevelt accomplished more than most of us could imagine in several lifetimes. But along the way, he played several roles that hardly seemed on a direct route to the presidency: he spent lengthy periods of time exploring the barely settled western territories, including South Dakota's Badlands, and partly as a consequence of his derring-do in unwelcoming terrains, he had several bouts of serious illness—one of which eventually killed him. By the time he attained the presidency, he had been an assembly member, a civil service commissioner, a police commissioner, assistant secretary of the Navy, and governor of New York—but he had also been a rancher, a somewhat rootless traveler, a historian, and a writer.

His nephew Franklin Delano Roosevelt took full advantage of his inbred gifts and privileges en route to the presidency—but he also spent a lengthy period in the 1920s quite literally flat on his back recovering (only partially, as it transpired) from the devastating effects of infantile polio. Almost the same could be said of John F. Kennedy, who suffered both from severe wartime injuries and chronic illness throughout his otherwise gilded political career, which ended in tragedy.

The second observation is that many of our most revered leaders have been people of very considerable breadth—as reflected in their life experience, their intellect, and their range of interests. More than a few could be defined by the word "polymath"—which literally means "having learned much." Its dictionary definition is "a person whose expertise spans a significant number of subject areas; such a person is known to draw on complex bodies of knowledge to solve specific problems." It is a term rooted in the Renaissance and the Enlightenment, used to describe thinkers who excelled at several fields in science and the arts. But the term really only entered the lexicon in the twentieth century and has now been applied to great thinkers and doers of any age. These polymaths pepper our history, providing us with inspiration and insight.

In the theatrical adaptation of Hilary Mantel's *Wolf Hall* novels, there is an unusual sort of job interview—a beautifully whimsical and rather coy exchange—between King Henry VIII and Thomas Cromwell, who is about to become his chief minister.

HENRY VIII: You see, I bear you no ill will, Cromwell. And I fear you have no experience in policy and in the direction of a campaign.

CROMWELL: None, Sir.

HENRY VIII: But you do understand money, don't you? Wolsey tells me you know what every monastery in my realm is worth.

CROMWELL: Well, monks can be very cunning when it comes to hiding their wealth, Sir. But the full amount could be brought to light.

HENRY VIII: And that total would be?

CROMWELL: [Pause—interrupted by the King]

HENRY VIII: I would be interested to know.

CROMWELL: Yes, you would, Majesty.

HENRY VIII: Let's see how you make the calculation.

CROMWELL: I trained in the Florentine banks and in Venice.

HENRY VIII: The Cardinal told me you were a common soldier.

CROMWELL: I was that too.

HENRY VIII: Anything else?

CROMWELL: What would your Majesty like me to be?

Although Cromwell was indeed being deliberately evasive, he was not exaggerating his experiences and capabilities. By the time he became chief minister in 1532, he had already lived a full and adventurous life. He had been a mercenary in Europe, a banker in Italy, a clerk in the Netherlands, and a lawyer in England. This was all before he became secretary to Cardinal Wolsey, himself a man of eclectic experiences and interests—whom the historian Diarmaid MacCulloch describes as "a fine instructor in the art of doing everything and missing nothing." MacCulloch goes on to characterize Cromwell himself as "an all-seeing polymath," with a seemingly conflicting set of personal characteristics—"witty, reflective, affectionate and calculatingly brutal."

Among more recent leaders, Theodore Roosevelt exemplified the "all-seeing polymath." One of his most distinguished biographers, Doris Kearns Goodwin, notes that his own writing included narratives of hunting expeditions; meditations and natural histories on wolves, the grizzly bear, and the black-tailed deer; biographies of public figures; literary essays; commentaries on war and peace; and sketches of birds. "Everything was of interest to him," remarked the French ambassador Jean Jules Jusserand, "people of today, people of yesterday, animals, minerals, milestones, stars, the past, the future."

The British statesman Viscount Lee observed of Roosevelt, "Whether the subject of the moment was political economy, the Greek drama, tropical fauna or flora, the Irish sagas, protective coloration in nature, metaphysics, the technique of football, or post-futurist painting, he was equally at home." These eclectic interests and experiences were integral to his success as a political leader. They "passionately linked" him with all manner of people—"western bullwhackers, city prize-fighters, explorers, rich men, poor men, an occasional black man, editors, writers." They also gave him what we have come to think of as a *political hinterland*—a set of intellectual interests into which happy retreat was always possible.

Like Theodore Roosevelt and John F. Kennedy, Barack Obama was first elected president in his forties. Although he had had a more conventional political ascent, with less obvious "wandering," he had a much more eclectic and diverse cultural heritage and upbringing, which he captured powerfully in his best-selling memoir of early life, *Dreams from My Father*. Writing shortly after his 2008 election to the presidency, the novelist Zadie Smith says of Obama's personal story, "The tale he tells is all about addition. His is the story of a genuinely many-voiced man. If it has a moral it is that each man must be true to his selves, plural." She suggests that Obama embodies a mythical place called Dream City—"a place of many voices, where the unified singular voice is an illusion." And she says of the newly elected president, "He had the audacity to suggest that, even if you can't see it stamped on their faces, most people come from Dream City, too. Most of us have complicated back stories, messy histories, multiple narratives. [We] conjure contrasting voices and seek a synthesis between disparate things."

Britain's iconic wartime leader Winston Churchill also served in a broad variety of roles along his circuitous and often seemingly quixotic journey to political leadership. Not a few of these roles seemed like the very definition of "dead-end jobs"—and for much of the 1930s his career seemed destined to end in political irrelevance. During his "wilderness years," Churchill cultivated the numerous aspects of his own political hinterland, so that by the time he became Britain's most celebrated wartime prime minister, he had not only been an officer in the British army but a historian, a writer, and an artist—as well as an amateur bricklayer and butterfly breeder. And by the time of his death at the age of ninety, his writings included a novel, two biographies, three volumes of memoirs, and several histories—all of which, as I pointed out in the prologue, won him the Nobel Prize in Literature.

In the same way, breadth of experience and perspective has been a characteristic of many iconic business leaders through the ages— from Andrew Carnegie and Andrew Mellon to George Shultz and John Whitehead; from Michael Bloomberg and Hank Paulson to Steve Jobs, Bill Gates, Jeff Bezos, and Mark Zuckerberg.

But none of these political and business leaders could match Benjamin Franklin, who by the time of his death could lay claim to being an author, printer, political theorist, politician, postmaster, scientist, inventor, civil activist, statesman, and diplomat. In his biography of

Franklin, Walter Isaacson suggests the relevance to today's world: "Benjamin Franklin would have felt right at home in the information revolution. The essence of Franklin's appeal is that he was brilliant but practical, interested in everything, but especially in how things work."

———

As INDIVIDUALS AND AS A society, we cannot afford to be so prone to the perils of depth. We do need a pronounced swerve toward greater breadth—drawing upon the inspiration of those who have success-fully shaped their lives in that direction. But the question is how—what does it take to build a remarkable life of breadth and diversity? How can you achieve the multifaceted unity of the Mosaic Principle?

The answer, I believe, lies along six dimensions—the six most important skills, capabilities, and characteristics that determine success in building such a life and career. The experience and research recounted in this book suggest that you are most likely to build a remarkable life of breadth and diversity if you apply a strong moral compass, define an intellectual thread, develop transferrable skills, invest in contextual intelligence, build an extended network, and maintain a prepared mind. In the chapters that follow, I explore each of these dimensions of the Mosaic Principle—starting with the foundational concept of a moral compass.

PART 2

THE SIX DIMENSIONS OF THE MOSAIC PRINCIPLE

3

DOING WHAT SEEMS RIGHT
Applying Your Moral Compass

God is sitting here, looking into my very soul to see if I think right thoughts. Yet I am not afraid, for I try to be right and good; and He knows every one of my struggles.

—Emily Dickinson, letter to Abiah Root, 1858

Organizations endure in proportion to the breadth of morality by which they are governed. Thus the endurance of an organization depends upon the quality of leadership; and that quality derives from the breadth of the morality upon which it rests.

—Chester Barnard, *The Functions of the Executive*, 1938

AREAS OF MORAL COMPLEXITY

In the early days of creating Partners in Health, Paul Farmer and his young, ambitious colleagues in Boston would sit around and debate for hours what they wanted to do with their lives and how they could best apply their very considerable skills. They decided that what they most craved were *AMCs—areas of moral clarity*. They wanted to be sure they were making the highest and best use of their talents and that they were always doing the right thing. So, they chose the field of public health with a "preferential option for the poor." They would save lives, restore the sick and wounded to good health, and help the poor live lives of dignity and hope. They would do so initially in Haiti—persistently the poorest country in the Western Hemisphere. That seemed as close to an AMC as they could possibly find.

And yet, as they soon discovered, even this seemingly unimpeachable choice would turn out to be an AMC of a different kind—an *area of moral complexity*. That was partly because of another choice they made at the same time—that in addition to providing medical care to the poor amid the systemic poverty and periodic chaos of Haiti, they would continue to practice and develop their professional skills in the United States, working in some of the world's leading medical schools and hospitals, surrounded by considerable wealth and prosperity. Half the year they would operate out of makeshift facilities in Cange, but the rest of the time they would work in pristine and gleaming operating rooms in Boston, benefiting from a well-resourced health-care system. How could they reconcile themselves to this contrast in context and motivation?

Farmer himself recognized the moral complexity in this situation. He would later say that "if you're making sacrifices (such as working in a place like Haiti), unless you're automatically following some rule, it stands to reason that you're trying to lessen some psychic discomfort." That is what it felt like to him to "sell" his medical services for money in a world where some can't buy them. This was the moral complexity of his caring profession, and he found it very uncomfortable. He would add, "You *can* feel ambivalent about that, because you *should* feel ambivalent about that." His decision to be a doctor for part of the time to people who wouldn't otherwise have medical care, living in tough conditions, could be regarded as a self-sacrifice; but it could also be regarded as a way to deal with this moral complexity—perhaps even a way of salving his conscience.

Paul Farmer has very consciously chosen to shape his life in a certain way—to hone his professional skills in the most sophisticated of environments, but also to apply those skills in some of the most troubled and demanding of environments. Instead of single-mindedly operating in an area of moral clarity, he has chosen to wrestle year after year in an area of moral complexity. He has had to make choices and trade-offs—sometimes even to resolve apparent conflicts of interest. And each time he has asked himself the same question: "What's the right thing to do?"

This is what happens when you try to build a broader life and career. You may yearn for areas of moral certainty, but more often you'll be dealing with areas of moral complexity. When you meet people who have shaped their lives in this way—who have chosen breadth over depth, or at least breadth alongside depth—they rarely talk about their certainty that they have done the right thing. More often, they openly wonder whether they have chosen the correct options and whether they would have been better advised to go a different route. They feel an almost permanent sense of ambiguity and uncertainty, and occasionally even underlying guilt.

This is what makes a broader life so difficult. Nearly a hundred years ago, Walter Lippmann—the American writer, reporter, and political commentator, one of the founders of the *New Republic*—wrestled with the apparent contradictions between liberty and democracy in a complex modern world. "Above all the other necessities of human nature," he wrote, "above the satisfaction of any other need, above hunger, love, pleasure, fame—even life itself—what a man most needs is the conviction that he is contained within the discipline of an ordered existence." But where to find that ordered existence amid the complexity and ambiguity that are inherent characteristics of a broader life in today's world?

The solution for many lies in finding and applying a strong *moral compass,* an "inner sense" that distinguishes good choices from bad—an implicit ethical code and a guide for morally appropriate behavior. This is more than what society deems right and wrong through laws, regulations, and conventional social mores. It is a more individual and personal framework for how you make decisions about the direction of your life—decisions that sit well with the kind of person you are or want to be. As Carl Rogers, one of the most influential psychologists of the twentieth century, writes optimistically, "Man's behavior is exquisitely rational, moving with subtle and ordered complexity towards the goal his organism is endeavoring to achieve."

The philosopher Charles Taylor takes a similar view in describing what he calls the "culture of authenticity." He says, "Our moral salvation comes from recovering authentic moral contact with ourselves." He adds that there is an innately good True Self that we each need to tap into—so that we can stay true to our inner voice and not follow the distortions of a corrupting world. And he adds, "There is a certain way of being that is my way. I am called to live my life in this way, and not in imitation of anyone else's. If I am not, I miss the point of my life. I miss what being human is for me."

A strong moral compass is the first dimension of the Mosaic Principle. This is the full range of virtues, vices, or actions that are available to you as a person—that determine how you behave toward others, how you shape your life. Once fully developed, your moral compass can give your life a sense of mission and purpose that goes well beyond just doing what seems right or avoiding what seems wrong. It can enable you to tackle the complexities of a broader life, to do the right thing, and to live your life purposefully. Even if you choose to live a deep and narrow life, a strong moral compass is helpful; if you live a broader and more complex life, it is essential.

THE REVOLVING DOOR

If you try to build a broader life—especially if you do so at the intersection of business and government—the chances are that sooner or later you'll have the term "revolving door" thrown at you, and it probably won't be a compliment. That's certainly what happened to me.

My three decades at McKinsey afforded me plentiful opportunities for breadth and variety of experience—all of which I tried to take. I worked in a wide range of industries—from mining to media, from beverages to construction, from retail to technology. I helped my clients wrestle with big strategic issues and major organizational change programs, but I also helped them deal with the everyday operational challenges of how to make things work better. I drew upon my professional training in business management, economics, and finance; but sometimes I remembered that I had first been a history major in college, and I found that the most valuable thing I could do was to construct a coherent and articulate narrative that explained the past and anticipated the future, supported by the available facts and evidence. I worked all over the world for my clients, many of which were multinational corporations; and when later on an opportunity arose to move to the United States, I took it—along with my wife and four children, who fortunately decided to come with me!

All of that was great—but it wasn't really enough for me. Most of McKinsey's clients were large corporations, and I certainly enjoyed the world of business. But I was also fascinated by politics, public policy, social change, sports, the arts, and culture—and a lot else besides. It was difficult to cultivate all those interests within the confines of a conventional McKinsey career, so at first I found ways to pursue my "side interests" almost as hobbies or pastimes, especially as a volunteer in the nonprofit world. I helped set up a nonprofit educational enterprise, TeachFirst, focused on the professional development of teachers (motivated in part by the fact that both my parents had been teachers); as a member of the board, I worked on the transformation of the Royal Shakespeare Company (RSC), one of the world's leading theater companies; and when I moved to the United States, I worked with nonprofits such as Venture Philanthropy Partners and the Shakespeare Theatre Company in Washington.

In addition, for most of the 1990s I had the BBC as a client, which enabled me to work with one of the world's leading broadcasters on how to meet the early challenges of the digital world—within the constraints imposed on a public service organization, funded by a universal license fee. I helped the BBC design and launch new digital television and radio stations, diversify its programming to address new audience needs, build its initial presence on the rapidly emerging Internet, and articulate to the British government why there should be an increased license fee to pay for all this. This placed

me in frequent contact with the senior ranks of the British establishment, and I built a robust and broad network of friends and colleagues in the world of politics and government.

Eventually, in 2001, I had the opportunity to work in government
itself—as a special adviser in the Prime Minister's Strategy Unit at
No. 10 Downing Street. Tony Blair had just won a second landslide
election victory, and he was more determined than ever to reform
Britain's tradition-bound and often sclerotic public services such as
health care, transport, prisons, and education. So, for three years I
worked alongside other would-be policy advisers at No. 10 to develop long-term strategies for public-sector reform—while in a separate part of the building Blair was making the decisions to participate
in the Iraq War that would ultimately contribute to his downfall.

During those three years I learned a lot about how things work—
and don't work—in government. And when early in 2004 I refo-
cused exclusively on my McKinsey career, it made sense to try to
build a government practice at our firm. We had done bits and
pieces of work for governments in the past but never in a sustained
and focused way—so I decided that it was about time we did. I and
a small band of like-minded colleagues started applying for government consulting contracts—and gradually we started winning some,
first in the Home Office, then in the Departments of Education, Defense, and Work and Pensions—and especially in the Department of
Health, which oversaw Britain's monolithic but treasured National
Health Service.

By the middle of 2005, things seemed to be going well—we had
a number of projects underway, a growing number of relationships
across the government, and we were excited about the impact that
our work was starting to have. That's when I got into trouble.

"Fears Grow over Management Consultant's Role in No. 10." That
was the headline in the *Guardian* newspaper on Monday, June 13,
2005. A quick reading of the article revealed that the management
consultant in question was me. And in the days that followed it became apparent that the left-of-center antiestablishment *Guardian*
was not alone in its "fears." From the other side of the political spectrum, it was joined by the *Daily Mail,* a popular right-wing tabloid

newspaper. The *Guardian* and *Daily Mail* can rarely agree about the time of day, but on this occasion they were aligned in their mistrust of me and my firm. They were joined—indeed egged on—by Conservative Party politicians in the British Parliament, who were motivated principally by a desire to embarrass Tony Blair and his Labour Party government but didn't mind if there was collateral damage to the "secretive" high-end consulting firm that was apparently so popular with the government.

Our sin in the eyes of these politicians and media commentators was to have gained "inappropriate access to and influence over" the higher reaches of the British government. Another newspaper, the *Independent*, summarized this concern as follows:

> The links between No.10 and McKinsey, and the movement of partners and civil servants between the company and Downing Street, have led to suggestions that there is a revolving door between them.

Yet another newspaper, the venerable *Times* of London, printed a cartoon that visualized this so-called revolving door between the Prime Minister's Office and McKinsey.

FIGURE 3.1. Cartoon in the *Times* (London), August 2, 2005. Reprinted with permission of News UK & Ireland Ltd.

The media's concern was not just over our seemingly close relationship with the government but with what we would do with it. For instance, one newspaper speculated that McKinsey—sometimes dubbed the "Jesuits of capitalism"—would press civil servants to become more "business-like and entrepreneurial" and to push through a private-sector-inspired electronic revolution in the delivery of all services. The McKinsey slogan, it asserted, is "everything can be measured, and what gets measured gets managed." It added that such a reorientation of the government's approach to the management of public services could lead to further job cuts—on top of many that have already been announced—and would place the government on a collision course with the public-sector unions, whose resentment was already high about the appointment of people with business backgrounds to government roles.

I found this unsolicited media notoriety personally uncomfortable. I had typically been one of the "grey men," used to operating in the background, even in the shadows—and unused to the public spotlight. Only once before had I attracted any significant media attention—ten years earlier in 1995 when the *London Evening Standard* accused me of having too much influence over the leaders of the BBC. Because these were the very early stages of the Internet, the media didn't have a digital photograph of me on file. So instead they illustrated the story with a mocked-up silhouette of an anonymous business executive, complete with a bowler hat—then the symbol of the City of London financial center. Although I had no meaningful connection with the City of London, the implication was clear—the "money men" were taking over our traditional way of life.

Of course, this periodic media accusation of "too much influence" was an area of moral complexity for a management consultant like me. In common with any professional adviser, my objective absolutely was to gain access to and influence over my client—so that I could help him or her, and of course so that I could secure more business for myself and my firm because of the high quality of our work. So it felt odd to be impugned for being successful in that objective. I was also happy to be helping a reform-minded government achieve its declared objectives of improved efficiency and effectiveness in the management and delivery of high-quality public services. I did indeed believe that the government could benefit from more of a business mind-set and tool kit in the design and delivery of these services—and I was happy to be part of that process.

All of that said, I was well aware that the concept of the "revolving door" between business and government—as illustrated in the *Times* cartoon—had taken on a pejorative meaning. More often than not these days, it is used to imply an ignoble or even immoral motivation whenever a businessperson goes into government or a government official goes into business. The more or less explicit assumption is that people who make this kind of transition are doing so in order to enrich themselves personally through their access, influence, and knowledge—now or later, and at the government's and taxpayer's expense. Tony Blair himself would later bemoan the fact that every time he sought to bring a businessperson into the British government, he was accused of fostering some form of implied corruption. "Cronyism" was, and remains, the tabloid term of preference for this phenomenon—so people like me were "Tony's Cronies."

In the United States, concern about the revolving door has intensified since the 2008 financial crisis. Prior to that, as Andrew Ross Sorkin writes in the *New York Times,* "there had been a well-worn path of Wall Street executives going to work in Washington." He cites a series of treasury secretaries with that heritage—Douglas Dillon of Dillon, Read for President Kennedy; Donald Regan of Merrill Lynch for President Reagan; and of course, Hank Paulson of Goldman Sachs for President George W. Bush. "But," he adds, "in recent years Wall Street executives have either shied away from working in Washington or been impeded by lawmakers hostile to their nominations. In a post-financial-crisis world, most bankers have avoided Washington either by choice or by default." For instance, in 2014, Antonio Weiss, a senior banking executive at Lazard, was nominated by President Obama for deputy secretary of the treasury; but when Senator Elizabeth Warren threatened to block his confirmation, he withdrew his name and instead became a special adviser to the treasury secretary, a job that did not require Senate confirmation.

Nowadays the "revolving door" has come to represent one of the most acute areas of moral complexity at the intersection of business and government. I knew this, and like anybody who operates at that intersection, I needed to be confident of my moral compass—that I would always do the right thing, or at least what seemed right at the time. But as the newspaper reports accurately implied, my moral compass had actually gone awry at a crucial moment.

A few years earlier, I had invited the former director-general of the BBC, John Birt, to become a part-time adviser to McKinsey's media practice. He had previously been one of my clients before his retirement from the BBC, so I knew that he was an experienced media industry expert and a more than capable strategist. I was confident that he would be an enthusiastic adviser to our clients and teams—and so it proved, as we built a mutually productive relationship. But some time later, he had taken on a part-time, unpaid role as a strategic adviser to the prime minister—a position of some influence. He had no direct, or even indirect, say over who won consultancy contracts with the government—but it was easy to assume that he might have some. If not an actual conflict of interest, it could certainly be perceived as one.

My moral compass should have told me to suspend the relationship between McKinsey and John Birt as soon as we started to apply for government contracts. But it didn't and neither did his. As a result, I found myself having to fend off media criticism for what I soon came to realize was a legitimate concern. I was morally compromised and I had to acknowledge it.

Much later than I should have, I did ask John Birt to step down from his part-time role with McKinsey, which he did with some reluctance—because he enjoyed the work. He subsequently took on a similar role with another management consultancy, who were apparently less concerned about the perceived conflict of interest—and in any case had a lower public profile. We explained our change of tack to the newspapers and politicians, and soon enough the media frenzy died down—overtaken by other much more important stories. In the process, we learned some valuable lessons about the need to engage constructively with the media—and I learned some even more important lessons about the need to maintain my moral compass amid the complexity and ambiguity of my life.

FINDING YOUR MORAL COMPASS

What defines a person? Is it their expertise, their memories, their hobbies, their family and friends? Are these the things that define personal identity—that make you *you?*

Look deeper, argue researchers at Yale School of Management— into the soul. According to their work, kindness, loyalty, empathy, politeness, and other moral traits are really what constitute someone's being. They tested this hypothesis in the most challenging of real-world contexts, that of radical mental change—so-called neurodegeneration. Specifically, the researchers (Strohminger and Nichols) focused on three neurodegenerative diseases: frontotemporal dementia (FTD), Alzheimer's disease, and amyotrophic lateral sclerosis, better known as ALS or Lou Gehrig's disease. ALS served as a control because it primarily affects movement, and not memory or moral behavior. Alzheimer's primarily affects memory but also has some effect on moral behavior. But FTD is the one most likely to have a moral impact—its symptoms include a loss of empathy, poor judgment, and increasingly inappropriate behavior.

The researchers recruited people from online support groups for friends and family of patients suffering from FTD, Alzheimer's, and ALS, and they asked questions like "Do you feel like you still know who the patient is?" using 5-point scales. Friends and family of ALS patients averaged about 4.1 points on that scale, but the number dropped to 3.8 for Alzheimer's and to 3.4 for FTD, suggesting that morality was indeed at the core of how people conceived their loved one's identities, even more than memory. With more detailed analysis, they concluded, "Contrary to what generations of philosophers and psychologists have thought, memory loss doesn't make someone seem like a different person. Rather, morality . . . played the largest role in whether someone comes across as themselves or whether their personal identity has been swallowed up by the disease."

Observing or experiencing a neurodegenerative disease is obviously an extreme way to define somebody's identity, to identify their moral compass. But in more normal conditions, when you have more control over what is happening to you, how *do* you find your moral compass? For most of us, this is the first critical step in shaping our life and career—especially if we want to live a broader life. We know that such a life will involve many choices and trade-offs, pervasive ambiguity, and occasional conflicts of interest. We will be motivated by lots of different things, and we will have to decide which ones matter more than others. We will spend more time in areas of moral complexity than in areas of moral certainty. We will find ourselves frequently thinking, "If I choose to meet this need, then by definition I am choosing not to meet this other need. How can I feel good about that?"

So, we need some way to define our approach to moral complexity. As David Brooks observes, "If the outer mind hungers for status, money and applause, the inner mind hungers for harmony and connection—those moments when self-consciousness fades away and a person is lost in a challenge, a cause, the love of another or the love of God." We need a moral compass to sustain what he calls "the idea that we have multiple selves over the idea that we have a single self," to enable our "unconscious, that inner extrovert . . . to achieve communion with work, friends, family, nation and cause."

For some people, finding their moral compass will be relatively straightforward—they will find it by the approach that Paul Farmer calls "automatically following some rule." This may be an organized religion or highly structured philosophy that has predetermined requirements—or at least guidelines—on how to behave.

As it happens, Farmer himself has followed a more or less organized religion or governing philosophy. Although he is not the kind of person to "automatically follow some rule," a key element in his professional and personal journey was his early adoption of a religious philosophy called "liberation theology"—which became a defining element of his moral compass. He explains, "Over the course of my 20s, the slender, frayed thread of my own (Catholic) faith, which I had believed cut, slowly came back into view. There was a filament a bit stronger than imagined, made visible in part by my Haitian hosts and patients and friends, and in part by Catholic social activists working against poverty in settings as different as tough neighborhoods in Boston, the farms of North Carolina, and the slums of Lima."

He specifically attributes this spiritual awakening to the work of Father Gustavo Gutierrez, a "diminutive and humble Dominican priest," who like Farmer now divides his time between an American university (Notre Dame) and a Latin American country (Peru), and who established through his writings the core principles of liberation theology—the preferential option for the poor; the notion that "structural violence" is inflicted through poverty, racism, gender inequality, homophobia, and xenophobia; and the third notion of "accompaniment." Applying this concept to medicine—and especially medicine for the poor—he asks, "How can we accompany our patients on the road to cure or wellness or a life with less suffering due to disease?"

Even if you don't have an "organized body of thought," you can define your moral compass in clear and simple terms. Some define this as *integrity*—a moral or ethical code. Michael Wilson became Canada's minister of finance after a distinguished career in banking and then went on to lead important social initiatives in mental health research. In answer to the question, "Where do you find your moral compass?" he says, "I cannot have my integrity put in question by something I have done. So my north star is the mirror. I look into it to ask myself, 'Are you comfortable with doing this?' You have to understand that cutting corners in life is going to get you into trouble. Whether it's tomorrow or a month or five years from now, you've got to be careful, and unfortunately that's not an easy thing to do. The more you base decisions on the ethics of the situation, the better off you'll be in practically everything you do."

For many, the flywheel of their moral compass is just this kind of integrity, which is underpinned by personal commitments to truthfulness, honesty, and a desire to do the right thing, even at personal risk. At minimum, this can be viewed as self-protection, because a person of integrity—and with a reputation for honesty—is most likely to stay out of trouble. Jeff Skilling found that out the hard way, and a few years later so did two other distinguished former colleagues of mine.

Rajat Gupta had been the worldwide managing director of McKinsey for nine years and a partner and colleague for a lot longer than that. Although he had subsequently retired from the firm and taken on a series of nonexecutive roles in the corporate and nonprofit worlds, he nevertheless remained a highly respected and influential figure among those of us still at McKinsey. We certainly thought of him as "one of us"—and for many he had been an important personal mentor. One of the people he had most closely mentored was Anil Kumar, a partner of McKinsey who introduced the firm as an institution and Gupta as an individual in what became known as the "Galleon Scandal."

Kumar's Wharton business school classmate Raj Rajaratnam had founded and built an extremely successful hedge fund in New York called the Galleon Group, which had more than $7 billion under management at its peak. It achieved exceptional returns for its investors by drawing upon a variety of information sources—some of them, it transpired, of dubious legitimacy. As we all learned later, Galleon was able to employ inside information gleaned from Anil Kumar about his clients at McKinsey, and later from Rajat Gupta's direct participation in Goldman Sachs board meetings. This seemed like a classic case of "insider trading"—and Rajat Gupta was eventually convicted and sentenced to two years in federal prison. Anil Kumar, who (unlike Rajat Gupta) had apparently been paid directly by Rajaratnam for his information, secured a noncustodial sentence in return for his prosecution evidence.

When two of your colleagues—one of them the former head of your firm—are convicted of serious federal crimes, it definitely makes you think. Would I have done the same thing in their place? I hope not—but we all grew up in the same institution, and you're bound to wonder whether there was something about our shared professional upbringing that led to this outcome. And you're also left wondering whether your moral compass is robust enough to avoid getting caught up in this kind of situation yourself.

This is one way of thinking about the concept of the moral compass—as a means of avoiding crime and punishment in conditions of extreme moral complexity. But many people think of their moral compass as more than a way to stay out of trouble. They think of it much more positively as a way to find *meaning and purpose* amid the complexity of their lives—sometimes through trial and error, sometimes through practical experience.

Viktor Frankl, the Austrian neurologist and psychiatrist, found his moral compass in the most extreme of circumstances—the Nazi concentration camps of Auschwitz and Dachau, in which he was imprisoned for the last two years of World War II. Frankl himself survived to resume his career—although his wife and mother did not. He went on to establish what became known as the Third Viennese School of Psychotherapy, founded on the principles of *logotherapy*, a form of existential analysis of what matters to people, the science of motivations.

In his landmark work, *Man's Search for Meaning*, he tells the story of his time as a concentration camp inmate, which led him to discover the importance of meaning in all forms of existence, even the most brutal ones, and thus a reason to continue living. Terrible as it was, his experience in Auschwitz reinforced what was already one of Frankl's key ideas: life is not primarily a quest for pleasure, as Freud believed, or a quest for power, as Alfred Adler taught, but a quest for meaning. The greatest task for any person is to find meaning in life. You cannot always control what happens to you, but you can control what you will feel and do about what happens to you. I have personally found this a critical concept in handling the inevitable ups and downs of my own life and career.

Frankl expands upon the significance of meaning—of intrinsic motivation and of a moral compass. "Man's search for meaning is the primary motivation in his life and not a 'secondary rationalization' of instinctual drives. This meaning is unique and specific in that it must and can be fulfilled by him alone; only then will it achieve a significance that will satisfy his own will to meaning." And he quotes Nietzsche: "He who has a *why* to live for can bear almost any *how*."

But although the search for meaning is all-important as you seek to shape your life, this is not necessarily a search for resolution and inner peace. Frankl addresses the ambiguity and ambivalence that seemingly afflict many people as they seek to balance and reconcile their varying motivations—he says that this is in fact our natural and desirable state. It is a dangerous misconception of mental hygiene to assume that what people need in the first place is equilibrium or, as it is called in biology, "homeostasis," which is to say a "tension-less state." What people actually need is not a tensionless state but rather the striving and struggling for a worthwhile goal, a freely chosen task.

And in the preface to the 1992 edition—written nearly fifty years after the events that inspired it—Frankl writes, "I want you to listen to what your conscience commands you to do and go on to carry it out to the best of your knowledge. Then you will live to see that in the long run—in the long run, I say!—success will follow you precisely because you had forgotten to think about it."

This is a much more positive and hopeful way to view the concept of a moral compass—as a critical tool in the search for meaning in areas of moral complexity. And it leads directly to the importance of breadth. For it intuitively seems improbable that we will satisfy this search for meaning if we look in only one place, using only one search methodology. That would be like trying to find the answer to all our most important questions by reading only one book or looking at only one website. Even the most devoted Bible scholar might find that a little too narrow an approach. It makes much more sense—we are much more likely to succeed in our quest—if we broaden our search field and diversify the search tools at our disposal.

If our moral compass can help us to find meaning, then we might also hope that it will help us to find *happiness* for ourselves and others—which we might think of as the highest objective of all. In *Conscious Business,* Fred Kofman asks, "What is the ultimate goal of human life? Happiness. You seek other basic goods such as money, fame, or power because you think they will make you happy, but you want happiness for its own sake. Everything you do—work, play, pray, study, marry, have children—is a search for happiness."

Using chess as a metaphor, Kofman talks about what it takes to "win the real game," which can only happen if you are willing to make sacrifices. He argues that when you make a sacrifice—which means literally "to make sacred"—you relinquish a lower goal in order to pursue a higher one. Just as in chess, so in life: if you forget the hierarchy of goals, you will make stupid mistakes. To play chess consciously you need to keep in mind the hierarchy of means and ends. You make sacrifices and avoid sacrileges. In other words, pursue your meaning and purpose, and preserve your integrity.

Beyond choosing what you do, the conscious pursuit of happiness entails choosing *how* to do what you do. Although the outcome is important, happiness depends more on the process. Happiness comes from integrity and meaning rather than from success in achieving a goal, from behavior in alignment with essential values rather than from winning or losing. This is a variation of the Olympic motto that the winning is less important than the taking part—even if that principle rarely seems to apply in the modern world of sports, least of all in the Olympics. Kofman concludes, "If you want to do business consciously—if you want to live consciously—you need to enact the universal virtues of wisdom, courage, love, justice, temperance, and transcendence and seek success beyond success."

Perhaps more than any other business thinker, Clayton Christensen has sought to reconcile these dimensions of ethical conduct, meaning, purpose, and happiness for successful leaders—especially for the prospective business leaders who are seeking to build and sustain a successful enterprise, the focus of his foundational MBA course. In his writing and teaching, Christensen has been especially influenced by the frustrations and disappointments of his own friends and peers—as well as by recent brushes with mortality.

Reflecting upon recent Harvard Business School reunions, he states that when he first knew them "my classmates were not only some of the smartest people I've known, but some of the most decent people, too. At graduation they had plans and visions for what they wanted to accomplish, not just in their careers, but in their personal lives as well. *Yet something had gone wrong for them along the way.*" In particular, he notes that for more than a few their personal relationships had begun to deteriorate, even as their professional prospects blossomed. "I sensed that they felt embarrassed to explain to their friends the contrast in the trajectory of their personal and professional lives." You will recall from Chapter 1 that one of his classmates was Enron's Jeff Skilling, who had obviously experienced a particularly dramatic fall from grace.

Observing the travails of his own classmates—their personal dissatisfaction, family failures, professional struggles, even their criminal behavior—was one trigger to take a closer look at individual motivation and behavior. The other was the discovery in 2009 that he had contracted the same kind of cancer that had killed his own father—a discovery that he shared with his MBA students, to concentrate his and their minds. Drawing upon these sources of motivation, he developed a way of defining his moral compass based upon the answers to three fundamental questions: How can I be sure that:

- I will be successful and happy in my career?
- My relationships with my spouse, my children, and my extended family and close friends become an enduring source of happiness?
- I live a life of integrity—and stay out of jail?

One suspects he wouldn't have mentioned jail if it weren't for Jeff Skilling—but speaking personally, with Jeff Skilling and Rajat Gupta in mind, I would take nothing for granted.

He notes that for many of us, one of the easiest mistakes to make is to focus on trying to oversatisfy the tangible trappings of professional success in the mistaken belief that a better salary, a more prestigious title, a nicer office will make us happy. "But as soon as you find yourself focusing on the tangible aspects of your job, you are at risk of becoming like some of my classmates, chasing a mirage. The next pay raise, you think, will be the one that finally makes you happy. It's a hopeless quest."

Christensen prefers a "theory of motivation" that encompasses a different set of questions that are more likely to yield productive answers: "Is this work meaningful to me? Is this job going to give me a chance to develop? Am I going to learn new things? Will I have an opportunity for recognition and achievement? Am I going to be given responsibility? These are the things that will truly motivate you." They provide a moral compass that can help to shape your life—and to navigate your motivation map.

NAVIGATING YOUR MOTIVATION MAP

In the physical world, a compass is most useful when used in conjunction with a map that tells you exactly where you are and where you're trying to get to. In the same way, a moral compass becomes all the more useful when used with a *motivation map*—both to understand where you are now and where you are seeking to go with your life, and to make sense of the inevitable complexity and ambiguity of a broader life.

What motivates you? Do you want to save the world, to make lots of money and be recognized and rewarded for your achievements, to change the organization in which you work, to have power and influence over others, to enhance your skills and capabilities, to do things that interest and excite you, to work with enjoyable colleagues, or to have a lifestyle that suits you?

My guess is that your first instinctive answer is, all of the above— or at least most of them. You have multiple motivations—there isn't just one thing that matters to you while nothing else matters at all. Moreover some of these motivations are—or can be—mutually compatible. For instance, you're more likely to "save the world" or at least to change it in some material way if you have power and influence over others—and in the process you may find yourself doing very interesting work with colleagues whom you like and respect.

In today's business world, there are more than a few opportunities to "do well by doing good"—and the search for them is a priority for many. Craig Newmark, founder of Craigslist, likes to say that he is motivated by "nerd values": "First I need to earn an okay living, then change the world." He started Craigslist as a hobby, while working at a bank, simply highlighting interesting events in the San Francisco area. So he is able to advise that "first, you have to run and persist in running a site that's a genuine community service, without specifically intending to get rich at it." Although eBay owned a substantial minority stake for more than a decade, Craigslist has remained essentially independent and privately owned—now helping millions of people in cities all over the world find everything from used cars to romance.

Of course, Craig Newmark has gotten rich, as have many in the world of digital technology and the Internet. But more than a few Silicon Valley companies and leaders have nevertheless positioned themselves as almost anticorporate or postcorporate—emphasizing that they have a sense of purpose beyond making a profit. For instance, Mark Zuckerberg says of Facebook that it "was not originally created to be a company. It was built to accomplish a social mission—to make the world more open and connected." In his letter to potential investors as part of the filing for an initial public offering in January 2012, Zuckerberg writes, "Facebook aspires to build the services that give people the power to share and help them once again transform many of our core institutions and industries. We don't build services to make money; we make money to build better services."

We might all aspire to do well by doing good—especially if we can follow in the footsteps of Craig Newmark and Mark Zuckerberg. But let's be honest—some of the most significant motivations are likely to conflict with each other. It may be difficult to make lots of money if you're trying to save the world, or to have a sustainable lifestyle if you have power, influence, and responsibility over lots of other people. The likelihood is that you will have to make some choices, some trade-offs—to resolve what really matters to you. That's why you need a moral compass and a motivation map.

So let me ask the question in a different way: Which of these motivations matter most to you, which matter least—and by the way, which don't matter to you at all? In other words, what is your hierarchy of motivations? And while I'm asking questions—how do you balance and reconcile your motivations in order to make sense of your life?

If you want to have a broader life and career, you're going to have to wrestle with these questions—as you resolve which options to pursue at each stage of life. You will especially have to wrestle with the "money question": How much money, how much income, are you prepared to sacrifice if you are motivated by public and social goals that are typically not well remunerated? How much wealth will you trade off for power and influence? This is a really important question to be honest about—especially with yourself.

Bill Novelli has been an executive in a large multinational corporation (Unilever), created and built his own public affairs advisory firm (Porter Novelli), led AARP—the largest nonprofit membership organization in the United States—and now in his early seventies leads the Global Social Enterprise program at Georgetown University's McDonough School of Business. Many of his talented and energetic business school students, he believes, would make wonderful social entrepreneurs—founding and leading enterprises aimed primarily at the public good. But he tells me with a tinge of irony and sadness, "I've come to realize that there are two kinds of students at business school—those who say that they don't really understand what I'm talking about in my social enterprise classes and who go off to work in investment banking or consulting; and those who say they do understand and love what I'm talking about—but more than a few still go off to work in investment banking or consulting! It might not be what they really want to do, but they find it hard to turn down that kind of money—especially when they're worried about paying off their student debts."

As David Brooks observes, "The cultural, technological, and meritocratic environment in which we now live has not made us a race of barbarians. But it has made us less morally articulate. Many of us have instincts about right and wrong, about how goodness and character are built, but everything is fuzzy."

So how do you make things less "fuzzy" and address the choices—even the apparent conflicts of interest—that accompany a broad life and career? The answer is that you use your moral compass to navigate your motivation map—seeking to understand, evaluate, and reconcile your own motives. As Craig Newmark observes, "The biggest entrepreneurial lesson I've learned has been that you really do need to follow your instincts. Trust your instincts and your moral compass." And he adds, almost to encourage us, "What surprises me, in a way, is how almost universally people are trustworthy and good."

In navigating the map, you will place comparative weights on different motivations—determining which matters most to you and charting a course that reflects this weighting. Developing and navigating this motivation map will be the work of a lifetime, not just of a moment—for the simple reason that your motivations will change as your circumstances change. Nothing is forever, least of all what matters most to you.

We are all different, but typically you will need to ask yourself at least eight interrelated questions as you navigate your motivation map:

1. *How much do you want to do good?* Many of us aspire to do good and admire it in others—but only a select few place doing good unequivocally at the top of their hierarchy of motivations. Those who do are the kind of people who aspire to change—or even save—the world, who are driven by an intense desire to serve the needs of the poor or vulnerable, to protect and preserve the environment in which we all live, or to pursue some other altruistic objective. They are "mission driven," motivated by passionate belief in a cause, and often inspired to build a movement for change. Despite their self-reported ambivalence and "psychic discomfort," Paul Farmer and his colleagues at Partners in Health have clearly placed doing good at the heart of their motivation map. They are willing—even enthusiastic—to bear material physical and emotional hardship to achieve significant social good.

Some people find a way to do good early in their lives and stick with it as a vocation or calling. Brett Wigdortz discovered his calling when he was working for me at McKinsey on a pro bono project. Our aim was to identify ways in which local businesses could help strengthen education for underprivileged kids in London. The project yielded a very practical idea—to create a nonprofit social enterprise called TeachFirst that would enable talented graduates of excellent universities to enter the teaching profession for a prescribed period of time without the usual lengthy professional apprenticeship that put so many off. This would enhance the quality of teaching in deprived inner-city neighborhood schools by addressing the most urgent of needs—the recruitment and professional development of talented teachers.

At the time, Wigdortz was just the junior analyst on the McKinsey team, an American from Ocean Township, New Jersey, who had recently transferred to the London office after a series of early professional experiences in the United States and Far East, and who had been almost randomly assigned to this engagement. But at the end of the project, he came to me and said, "This is what I want to do. If TeachFirst is going to happen, it's going to need an entrepreneurial leader, and I think that could be me." Of course, I said yes— little thinking that he would be able to make much of it, because it was just a fledgling untested idea. But thirteen years later, TeachFirst is now a significant feature of the British educational landscape with thousands of "alumni," including many who have gone on to make teaching their life's work, and others who are building successful careers in other walks of life.

Brett Wigdortz has been motivated throughout these thirteen years by an unbridled aspiration to do good—and to change the education system in his adopted country. Along the way, he has teamed up with Wendy Kopp, the celebrated founder of Teach for America, who was already pursuing a similar aspiration in the United States— and with distinctive success. Through their shared platform, Teach for All, they have taken around the world the concept that they had first developed independently, to expand educational opportunity "by recruiting each nation's most promising future leaders to commit two years to teach in high-need areas and become life-long leaders for educational excellence and equity."

Not everybody finds their calling to do good as early as Brett Wigdortz and Wendy Kopp—but they might find it later. Bill Drayton had trained as a lawyer, spent ten years at McKinsey, and served for four years in the Carter administration as assistant administrator of the Environmental Protection Agency (EPA). It was only then—in 1980—that Drayton launched Ashoka, the organization that he still leads, which over the past three decades and more has become the largest network of social entrepreneurs and what he calls "change-makers" around the world.

2. *How much do you want to do well?* Is creating wealth a primary route to meaning and happiness for you and your family? Is this a primary motivating force in your life? For most, the answer to this question is yes—at least to some degree. And for some this is an easy question—they want to make as much money as possible as quickly as they can. Clearly and definitively it's the aspiration of those who set up or work for a hedge fund or any kind of money management enterprise. There may be a public positioning statement about the value of liquid markets to the functioning of our free enterprise system—or something like that. But who's kidding whom? The aim is to make money—to do well in everything that is financial and material.

For others of us, the answer to this question is a little more nuanced and even ambiguous. We want to do well—for sure. But we don't necessarily define that purely in terms of money—we might be as interested in stature, prestige, and respect. And when it comes to doing well financially, our aspiration may be to "make enough money"—whatever that means to each of us. For some, it just means making enough that we don't have to think about money too much—so that it doesn't become our primary motivation. We don't necessarily want—or at least have any reasonable expectation—to become superrich, but we do want to support our families and achieve some measure of financial security. In the language of business, we are not "profit maximizers"—but we want to achieve decent financial returns on our investment in life.

The research suggests that as a society we have become inexorably more materialistic at an earlier and earlier stage. UCLA conducts an annual survey of college freshmen to understand what they think is important and how they want to live their lives. In 1966, 80 percent of freshmen said that they were strongly motivated to develop a meaningful philosophy of life; today less than half of them say that. In 1966, 42 percent considered becoming wealthy an important personal objective; by 1990 that number was 74 percent. Financial security, once seen as a middling priority, is now tied as students' top goal. Today, even students who are just getting started at college are willing to express the view that making money is a high priority.

The problem, though, is that this motivation often appears in conflict with the aspiration to do good—whether in government or in the nonprofit sector. That's the result of the widening gap between private-sector and public-sector compensation. To take one illustrative sample, fifty years ago the pay of presidential appointees in the federal government was, if less than lavish, in the same general league as that of a successful professional in the private sector. Today's salary for a leading government official (even a cabinet member), although several multiples of the average family income, is roughly equivalent to starting pay for graduates of top law or business schools and a small fraction of a law partner's or CEO's compensation. In part because of this widening disparity, as Jack Donahue and Richard Zeckhauser of the Kennedy School at Harvard wryly observe, "Government is impermeable, and business is sticky."

More significantly, income inequality has become a pervasive feature of modern society, and it creates complicated moral trade-offs for many of us. The most tangible constraint on building a broader life and career is often financial—the constraints of income and financial security. In the early years of our professional lives, we have to pay off student debts. Several recent US presidential candidates have made a campaign feature of the fact that they have only just paid off their student loans in their early forties—notably Barack Obama in 2008 and Marco Rubio in 2016.

That obligation, along with the demands of a growing family, persuade many to place making money high atop their hierarchy of motivations. And once you start on the road to substantial wealth, it can be hard to change paths—you get used to the money and the accompanying lifestyle, you have continuing financial obligations to support your children and sometimes older family members, and you're just not willing to scale back the life you've gotten used to.

3. *How much do you want to have power and influence in society?* For some of us the primary motivation is to make a difference—and we can only do that if we have some degree of executive authority, or at least pronounced influence over those who do. The pursuit of power and influence in society is most evident in those who move from business into government. After all, why else forgo income and privacy—especially to go into the rough-and-tumble world of electoral politics? But there have always been people willing to make this choice in pursuit of power and influence.

In their 2011 biography of Mitt Romney, published before he became the Republican nominee for president, Michael Kranish and Scott Helman of the *Boston Globe* recount this vignette from the 2008 election campaign: When a young girl asks Mitt Romney during a New Hampshire gathering what he would tell her class to make them want to be politicians, he deadpans at first, saying, "The answer is: nothing. Don't do it. Run as far as you can." But when he turns serious, he invokes the advice he says his father offered years ago: "Don't get into politics as your profession . . . get into the world of the real economy. And if some day you're able to make a contribution, do it." This is the essence of Romney's pitch, and it has been ever since his days as a deal maker in the 1980s and the 1990s. He's made his money—a mountain of it, in fact—and believes, as his father did, that he now owes a debt to the country that made a place for him.

The pursuit of power and influence is not confined to those who have made a lot of money. In the midst of a flourishing academic career, Michael Ignatieff, then a professor at Harvard's Kennedy School, was persuaded by the Liberal Party in his native Canada to return to his country of origin, run for political office, and ultimately lead his party into the 2011 parliamentary election—which he and they humiliatingly lost. I recount more of this story later—but for the moment, it's worth reflecting on one of the observations from *Fire and Ashes,* Ignatieff's narrative of his brief and thwarted political career. He writes, "I have always admired the intellectuals who have made the transition into politics: Mario Vargas Llosa in Peru, Vaclav Havel in the Czech Republic, Carlos Fuentes in Mexico. Politics was the big arena, *the place where you lived a life of significance.*"

4. *How much do you want to drive change?* Are you naturally impatient, frustrated by the shortcomings of what you see around you, determined to make it better—no matter what the obstacles or short-term sacrifices? If so, does your primary motivation come from moving the needle on a complex, multistakeholder problem—the more difficult and previously intractable the better? Are you unimpressed by traditional ways of doing things, quite content to break conventions, to develop new approaches, to build a movement for change?

David Burstein is a natural change agent—and he is only just in his thirties. The thing he wants to change and to advance is the political engagement and influence of his own generation—the so-called millennials. He has already used multiple mechanisms to advance this cause. He was the founder and executive director of the youth voter engagement organization Generation 18, he directed the documentary films *18 in '08* and *Up to Us,* and he has written a book whose title speaks for itself: *Fast Future—How the Millennial Generation Is Shaping Our World.* Now he has started another new organization, Run for America, the objective of which is to recruit, train, and support millennials who want to run for political office.

Burstein issues a rallying cry for the change agents in his own generation: "In reality and in our own perception, we are the most global generation. We can be in touch with our peers anywhere in the world and with just one click. Because Millennials have grown up in the fast future, we think of the world practically and pragmatically. The problems we face seem bigger and more global, and the solutions we envisage are both longer-term and more structural—and yet at the same time, more urgent than ever. We know we'll be working on solutions to these problems for our whole lives—and we also know that we need to start now."

5. *How much do you want to do interesting work?* Some of us are wary of declaring lofty aspirations for our lives, although we may nevertheless end up doing lofty things. Tim Geithner says of his career, "I didn't go into government to be a reforming crusader. I just wanted to do interesting and consequential work." Nevertheless, he ended up being president of the New York Federal Reserve and US secretary of the treasury in the midst of the worst economic crisis of our lifetime. That would probably qualify as "interesting and consequential work"—and maybe a bit more than that!

For many of us, the pursuit of "interesting and consequential work" is indeed our core aspiration. We don't have to be saving the planet or transforming an enterprise—but we do have to be doing something that we find inherently interesting and challenging, preferably in conditions that we find pleasant. Talking about an earlier stage of his career, Geithner describes his frustration at operating in different, and for him much less congenial, circumstances: "The IMF was a more formal and less fun place to work than the Treasury. The meetings were endless, with crushing bureaucracy, an intrusive and fractious board, an appalling amount of paper, and a lot of factional conflict among various fiefdoms."

This is a primary motivation for people like me—advisers and problem solvers who are attracted by the range and variety of challenges in that profession. We have butterfly minds, low boredom thresholds, and the question we ask most often is, "What's next?" We like to be challenged in new ways, to confront difficult and novel problems in high-paced work environments, to allow our brains to stretch—even to wander.

6. *How much do you want to have enjoyable colleagues?* How much of your other motivations would you sacrifice if it enabled you to work with people whom you like and respect? What kind of prominence do you place on the intrinsic quality of your colleagues and your relationships with them?

This is not such an unusual thought. How often do you hear somebody say, "I joined this organization because I really liked the people whom I met in the interviews," or "I was inspired by the leaders, who seemed very compelling"? Many of us make important career choices on that most personal of organizational attributes—the people with whom we will work.

And once we have joined, it is often the people who persuade us to stay—either indirectly or directly. After all, we have built up social capital, developed relationships, created a sense of mutual understanding and shared commitment. So, having committed to an organization once because of the chance to work with enjoyable colleagues, we recommit again and again for the same reason. We say to ourselves, "I'm going to stay because my colleagues have become my friends." That's certainly one of the principal reasons why I stayed with the same firm for such a long time.

7. *How much do you want to improve yourself?* What are you willing to do in order to make yourself a better professional and person? Would you take the time to go back to school to enhance your capabilities and credentials? Would you invest in self-directed learning, even if that provides some distraction from immediate priorities and opportunities? Many of us recognize that we have a lot to learn—and indeed that life is a continuous learning process. So we place a high priority on placing ourselves in settings where we can learn a lot.

8. *How much do you want to have a sustainable lifestyle?* How important is work to you? And how important are all the other aspects of your life—family, friends, extracurricular interests, causes and beliefs, and personal health? How do you decide which of these priorities should take precedence at any one time?

This eighth and final question stems from a conscious acknowledgement that our professional lives don't entirely define us and that our aspiration for breadth applies to our personal as well as our professional lives. It also reflects the fact that achieving balance and sustainability in our lives can be extremely difficult—especially in this "always on" world, where the demands of a successful professional career can be so intense.

NAVIGATING IN SEQUENCE

If we have all eight of these different motivations and if some of them conflict with others, how do we make choices among them—how indeed do we navigate our motivation map? Some people have a clear and specific answer to this question.

Peter Thiel is one of the most successful—and wealthy—Silicon Valley entrepreneurs and venture capitalists. In his book *Zero to One,* Thiel argues strongly for singularity of purpose and against multiplicity of motivations. In a section entitled "Can You Control Your Future?" he argues that the answer to the title question is yes—but only if you make a clear and explicit commitment to a *single* career objective. He calls this *definite optimism*—and explains that if you treat the future as something definite, it makes sense to understand it in advance and work to shape it. He adds, "A definite view . . . favors firm convictions. Instead of pursuing many-sided mediocrity and calling it 'well-roundedness,' a definite person determines the one best thing to do and then does it. Instead of working tirelessly to make herself indistinguishable, she strives to be great at something substantive—to be a monopoly of one."

Thiel has backed up his enthusiasm for definite optimists with action and money. In 2010, he created the Thiel Fellowship, which awards $100,000 to twenty people under twenty years old, in order to spur people to stay out of college and create their own ventures. In support of his fellowship, he argues that for many young people, college is the path to take only when they have no idea what to do with their lives. He says, "I feel I was personally very guilty of this; you don't know what to do with your life, so you get a college degree; you don't know what you're going to do with your college degree, so you get a graduate degree. In my case, it was law school, which is the classic thing one does when one has no idea what else to do. *I don't have any big regrets,* . . . but if I had to do it over I would try to think more about the future than I did at the time."

This is a definitive thesis. But Thiel's own life story so far is at least as instructive as the opinions he expresses. His success as a technology entrepreneur and investor is almost unmatched. He co-founded PayPal with Max Levchin and Elon Musk and served as its CEO. He also cofounded Palantir, of which he is chair. He was the first outside investor in Facebook, acquiring a 10.2 percent stake for $500,000, and now sits on the company's board. He also runs a series of investment firms, as well as a slew of philanthropies under the umbrella of the Thiel Foundation. He was ranked number four on the 2014 Forbes Midas List of the megarich, with a net worth of $2.2 billion.

But what did he do before all this? He studied twentieth-century philosophy as an undergraduate at Stanford University and then acquired a law degree from Stanford Law School. He clerked for a judge on the Eleventh Circuit of the US Court of Appeals, and from 1993 to 1996 he traded derivatives for the Credit Suisse Group—leaving to found Thiel Capital Management, a multistrategy fund, which led by 1998 to the creation of PayPal as a pioneer among online payment systems.

Peter Thiel is right. You do need to make a choice—even at the extreme to "choose the one best thing to do and do it." But do you really need to make that choice so early in life—even before college, even precluding the option of going to college; and does such a choice really need to last a lifetime? He certainly hasn't lived his own life that way. He went to college, even studying philosophy, which doesn't sound like an obvious route to commercial success. He studied and practiced law and investment management before he found the business opportunity that would transform his life. And even now—$2.2 billion to the good—he lives a life of breadth and diversity, continuing to make choices among a wide variety of options.

He may express skepticism about a broader life and career, but as far as his own life is concerned he has "no big regrets." He has navigated his motivation map in a way that works for him—sequentially, taking his life in stages. Thiel may not have known what he wanted to do when he went to college or when he chose to go to law school or even when he clerked for a judge or traded derivatives in the financial markets. But sooner rather than later, he figured it out. And there must be at least a possibility that he figured it out because of, rather than despite, the breadth and diversity of his educational and early career experiences—that he is one of those people who are successful because of their breadth, at least as much as because of their depth.

Navigating your motivation map is the work of a lifetime, not of a moment. The nature and weighting of your motivations change, because your circumstances change—and because you change. Sometimes you look back and you think, "What was I thinking when I made that choice? What was motivating me then?" Or even, "How could have I been so silly and stupid? If I had known then what I know now, I would never have made that choice." But when you reflect upon it, you realize that what motivated you then was different from what motivates you now. After all, you're on a journey, and you're doing your best to navigate along the way. You live your life in sequential chapters.

Jennifer Pryce has been navigating her motivation map in sequential chapters for the past twenty years. She is now chief executive of the Calvert Foundation—a nonprofit organization that connects individual investors with organizations that work on affordable housing, job creation, environmental protection, and other social interest objectives. Her route there has been complicated, winding, and messy, navigating her motivation map to make unusual choices and, when necessary, using her moral compass—her "inner voice"— to figure out what's the right thing to do next.

Pryce studied mechanical and biomedical engineering at Union College in upstate New York—as she observes, "a female in a male-dominated discipline." "I really enjoyed the quantitative elements of it—and it also taught me a general thought process. I enjoyed finding a methodical way to break down complex problems, and it was interesting work." That was her primary motivation at the time—to do interesting work. But things changed, and as she approached graduation she realized that the more immediate career opportunities weren't for her.

> I knew that following a traditional path to enter the engineering field, and refining those skills to become a professional in that area, just wouldn't make me happy. So when the Peace Corps came on campus in May—and I was graduating in June—that seemed like an intriguing opportunity.
>
> What was running through my mind was that I had never left the United States, I didn't speak another language—and that seemed a

shame. I wanted to explore and broaden my horizons, so I told them when I applied that I'd go anywhere in the world.

For the next two years, Pryce worked in the small African country of Gabon as a math teacher. "I was lonely at times, and it was very difficult—but it was extremely satisfying. I did learn a new language (French), and I also learned to live and function effectively in an unfamiliar environment. I also got to help people who needed help; and I learned how much I like working alongside other people." This was certainly a period when doing good and working with enjoyable colleagues were the top priorities.

But when she came back to the United States and to her hometown of New York, she was "a little lost." She took a long-term, albeit temporary, assignment with a socially responsible investing firm. That led her into the financial world—initially as an equity researcher and then after completing an MBA as an investment banker. As a researcher for about three years, she supported analysts in different industries like car manufacturing and semiconductor research. She joined Morgan Stanley as an investment banker, and the engineer in her loved the quantitative aspects of finance. She also liked being "at the center of the action on important deals and transactions." She moved to London and seemed set on a successful and lucrative career in banking, in which she would have considerable power and influence.

But after two years in London, she had had enough—she was struggling to feel in control of her life and health, not least because she discovered that she had a chronic medical condition. She recalls, "I had become ill and tired, and I really wasn't sure about my future in banking. I had to take care of myself—I just didn't feel that banking was going to make me happy for the long run; and I didn't want to feel regretful five years down the road. It was an unusual decision—I certainly gave up a lot of money. But I decided that's what I wanted to do, and I did it." What was so unusual was not just that she left a successful and lucrative career, but what she did next. She moved to the other side of the world, to Australia—and while she was there she trained to become a certified yoga instructor, turning something that she had always liked to do as a pastime into her job. She was putting her lifestyle at the top of her priority list—at least for a while.

"By this stage, I was clearly on a nontraditional path—I wasn't even on a career ladder, let alone moving up it seamlessly. But I did use the time to reflect and reprioritize; and when I came back to the United States, I found the professional arena that really suited me." She reflects more broadly on this unconventional approach: "I've learned in my life that by not being on a clear path and a clearly defined organizational ladder, it's not easy to know where to move on to. So I've taken sideways breaks to get clarity about what skill set or environment I want to go into next to be happy and excel. When you do that, it's difficult for mentors to help—you really have to understand and help yourself."

Back in New York, she found a role at the Public Theater—"to understand how nonprofits worked." She built connections in the burgeoning field of community- and socially directed finance (now drawing upon her investment banking experience) and became a director for the Nonprofit Finance Fund. "I moved to Washington and began leading efforts there to finance community facilities such as healthcare clinics, and it was a great time. I saw transformative outcomes working with governments and banks, structuring transactions that wouldn't normally make financial sense at all." She adds, "It was one of those moments in life where I enjoyed my work so much that it seemed easy. I had an understanding of how finance works, and enough understanding of government and nonprofits. I sat on the board of a charter school, and learned more about how it all fits together, the key patterns that I needed to apply."

And that led her to a series of roles at the Calvert Foundation—first as US portfolio manager, then as chief strategy officer, and now as president and CEO. In appointing her, the Calvert Board applauded her "decades of experience and innovative spirit." As Jennifer describes it:

> The Calvert Foundation is a unique asset in the financial universe—
> it goes beyond impact investing, giving investors an easy, accessible

way to invest their money with intentional social impact. We support the raising and delivery of capital that creates opportunities and equality for all. Our world needs ideas like Calvert Foundation to succeed.

For me personally, I seem to have found my perfect role. I am leading an organization with big goals and aspirations. I am working with colleagues that I like and respect. And I am applying my financial and business experience to the field of impact investing, which I think is so important. A lot of things have come together for me for this to be possible.

At various stages, Jennifer Pryce has prioritized interesting work, self-improvement, enjoyable colleagues, doing well, having power and influence, maintaining a sustainable lifestyle, driving change, and doing good. She has applied her "inner voice," her moral compass, to navigate her motivation map sequentially in a way that has made sense to her—and along the way she has built a broad life and career. She has exemplified the first dimension of the Mosaic Principle. And the reason why she has ultimately been able to resolve the long-term direction of her career—the reason why "things have now come together"—is that she has also found an intellectual thread to underpin the breadth of her life experiences.

4

ON BEING T-SHAPED
Defining an Intellectual Thread

The more we progress, the more we tend to progress. We advance not in arithmetical but in geometric progression. We draw compound interest in the whole capital of knowledge and virtue which has been accumulated since the dawn of time.

—Sir Arthur Conan Doyle, *The Stark Munro Letters*

IN THE SPRING OF 2010, just a few months after being appointed by President Obama, David Hayes faced the worst crisis ever confronted by somebody in his position. An explosion aboard BP's Deepwater Horizon oil drilling rig in the Gulf of Mexico had killed eleven crew members and ignited a seemingly inextinguishable fire. On April 22, Deepwater Horizon sank, leaving the well gushing at the seabed and causing the largest offshore oil spill in US history.

The oil flowed continuously from the ruptured well for more than three months, polluting the coastlines of Florida, Alabama, and Mississippi and causing extensive damage to marine and wildlife habitats and to the gulf's fishing and tourism industries. David Hayes recalls the horror of it all: "For 63 consecutive days the Deepwater Horizon story led the evening news on television. The cable news channels had a continuous graphic of oil spilling into the ocean—hour after hour, day after day. It seemed like it was never going to end."

As US deputy secretary of the interior Hayes was put in charge of coordinating the government's response. He had to work with the US Coast Guard (whose former head, Thad Allen, took operational command in the gulf); with the Department of Energy and several parts of the government; with BP, Transocean, and Halliburton—the owners, designers, and operators of the rig respectively—as well as with many other private-sector companies involved with the rig or rescue; and with Greenpeace and dozens of national and local pressure groups, including fishermen's volunteer associations and local parishes.

Nobody could really control a situation like this, but Hayes was better qualified than most to coordinate the response. Unusually, he had played his current role at the Department of the Interior once before—in the Clinton administration. So he had served for several years as the "chief operating officer" of the department that includes the National Park Service, the Fish and Wildlife Service, and the troubled Minerals Management Service, the agency that had been responsible for the regulation and oversight of offshore drilling. He knew all the levers to pull within his own department and across the federal government. But he could also draw upon more extensive experience than just his two terms in government. His life had been much broader than that.

Sitting in his office on the sixth floor of the Interior Department's art deco headquarters—a building that stands almost as a monument to President Theodore Roosevelt and his love of nature and the wilderness—Hayes recalls of the crisis, "It was definitely the most complex situation that I have ever had to deal with—but I did have an advantage. I had spent much of my career outside of government as an environmental lawyer and advocate, representing companies and individuals who were dealing with the government on regulatory issues. I knew many of the people involved in the Deepwater Horizon crisis personally, and I could stand in their shoes. That gave me something of a head start as we sought to get to grips with the crisis."

Either side of his two spells in government, Hayes had spent many years with the law firm Latham & Watkins, where he had headed up the Environment, Land and Resources Department. He had also held several similar positions in the nonprofit sector—as chair of the Environmental Law Institute, senior fellow for the World Wildlife Fund, a consulting professor for Stanford University's Woods Institute for the Environment, and vice chair of the American Board of Rivers. He had built a broad career that straddled government, business, and the nonprofit world—but it was all underpinned by his deep knowledge of environmental law and policy. He had developed a robust intellectual thread.

The same was true of his day-to-day counterpart in the White House—Carol Browner, who had been appointed by President Obama as his director of energy and climate change policy (often referred to as the "environmental czar"). Carol Browner had also been an environmental lawyer—although that wasn't the way she started her career. She actually started as a civil rights lawyer in Florida, representing battered women—which led her into the policy world. It seemed that every one of her clients ended up going back to her batterer. It made her realize she could not change the world case by case. She would need to try to change it policy by policy.

She first moved to Washington with Citizen Action, an activist group that drew her into the policy issues around the 1986 Superfund environmental legislation, and then into Congress as a legislative assistant first to Senator Lawton Chiles and then to Senator Al Gore. "I liked working with people to effect change in Congress. It was a very exciting time. Environmental and citizens groups had huge ability to affect debate at that time. Things were not as polarized as they are today. There was a lot more bipartisan policymaking."

Her opportunity to serve in the Clinton administration came almost by chance. She had gone back to Florida to work for the governor as secretary for the environment. In August 1992, Hurricane Andrew devastated South Florida. Bill Clinton was in the midst of his presidential campaign and came to visit—so Browner met him alongside the governor. When Clinton won, he invited her to Little Rock, and she interviewed for the EPA job—and got it.

Browner became the longest-serving administrator of the EPA, staying through all eight years of the Clinton presidency. During her tenure, she reorganized the agency's enforcement structure and oversaw two new programs designed to create flexible partnerships with industry as an alternative to traditional regulation. She also started a successful program to deal with contaminated lands in urban areas, and she took the lead within the administration in protecting existing laws and budgets and in designing a stringent set of air quality standards.

Browner's policy-making and enforcement programs at the EPA positioned her right in the middle between environmental activists (of which she had been one) and business leaders. "I decided to lean heavily upon the science and the scientists in EPA and beyond. My mantra to environmentalists was, 'I will give you the level of protection that the science dictates should be given to air and water.' I would say to the business community, 'I am not going to debate you on the science, but I am happy to give you the flexibility you need to meet the standards.' I would use the argument of legitimate competition to make my case: 'If you're leading a business that makes a half billion dollar investment to meet an air or water quality standard, and your competitor doesn't, that's not fair. I want that regulation there, so that you are both forced to comply—after all, you're both selling to the same utility market.'"

Her time at the EPA was far from tranquil as the political environment in Washington grew more and more contentious. "Newt Gingrich came after us as Speaker of the House. Under the rubric of the Contract for America, we were the proximate cause of government shutdown. I had to build an argument for why you want and need an EPA—even while the White House was in something of a defensive crouch."

During the Bush years, Carol became a founding member of the Albright Group, a consulting firm focused on commercial diplomacy—as well as serving on several boards and think tanks focused on environmental issues. She went back into government in 2009, leading the Obama administration's initial efforts to formulate a comprehensive energy and climate change program.

Alongside David Hayes, Carol Browner brought to government—and specifically to the Deepwater Horizon crisis—a distinctly broad range of experience, underpinned by a directly relevant intellectual thread in environmental law and policy. She herself observes why this matters: "I have this interesting experience of having affected environmental legislation as a civic activist, having written environmental legislation as congressional staff, and having worked within the executive branch to help implement the environmental laws that I had actually written—and now advising companies on how to work effectively within them. I have been able to see things from the activist side, the legislative side, the administrative side, and the business side. I view them as all part of the environmental movement that we have built—and we have never needed it more than today."

Taking such a broad approach to building the environmental movement has challenged some of the relationships that she holds dear. "When I went from social change to government, I came under a lot of pressure from friends who questioned my motives. I had to say, 'I still believe in the same things; but I am trying to figure out how to do them in a different context.' The tools that I had at my disposal in government were just different from what I had had as activist. This was the hardest thing to explain—'I am still the same person, but I am doing what I believe in in a different way.'"

After a long and tortuous summer, David Hayes and Carol Browner ultimately coordinated a successful program to cap the oil spill, dissipate much of the oil, painstakingly restore the gulf to something approximating its previous state, and initiate a Spill Response Fund to compensate victims. Gradually, Hayes was able to refocus some of his energies away from the crisis, and back to the twenty-three agencies and 70,000 government employees for whom he was responsible. As he reflects upon the Deepwater Horizon crisis, he notes, "It certainly helped that I had relatively broad experience in the business and nonprofit sectors, as well as in government—and that I had an intellectual grasp of the environmental arena. It gave me a leg up in understanding their issues and incentives, and in helping the other interested parties achieve their objectives at the same time as mine."

THE T-SHAPED APPROACH

This book aims to capture and convey the virtues of breadth in building a life and career. But this should not be taken as a recipe for "randomness," for the professional dilettante, for being "jack-of-all-trades and master of none." You are much more likely to build a broader life and career if you also build a robust intellectual thread—a focused body of knowledge and experience that provides leverage and relevance to your breadth. That's why defining an intellectual thread is the second dimension of the Mosaic Principle.

Nowadays, whenever I am asked the question, "Should I be broad or deep?" or "Should I be a generalist or a specialist?" my answer is yes. I don't mean to be flip or disrespectful—it's just that I have come to believe that this is not really a meaningful question. More specifically, it is not an either/or question—it is a both/and requirement for success. The real question is, How can I be a broad specialist or a deep generalist? How can I be a successful hybrid between breadth and depth? And I ask a question in response: "What is your intellectual thread?" Or, to put the question more bluntly, "Why would anybody call you to help them? What is it you know better than most—maybe better than anybody?"

The dilemma that so many of us feel between breadth and depth of intellectual development goes back a long way. It was most vividly expressed—and rendered animate—by the philosopher Isaiah Berlin in *The Hedgehog and the Fox*. This famous essay is actually a reflection upon the novelist Leo Tolstoy and his philosophy of history, the subject of the epilogue to *War and Peace*. But since its publication in 1951, *The Hedgehog and the Fox* has been interpreted as a fundamental distinction between human beings who are fascinated by the infinite variety of things and those who relate to a central, all-embracing system—between the way of the far-ranging generalist and the way of the concentrated specialist, between breadth and depth.

The theme of the essay is set by the Greek aphorism, preserved in a fragment from the poet Archilocus: "The fox knows many things, but the hedgehog knows one big thing." Berlin expands upon this simple distinction to create a model of humankind:

> There exists a great chasm between those, on one side, who relate everything to a single central vision, one system, less or more coherent or articulate, in terms of which they understand, think and feel—a single, organizing principle in terms of which alone all that they are or say has significance—and on the other side, those who pursue many ends, often unrelated and even contradictory, connected, if at all, only in some de facto way, for some psychological or physiological cause, related to no moral or aesthetic principle.
>
> These last (foxes) lead lives, perform acts and entertain ideas that are centrifugal rather than centripetal, seizing upon the essence of a vast variety of experiences and objects.

They can do so because they feel no compunction to fit their varied ideas and experiences into "one unchanging, all-embracing, sometimes self-contradictory and incomplete, at times fanatical, unitary inner vision." Berlin uses another more humanist set of terms to ask whether Tolstoy belongs to the first category or the second—is he a monist or a pluralist, is his vision of one or of many, is he of a single substance or compounded of heterogeneous elements?

Many have asked whether Berlin himself favored the hedgehog over the fox. In a 1991 interview he tried to answer that question: "I've got no either envy of or obsession by or terrible interest in people with a single vision; on the contrary, I think them very grand, important geniuses, but dangerous. Human desire for certainty is unshakeable, incorrigible, highly dangerous." He did, however, have one big idea of his own—his own personal hedgehog—and it was paradoxical: beware of big ideas, especially when they fall into the hands of political leaders.

Berlin's predilection to categorize people into two extremes has elicited some ironic philosophical humor. The British philosopher

Bryan Magee said of him, "Berlin loved categorizing individuals in the spirit of a party game. . . . [M]ost often there were two categories and two alone: either you were, when it came right down to it, a conservative or a radical, shall we say; or you were either a hedgehog or a fox; or you were either a bishop or a bookmaker—he was inexhaustibly fertile in his 'two sorts of' distinctions. It gave rise to a joke against him: 'The world is divided into two sorts of people: those who think the world is divided into two sorts of people and those who don't.'"

But, of course, the world is not really divided into two sorts of people—and few of us are at one extreme or another. Most of us lie somewhere on a spectrum between the two extremes of almost any defining characteristic. For instance, as Susan Cain shows in *Quiet*, few of us are absolute introverts or extroverts. Many of us are somewhere in between—we are *ambiverts.* In the same vein, Adam Grant in *Give and Take* shows that many of the most successful people are neither absolute givers nor takers. They are what he calls "otherish givers"—they adopt a giving mind-set, but they still take care to look after their own interests.

The dichotomy between breadth and depth works in much the same way. For most of us it is neither necessary, nor wise, nor even possible to operate exclusively at either extreme—to be completely deep or completely broad. We are much better advised to occupy a middle ground that encompasses the most valuable elements of both breadth and depth. Although Isaiah Berlin's essay is an unparalleled portrait of human dividedness, he suggests that all of us should have elements of both fox and hedgehog within us. We are best advised to act as "hybrid engines"—occupying a position somewhere between the two extremes. Fortunately, there is a proven model of how to be both broad and deep, and it is represented by Figure 4.1.

The best model for success in work and life is the T-Shaped Approach. The *T* is a visual metaphor for a hybrid of breadth and depth—a broad generalist with a deep intellectual thread. The vertical stroke of the *T* represents a depth of skill or expertise—a specific intellectual thread that is typically gained through years of study and

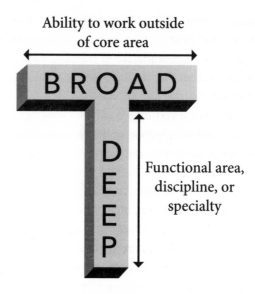

FIGURE 4.1. The T-Shaped Approach

practical experience. David Hayes and Carol Browner have just such an intellectual thread because of their decades of work in the energy and environment arena. They have both gained a theoretical and practical understanding of that field—the science, the law, the economics, the market dynamics, the politics, and the motivation of the key players. This depth of specific experience has enabled them to grapple with the complex legal and policy issues that typically arise in an environmental crisis like Deepwater Horizon.

But this kind of specific depth—the vertical stroke of the *T*—is often not enough to solve complex problems and to enable people to flourish in their lives and their careers. That is where the horizontal stroke of the *T* comes in. It represents the breadth and range of experience and perspective that enable and reinforce collaboration across different arenas. It reflects the empathy that enables people to imagine a complex problem from a completely different perspective—to stand in somebody else's shoes, as David Hayes and Carol Browner did with Deepwater Horizon. They could draw upon the experience they had gained from addressing complex environmental issues in the private and nonprofit sectors as well as in government. Because of that experience, they understood intuitively the perspectives of the people with whom they were dealing and could create solutions that met their needs.

If you have only the vertical bar of the *T*—the deep subject-matter expertise—you will be imprisoned by the narrowness of your experience and perspective. You will see an issue or a problem through a specific lens and find it difficult to understand what is informing and motivating your counterparts from other walks of life. But if you only have the horizontal bar of the *T,* you will struggle to make your way in the world. Nobody will call you for your expertise, because you will have none. You will lack the specific skills and knowledge to understand complex technical and operational problems and know how to address them. You will be overly dependent upon people with greater subject-matter depth, who may have the capacity to pull the wool over your eyes. That was what the technical specialists did in bringing Enron to its knees and later in creating the conditions for the global financial crisis.

In his book *Originals,* Adam Grant explains another benefit of mixing depth and breadth of expertise within a T-Shaped Approach—it is the best way of enabling creativity and entrepreneurial risk taking within a balanced risk portfolio: "Having a sense of security in one realm gives us the freedom to be original in another." He quotes Polaroid founder Edwin Land, who observed, "No person could possibly be original in one area unless he were possessed of the emotional and social stability that comes from fixed attitudes in all areas other than the one in which he is being original." Grant adds that successful innovators and entrepreneurs "take extreme risks in one arena and offset them with extreme caution in another."

BUILDING AN INTELLECTUAL THREAD

The T-Shaped Approach marries a broad, multidimensional mind-set with a sustained commitment to building an intellectual thread—an

area of subject-matter expertise. This blend of breadth and depth ac-
cumulates over time as a function of intellectual study and practical
experience. The combination can provide the hybrid fuel to drive a
long and distinguished career and to make a profound impact in a
variety of arenas.

That is exactly what has happened for Roger Sant. Now in his
mideighties, Sant has had a broad and distinguished career in government, business, and the nonprofit world. But he is distinctive
not just for the length and breadth of his career. Over more than six
decades, he has built an intellectual thread in energy efficiency and
environmental conservation that has enabled him to formulate policy, create and develop a successful company, and guide several nonprofit enterprises. He has come to embody the T-Shaped Approach.

I first met Roger Sant at a Board of Regents meeting for the
Smithsonian Institution—the umbrella organization that oversees
nineteen significant national museums and research establishments,
most of them located in and around Washington, DC—for whom we
were doing a strategic review. Being vice chair of the overall Smithsonian board was one of his many roles in the nonprofit world. But
as soon I spoke to him it was clear that his real passion lay in his role
as chair of the Smithsonian Museum of Natural History—the huge
facility on the National Mall committed to the preservation and protection of our environment and its many species.

Sant started to build his intellectual thread early in his career—
shortly after graduating from Harvard Business School and a string
of short-lived jobs in finance. He moved to Washington for a two-
year stint at the Federal Energy Administration—a then-unheralded
backwater of government, which gained greater prominence in the
teeth of the persistent energy crises of the 1970s—before being absorbed into the newly created Department of Energy by President
Carter. He recalls, "My motive was not just to spend some time in
government. I thought that the environmental problem and the related energy problem were very serious issues in which I wanted to
immerse myself. I thought that this was a good way of doing it—and
fortunately I got in at a time when they were really inventing policy,

so it was probably a better experience than anything else I could have done."

While in government, he had what he still describes as an "aha moment"—the "energy service notion" that what people would want was the "least-cost solution" that was relevant to their needs, irrespective of the precise source of that energy. Initially on leaving government, Sant created a think tank focused on how to shift energy investment to bring about more energy efficiency—but soon afterward he and his partner founded Applied Energy Services (now called the AES Corporation). "I remember writing an article for the *Harvard Business Review,* saying this is the way energy will be bought and sold in the future. We would pay very little attention to what kind of fuel it was and pay more attention to the efficiency and effectiveness of the system provider."

In reality, Sant acknowledges that the market never completely bought into his "aha" revelation—primarily because the regulatory structure remained siloed between different sources of energy. But by that time, "I decided my principal responsibility was to make the company successful under whatever the rules were." And he did. From an initial funding base of $1.1 million raised from family and friends, by 1988 AES was the largest independent power producer in the United States—and soon it was expanding internationally, buying up previously nationalized power plants and utilities. Sant confesses to some disappointment and regret: "So the company goes from all that high-minded doing good service for mankind to being a kilowatt hours provider. We did try to be the cleanest kilowatt hours provider—but we soon recognized that the only market of significance was selling kilowatt hours; and once we went abroad, trying to be the lowest cost producer."

AES was not an entirely smooth ride for Sant, especially after he formally retired from the company. When the collapse of Enron roiled the energy services market, AES itself faced the risk of collapse, and Sant came back from retirement to lead the company's revival. But by this time, his primary focus was—and has remained—on his nonprofit initiatives, most of which relate to the theme of energy efficiency and environmental conservation. He recalls, "I started with a little organization: the Environmental and Energy Study Institute—a little policy shop supplying information to Congress. At that time, my interest was in energy and urban systems; but as I got into it, I realized that I cared much more about nature, about what we now call biodiversity. So I transferred my attention to the World Resources Institute, which was a little broader focused—the first place I got exposed to the climate change debate; and then to the World Wildlife Fund, which was entirely focused on nature conservancy."

As chair of the World Wildlife Fund in the United States, he sought to apply the business principle of prioritization—although he consciously didn't call it that. "The most excited I ever got at the WWF was when the science guys started to focus and prioritize. They came up with an idea that just thrilled me—The Global 200. They looked around the world and said—'here are the 200 places in the world most important for us to focus on if we are to maintain the diversity of the planet as we know it—the best examples of ecosystems that people can come up with.' I just got blown away by it."

During his time at the WWF, and later the Smithsonian, Sant also pushed for metrics of success and failure. "It was very hard to know what kind of impact we were having—and for some reason, no one had ever asked! I think there's a clear explanation—most of us are trained not to achieve a goal, but rather to be specialists as biologists or botanists. But as hard as it was, we ultimately got widespread agreement that we could measure something on a scale of 1–10 on its relative health. It was hard, but as it turned out—not impossible."

THE POWER OF THE T-SHAPED APPROACH

As I argued in Chapter 2, the 2008 financial crisis was caused by deep specialists, aided and abetted by those who failed to supervise and regulate their activities. But the global rescue and recovery was led by a small band of people who individually and collectively exhibited the T-Shaped Approach—broad and diverse experience underpinned by a deep intellectual thread. By applying their hybrid blend of breadth and depth, they were able to steer the global economy away from the worst-case scenarios of catastrophic financial meltdown.

Initially the de facto leader of this group was Hank Paulson, who as President Bush's secretary of the treasury came back to Washington thirty years after he had begun his career as a liaison officer between the Treasury and Commerce Departments during the Nixon administration. In the intervening years, he had risen up the ranks at Goldman Sachs, becoming CEO from 1998 to 2006. When he took up his post at Treasury, he wryly observed that the global economy seemed in strong shape and he thought he would have a quiet time. But in reality he knew that there were warning signs, and early on told Treasury staff that it was "time to prepare for a financial system challenge."

The intensity of the financial crisis was such that there was little time to pause and reflect—decisions had to be made in real time and on the basis of intuition. But that was really the test of Paulson's intellectual thread in financial systems—that he was able to apply an intuitive frame of mind. The behavioral economist Daniel Kahnemann refers to this as "System 1" thinking—the kind of instinctive decisions you make when you don't have the time or need to pause and reflect. This was a full-blown crisis, and in crises there is rarely the luxury of more reflective and logical "System 2" thinking. As Paulson notes, "In a crisis, you have to weigh the cost of inaction against doing something that you know is imperfect." He adds, "We won't have a market left to protect if we don't take action"—referring to the government "bailouts" of the financial and automotive industries that underpinned the eventual recovery.

Paulson's intellectual thread was not abstract, based upon book learning; it was deeply practical and experiential. He had traded in the markets that were now under scrutiny, led one of the financial institutions that was now being recapitalized and placed under intensified regulations, and orchestrated large commitments across the investment spectrum as equity, debt, and derivative markets battled for survival. His T-Shaped Approach was then sustained by his successor as treasury secretary, Tim Geithner, who also had deep practical experience gained from previous financial crises in the Clinton administration and his time as president of the New York Fed—as well as by Ben Bernanke at the Federal Reserve and Christine Romer at the Council of Economic Advisors, both of them profoundly knowledgeable academics who had studied the Great Depression of 1929.

But the T-Shaped Approach might perhaps best be exemplified by two younger people who sequentially held the position of undersecretary of the treasury for international affairs—first David McCormick in the Bush administration, and then Lael Brainard in the Obama administration.

McCormick grew up in Pittsburgh in a middle-class family, graduated from West Point with a degree in mechanical engineering, became an army officer, and served in the first Gulf War. He worked briefly in the State Department and then completed a PhD at Princeton. He spent a brief time in consulting and then left to set up one Internet start-up, which he sold to another and became chief executive of the combined business, and then served for all eight years of the Bush administration in both the White House and Treasury.

McCormick's breadth of experience was evident from his spells in the military, academia, the commercial world—including the world of entrepreneurial start-ups—and in his extended government service. Taken together this range of experience constituted a robust horizontal stroke to his *T*. But of equal significance was his investment in building an intellectual thread in international economics— gained through his PhD in international relations, his commercial experience in running an international business, and his policy experience across government. Indeed he ascribes his initial interest in what he calls "international things" to his time abroad in the army— stationed in Saudi Arabia, as one of the first units into Iraq during the first Gulf War. So by the time of the financial crisis, the vertical stroke of his *T* was quite as pronounced as the horizontal.

The opportunity to apply and extend his intellectual thread came early in the Bush administration. He recalls, "The president's international economics guy resigned, and so I interviewed for the job, and to my surprise I got it. I moved from five concentric circles away from the president to working directly for the president, preparing the summit meetings on international economic issues with other heads of government." He spent two years as the White House's international economics "sherpa"—which also involved spending a lot of time with Hank Paulson at Treasury, and in 2006 Paulson asked him to take the treasury undersecretary role.

There he found himself as part of a Republican administration that was sanctioning and executing aggressive government intervention in private markets and enterprises. "Like all of us handling the crisis," he notes, "I was dealing with uncharted territory. So I tried to understand and make thoughtful decisions—not partisan decisions—but what-you-think-are-right decisions."

He is quick to point out that his T-Shaped experience did not qualify him to make all the decisions on his own. He recalls of that time, "At the Treasury and White House, there's this large and incredibly talented staff of people who have spent their lives on these issues. I didn't view it as my job to become the expert on all the most detailed policy issues; but I did aspire to being the convener, the sorter, and ultimately the recommender. In some cases I would be the decider—but I was never the person who was going to know more than the experts knew. My job was to get the right measure of intellectual challenge and debate around the choices. I sought to apply my professional background of seeing the problem at multiple levels, trying to be fact-based and logical, so that you can sort through all the choices and manage all the key stakeholders."

While the full extent of the financial crisis continued to reveal itself, the Bush administration transitioned over to the Obama administration in January 2009—and David McCormick handed over the Treasury's international brief to Lael Brainard. It was a relatively smooth transition, in part because Brainard had taken a very similar T-Shaped Approach to her career—albeit with more time spent in academic study.

After gaining an MS and PhD in economics from Harvard University—interrupted by a short period in management consulting—Brainard had been an associate professor of applied economics at MIT, before joining the Clinton administration in 1996 as deputy national economic adviser to the president. During the Bush years from 2001 to 2009, she worked at the Brookings Institution in Washington, where she was the founding director of the Global Economy and Development Program—before returning to the Treasury in a role that now included being the US representative to the G20 finance deputies and the newly created Financial Stability Board.

Brainard has consciously invested in building her intellectual thread—in the vertical stroke of the *T*. She observes, "I do think it helps to form intellectual foundations, rather than just go with the flow. That is why my time at Brookings was so important to me. You go out of government for a few years, and try to absorb what you have just learned and all the decisions you were party to." She adds, "I often find that when I am negotiating with my international counterparts, you can really tell which ones have an intellectual foundation, and which don't. Do they have a conceptual model of how financial markets function, and how fiscal and monetary policies interact with financial markets?"

She traces aspects of her intellectual thread way back: "When I was a young management consultant, I got to know how financial institutions operate across borders, and how they reacted to regulatory reforms. I was in Mexico recently for a G20 deputies meeting, and I was telling my Mexican counterpart that back in 1985 when I was a junior consultant I spent a lot of time in Mexico City helping a multinational financial institution that had had its assets frozen in their financial crisis at the time, and I came back later when I was at the White House as they went through another disturbance."

She particularly draws upon her experience of working with and for financial institutions: It helped that she had worked for an international firm, and that so many of her clients were multinational corporations. It made her understand the risks of "regulatory arbitrage"—that in response to the economic crisis, Washington could do one set of reforms, London would do a different set of reforms, Frankfurt and Paris would do theirs, and Singapore something completely different. Having worked for different kinds of financial institutions, she had seen that they're going to put a lot of resources into understanding the regulatory landscape, they're going to change their business models, and they're going to reallocate according to the incentives. It helped her to know all this, and she found it quite motivating when trying to negotiate level playing fields.

Lael Brainard believes strongly in the need for government to have people with practical experience of the arenas in which they're trying to set policy and impose regulatory restrictions: "We're going through a massive structural transformation in the U.S. financial sector right now—in collaboration with our international counterparts. It would be crazy to believe that we could get that right without some people being able to say with authority, 'Well, this is how you're going to behave if you're a trader; if you're CEO of a financial institution, this is what you're going to be thinking about.' You have got to have that perspective—just as when we were sanctioning investments in auto companies, we needed the perspectives of people who had made those kinds of investments in the private equity arena." In essence, she believes, we have to find a way to make the revolving-door concept work—practically and ethically.

Hank Paulson, Tim Geithner, David McCormick, and Lael Brainard all took a T-Shaped Approach to their professional careers and applied that approach in guiding the US government's response to the financial crisis. But one of their counterparts in Canada could make an even bolder claim—that he applied a T-Shaped Approach that helped his country avoid the financial crisis altogether.

Mark Carney, then the governor of the Bank of Canada, and now governor of the Bank of England, is one of a select group of economic regulators who transcend national boundaries because of the breadth of his experience and the depth of his expertise—and specifically because of his T-Shaped Approach. In his additional role as chair of the G20 Financial Stability Board, he applies his intellectual thread to address financial systemic risk wherever it occurs around the world.

Carney was born in Fort Smith, Northwest Territories. His father was a high school principal there and later a professor at the University of Alberta in Edmonton. Despite his Canadian roots, Carney went to Harvard University for his undergraduate studies in economics, and then to Oxford where he gained an MPhil and PhD for his thesis on the dynamic advantages of competition. He spent thirteen years with Goldman Sachs in its London, New York, and Toronto offices. His progressively more senior roles included cohead of sovereign risk; executive director, emerging debt capital markets; and managing director, investment banking. He worked on South Africa's postapartheid venture into international bond markets and on Goldman's response to the 1998 Russian financial crisis.

Always attracted to the policy environment, he left Goldman in 2004 first to become deputy governor of the Bank of Canada and then was seconded to become senior associate deputy minister and G7 deputy at the Canadian Department of Finance. He explained at the time, "I think you do have an obligation of citizenship to do something, some time, in the policy arena." At the Department of Finance, he led the government's $3.1 billion sale of its 19 percent stake in oil company Petro Canada, described by the finance minister as the "single most profitable transaction of its kind in Canadian experience." This largely reflected the distinctive arrangements that Carney orchestrated—floating the shares to the global financial market, while ensuring that nobody, especially no foreign interest, would be able to control more than 20 percent of the oil distributor's ownership rights.

While still at the Department of Finance, Carney laid the foundations for Canada's distinctive approach to the impending global economic crisis. The summer of 2007 saw early signs of slowdown in the market for asset-backed commercial paper (ABCP), a short-term debt instrument that is used by financial institutions to fund operations and other investments—leaving the holders of the $30 billion in ABCP notes stuck in limbo. The *Toronto Globe & Mail* observed that "the freeze-up hit hundreds of companies, pension plans, governments and more than 2,000 retail investors, many of whom had no idea that the ABCP they owned was stuffed not with plain vanilla debt, but with risky derivatives that lost most of their value in ensuing months."

In a marker of what was to come, Carney persuaded the government to intervene and provide a financial guarantee on these debt instruments so that they still had value and could be traded. This restructuring created a market for the paper, allowing owners who needed cash immediately to sell, though anyone who did would have to take a loss. Investors who bought the paper in the days after the restructuring profited handsomely as the fear came out of the market.

Carney was appointed as governor of the Bank of Canada in November 2007—serving as adviser to retiring governor David Dodge before formally assuming the role in February 2008 as the global financial crisis loomed. Relative to its Western peers, Ottawa owed less money per capita than any other G8 country, and none of its banks were insolvent. But markets were turbulent and no national economy was safe.

The defining act of his tenure as governor came very early on—in March 2008 when the Bank of Canada decided to cut the overnight rate by 50 basis points only months after he took office. The European Central Bank went in the opposite direction in July 2008 when it approved a rate increase, but Carney anticipated that the leveraged-loan crisis would trigger global contagion. When policy rates in Canada hit the effective lower bound (i.e., went as low as they could), the central bank came up with a new monetary tool: the "conditional commitment" announced in April 2009 to hold the policy rate for at least one year, in a boost to domestic credit conditions and market confidence. Ben Bernanke and the US Federal Reserve followed the same approach shortly afterward.

Meanwhile, Canadian output and employment began to recover from mid-2009, partly thanks to this monetary stimulus. The Canadian economy outperformed those of its G7 peers, and Canada was the first G7 nation to have both its gross domestic product and employment recover to precrisis levels. Late in 2009, *Newsweek* wrote, "Canada has done more than survive this financial crisis. The country is positively thriving in it. Canadian banks are well capitalized and poised to take advantage of opportunities that American and European banks cannot seize."

In November 2011 Carney was named chair of the Financial Stability Board, an international body created by the G20 to monitor and make recommendations about the global financial system. The board on Carney's watch initiated the designation of "systemically important financial institutions" and the guidance that they should face a higher regulatory burden than others—notably an additional capital buffer to ensure they had sufficient cash on hand under any conceivable scenario. Under attack for this approach—notably from Jamie Dimon, the CEO of JP Morgan—Carney responded that "the sad experience of the past few years shows that there is ample scope to improve the efficiency and resilience of the global financial system. By clarity of purpose and resolute implementation, we can do so."

On November 26, 2012, the British chancellor of the exchequer George Osborne announced the appointment of Mark Carney as the next governor of the Bank of England, succeeding Sir Mervyn King. It turned out that Osborne had been wooing him for some time—sounding him out in a Japanese restaurant on the sidelines of the G20 meeting of finance ministers in Mexico City a year earlier. He was the first non-Briton to be appointed to the role since the bank was established in 1694—and he took over at a time when the bank's powers were being expanded, including the power to set bank capital requirements. Despite Britain's characteristic skepticism about foreigners in positions of influence, there was no serious opposition to his appointment—rather like the feeling among Premier League soccer teams that the most important thing is to get the best people wherever in the world they come from (and whatever they cost)—and Carney was undoubtedly one of the best players.

Mark Carney's defining characteristic is his deep intellectual thread in financial systems and regulation—comparable to that of Hank Paulson and some of the other policy makers and regulators who dug the world out of the financial crisis. But he is just as notable for the breadth of his experience and perspective across sectors and countries—and the combination exemplifies the power of the T-Shaped Approach. This is reinforced by his socially empathetic approach to working with a variety of stakeholders. In January 2014, the *Financial Times* reported, "The change of style under the Bank of England's governor Mark Carney was on full display this week in

Davos. Although his predecessor Lord King spurned the Swiss gathering of billionaires, bankers and business people, Mark Carney used the World Economic Forum to full effect, giving views on topics ranging from Scottish independence to Bitcoins and bank bonuses in panel sessions and interviews."

FINDING YOUR INTELLECTUAL THREAD

The most common refrain of university commencement speakers is "follow your passion." Most famously, in his speech to Stanford University's graduating class in 2005, Steve Jobs advised, "You can't connect the dots [of your life] looking forward; you can only connect them looking backwards. So you have to trust that the dots will somehow connect in your future. You have to trust in something—your gut, destiny, life, karma, whatever. This approach has never let me down, and it has made all the difference in my life."

He went on, "You've got to find what you love. And that is true for your work as it is for your lovers. Your work is going to fill a large part of your life, and the only way to be satisfied is to do what you believe is great work. And the only way to do great work is to love what you do. If you haven't found it, keep looking. Don't settle. As with all matters of the heart, you'll know it when you find it. As with all matters of the heart, it just keeps getting better as the years roll along. So keep looking until you find it. Don't settle."

Jobs's speech inspired that class of graduating Stanford students and no doubt countless graduates elsewhere ever since—not to mention many people like me who had graduated decades earlier. But there is a challenge embedded in this masterpiece of inspiration: Just how do you find this passion, "the work you love to do"? How do you find your intellectual thread?

It's an especially challenging question for people—and I am one—who are instinctively drawn to the horizontal breadth-oriented stroke of the *T,* but who find the vertical stroke, the intellectual thread, harder to identify. We are the people whose intuitive approach to work and life is "please don't make me choose!" We're much more likely to pursue a slew of interests than to narrow our options to a single one. We typically exhibit some or all of the following dominant characteristics: the capacity to become excited by many things at once, often accompanied by difficulty choosing; a love of new challenges; once challenges are mastered, a tendency to become easily bored; a fear of being imprisoned in the same career or activity for life; a pattern of quick, sometimes unsatisfying flings with many pastimes; and career successes interspersed with periods of boredom or restlessness.

Eric Lander exhibited all these tendencies in his initially meandering journey to the discovery of his intellectual thread. Lander was raised by his mother in Flatlands, a working-class neighborhood in Brooklyn. His big early break was to be accepted by the elite Stuyvesant High School in Manhattan, where he joined the math team and loved it. He was chosen for the American team in the 1974 Mathematics Olympiad where the United States placed second behind the Soviet Union and where his roommate Paul Zeitz noted, "He was outgoing. He was, compared to the rest of us, very ambitious. He was enthusiastic about everything. And he had real charisma." They all agreed, he was the only one they could imagine being a US senator one day.

He was evidently a gifted mathematician—earning an Oxford PhD in record time, two years. But there was a problem—he couldn't imagine spending the rest of his life doing it. His PhD was in a subfield of pure mathematics so esoteric and specialized that, as he observes, "even if someone gets a great result, it can be appreciated by only a few dozen people in the entire world. . . . I began to appreciate that the career of a mathematician is rather monastic," he said. "Even though mathematics was beautiful and I loved it, I wasn't a very good monk." So he talked his way into a teaching program in managerial economics at Harvard Business School, which he was learning slightly ahead of his students. Initially, that seemed more practical than pure mathematics—but it soon turned out to be another field that didn't hold his attention for too long.

His innate scientific curiosity led him to start hanging around biology labs—and specifically around Robert Horvitz's worm genetics lab at MIT. Through a mutual friend, he was introduced to Dr. David Botstein, then a professor at MIT, who was looking for somebody who knew mathematics to take on a project involving traits like high blood pressure that were associated with multiple genes. As Botstein recalls, he was told, "There's this fellow, Lander, at Harvard Business School who wants to do something with biology." When they met, they "went to the whiteboard, and started arguing."

Soon Lander was immersing himself in the problems of mapping human disease genes—at a time when, as Dr. Botstein recalls, "talk of sequencing the human genome was beginning to gain traction." Lander wanted to know whether there was use for a mathematician in biology; when assured there was, he quit his business school job and found an assistant professorship at MIT's Institute for Biomedical Research. He started attending public debates on human genomics and quickly made his mark. He notes, "It's very easy to be an expert in a new field where there are no experts. All you have to do is raise your hand."

Despite his circuitous route to this point, Lander was still only thirty—an assistant professor in biomedicine and the recipient of a MacArthur Foundation grant. He was starting to become a central figure in the effort to sequence the genome. He combined his mathematics with the biology and chemistry that he'd learned hanging out in the labs. And he added insights about industrial organization from his business school days to streamline the effort and control costs. What he got from the whole experience was the sense of collaboration: "Something magical had happened. People were coming together and taking on really bold problems."

The "something magical" ultimately turned into the Human Genome Project—a fifteen-year program to map and sequence the genome. Along the way, Lander and his team investigated the distinguishing features of each genome by comparative analysis, they profiled the different genetic variations in the human population and explored how they affected our susceptibility to specific diseases, and they conducted the most comprehensive analysis to date of the genetic mutations underlying cancer.

In 2002, Lander approached the presidents of Harvard and MIT and proposed a permanent institute to perpetuate the cross-disciplinary approach that the human genomics project had pioneered. With their joint backing and a sizable gift from the Broad Foundation, he created an institute—located in a modern, custom-designed building near the main MIT campus—that today has about 1,800 collaborating scientists.

The evocative name of the Broad Institute of Harvard and MIT, of which Eric Lander is the founding director, is entirely coincidental—because it principally denotes the far-sighted philanthropy of Eli and Edyth Broad (pronounced "Brode"). But Lander and his team have embraced the accidental play on words, and the broad perspective of the T-Shaped Approach has become the de facto defining concept of the institute. The institute's website includes a section called the *Broad-Minded Blog,* and declares its commitment to creating a "unique cross-institutional and cross-disciplinary culture."

The institute's leadership team is "committed to empowering everyone here with the ability to contribute their diverse talents to the singular challenge of transforming medicine." Lander says of the institute, "This is in a sense a protected space. Half the place is devoted to finding the basis of disease and half is devoted to trying to transform and accelerate the development of therapeutics. It's different from what you find in many university settings where you have many labs, each of whom does its own thing."

To reinforce its broad-minded, cross-disciplinary approach, the Broad Institute has an artist in residence on staff, "because the interaction between artists and scientists—the sharing of views and the disparate approaches to solving problems—possess the potential to inspire both science and art." This marriage of science and the arts echoes the observation of the scientific philosopher Edward O. Wilson—that "the most successful scientist thinks like a poet—wide-ranging, sometimes fantastical—and works like a book-keeper. Sadly, it is the latter role the world sees." Wilson goes on to make the larger point: "If the heuristic and analytical power of science can be joined with the introspective creativity of the humanities, human existence will rise to an infinitely more productive and interesting meaning."

Today, Eric Lander is one of the most powerful and influential leaders in the worlds of molecular biology, medicine, and genomics—despite having no formal training in any of those fields. He leads a biology empire at the Broad Institute and raises money from billionaires. He advises the president of the United States on science and health-care policy. And he teaches freshman biology (a course he never took himself as a student) at MIT. How did all this happen? How did he go from the most solitary of sciences to forging new sorts of collaboration in a field that he never formally studied?

Lander himself is quick to ascribe most of this to the vagaries of chance. "I feel so incredibly lucky to end up here. I could not have planned this. What if I hadn't met David Botstein? What if I hadn't gone to a meeting where the human genome was discussed? I have no idea. This is as random as it gets. It's a very weird career."

Lucky he may well have been. But it's also apparent that Lander instinctively pursued a purposeful approach to finding his intellectual thread. First of all, he placed multiple bets rather than pinning all his colors to one mast. He tried mathematics, economics, biology, and medicine—before defining his chosen field of human genomics, effectively a blend of all four intellectual disciplines.

Implicitly, Lander was following the portfolio-of-options approach proposed by Margaret Lobenstine in her advice to people she calls "Renaissance Souls"—people who have the kind of intellectual and emotional restlessness that I described earlier. Specifically, he was following the "Renaissance Focal Strategy" that she recommends to the intellectually restless among us—to choose four key interests, rather like choosing four flavors at the ice cream store. Lobenstine suggests that four seems to be a "lucky number"—it strikes a balance between our love of variety and our need for concentration. It enables us to focus, but we don't have to choose—at least until the preferred choice becomes obvious. After all, for intrinsically broad people, choosing means losing. That's why it's better to focus instead—because focus enables us to do more, not less. Amid a world of possibilities, focus offers clarity and concentration. Where we might be tempted to apply our energies to keeping all our options open, now we can channel them into doing at least four things we love to do.

Second, Lander found untrodden ground at the intersection of established disciplines. He realized that in seeking your intellectual thread, you don't need to choose an established discipline, a known art form or science—indeed, you may be better advised not to do so. As Lander modestly observes, "It's easier to be seen as an expert when you're one of only a few people studying a given subject." Universities and think tanks around the world have embraced the pioneering significance of cross-disciplinary study.

Third, Lander appreciated that the process of finding your intellectual thread is a journey of self-discovery and that it does not always need to be planned. It may be as important to take stock from time to time of what you naturally find yourself doing. The human brain is so wired to our natural preferences that we instinctively gravitate to what we're passionate about. Given that context, the pattern of our preferences may naturally develop, and all we have to do is to reflect from time to time—usually when considering a change in educational or professional trajectory—on what we find ourselves naturally doing.

Nietzsche proposed just such a process of self-discovery when he said, "Let the young soul survey its own life with a view of the following question: 'What have you truly loved so far?' What has ever uplifted your soul, what has dominated and delighted it at the same time?" Line up these revered objects in a row, Nietzsche says, and they will reveal your fundamental self. That's how you will know what is your intellectual thread. It may also be how you will recognize and appreciate the set of skills that you can readily transfer from one arena to another.

5

THE FOUNDATION THAT
IS COMMON TO THEM ALL
Developing Transferrable Skills

Man is going to be replaced as a specialist by the computer. Man himself is being forced to re-establish, employ, and enjoy his innate "comprehensivity." Coping with the totality of Spaceship Earth and universe is ahead for all of us.

—Buckminster Fuller, *Operating Manual for Spaceship Earth*

THE MAKING OF A CAR CZAR

How does somebody without a day of experience in the car industry get to be named the government's "car czar"? And how does he then lead a complete turnaround in the fortunes of the US automobile industry in the midst of a full-scale economic crisis that threatens the future existence of the whole industry?

That's what happened to Steve Rattner in 2009, and it illustrates the capacity of some people to transfer critically important skills from one walk of life to another. Their ability to do so—especially in extreme circumstances like these—enables them to solve important problems for society and to build a more remarkable life and career for themselves.

There was nothing in Steve Rattner's early years that suggested he would one day end up saving the car industry. He started as a junior political reporter for the *New York Times*—indeed, his first job was as a news clerk to the legendary political columnist James Reston. He had two tours of duty in the Washington bureau during the late 1970s, covering the energy crisis as well as Paul Volker's leadership of the Federal Reserve during the inflationary crisis of that era, followed by a spell in London as European economics correspondent.

His coverage of complex economic issues attracted attention, and in 1982 he was recruited by Roger Altman—just coming out of the Reagan administration—to join the investment bank Lehman Brothers as an associate. He spent the next twenty years in investment banking and private equity, building a formidable reputation in the financial world. After Lehman was sold to American Express in 1984, he followed his boss Eric Gleacher to Morgan Stanley, where he cofounded the firm's communications group. In 1989, after Morgan Stanley filed for an initial public offering, he joined Lazard as a general partner. He became known as one of the principal deal makers in the media and communications sector, with highly acquisitive companies like Viacom and Comcast as his clients—and in 1997 he was named as the firm's deputy chair and deputy chief executive. He also became active in the nonprofit world—notably as chair of the Educational Broadcasting Corporation—and in politics as a prominent fund-raiser for the Democratic Party, especially for Bill and Hillary Clinton.

In March 2000, he and three Lazard partners left the firm to found their own investment and advisory firm, which they called Quadrangle Group, again focusing on the media and communications industry. It grew to manage more than $6 billion across several business lines, including private equity, distressed securities, and hedge funds. That was when Rattner first established his role as investment manager for Michael Bloomberg, for whom he now works as the director of his philanthropic investments. He also established the Foursquare media conference, which became a staple of the New York media landscape.

His time at Quadrangle was not without controversy—notably when the firm's 2005 payments to private placement agent Hank Morris to help raise money for its second buyout fund attracted unfavorable attention. Morris was also an adviser to Alan Hevesi, the New York State comptroller and manager of the New York State Common Retirement Fund. In 2009, Quadrangle and Rattner were investigated for what were deemed "kickbacks," and eventually they submitted to institutional and personal settlements with the Securities and Exchange Commission in April 2010 and with New York attorney general Andrew Cuomo in December 2010.

Meanwhile, Rattner had been drawn back to his first area of interest—politics and public policy—as the financial crisis coincided with the election of President Obama. Although he had flirted with government service in the past, the beginning of the new administration seemed like a compelling moment to step up. As he observes, "Our country was facing the greatest financial crisis since the Great Depression; when would the skills of a finance guy like me be more useful? If I hung back now, what would I be saving myself for?"

By his own account, he wasn't sure how he could best help, and he didn't want to be too prescriptive. He said to Tim Geithner and Larry Summers, who were formulating the new administration's economic team, "If I can help, I'd be happy to help." And they said, "We've got all of these problems—A, B, C, D, E, F—which one do you want?" He replied, "You choose," because he didn't want to box them in. And in December 2008, they called back and they said "Autos." Rattner replied, "Autos, I don't know anything about autos." And they said, "Well, you can figure it out."

The imminent collapse of the automotive industry was a looming disaster—second only as a matter of concern to the collapse of the housing credit market and the plummeting stock market, which were by then in full swing. General Motors and Chrysler were functionally insolvent, and the jobs of more than a million people in or connected to the automotive industry were at risk. This was the scenario that occasioned Mitt Romney to write his *Wall Street Journal* op-ed with the title "Let Detroit Go Bankrupt," which later came back to haunt him in his 2012 presidential campaign.

Rattner was appointed counselor and lead auto adviser to the Treasury (a.k.a. the car czar). Working with Ron Bloom, Diana Farrell, and the other members of the Auto Industry Taskforce, he helped engineer a remarkable "overhaul" (his word) in the fortunes of the US auto industry. The plan involved a total government investment of $82 billion in the sector, coupled with controlled bankruptcies for the two companies, as well as new management for both. It also involved the closure of 2,000 automobile dealerships, and tens of thousands of job losses—although many more would have been required without the rescue plan. By late 2009, GM and Chrysler had emerged from bankruptcy, had new management, and were on their way to profitability—a trajectory that has continued since. Ford, the strongest of the US automakers, had remained solvent throughout and did not need government assistance.

Rattner himself has reflected a great deal on this experience: "We didn't know it when we started, but it turned out that this was a problem we could fix; and the financial restructuring skills that I and others had brought to the government were directly relevant." He goes on, "I was certainly not hired for the auto job because of my auto experience, which was precisely zero; nor simply because of my financial and restructuring skills. I was hired because I had enough of the financial skills plus the advantage I had of knowing the political system, which gave me 'credit' as if I had been in government. I had spent time in journalism, fundraising, think tanks, policy stuff—and that's why they wanted me, because they thought I could navigate this sensitive set of issues."

That is what the government most needed at that time—the ability to *navigate a sensitive set of issues*. It was this broad and integrated combination of experience and skills—rather than a single dominant attribute—that was so valuable and transferrable. Rattner was also able to observe the similarities between his lives in business and government: "In a well-run administration, it's just like business. That part of it was strikingly familiar to me—you write memos, you have meetings, you assess options, you make decisions, you try to execute those decisions. The core activities and skill requirements are pretty much the same. That's why somebody like me, with no previous direct experience in government, could get something done while I was there."

Rattner has concluded one other thing from this remarkable experience: "What I have learned about myself is that I like having a portfolio approach. It may not be the best way to knock the cover off the ball in any one thing. But it allows you to leverage what you've learned in one arena into another. And you get to serve."

THE MAKING OF A CULTURAL LEADER

How does somebody who also spent his formative years as a political journalist get to lead two of Britain's leading cultural institutions? And how at both institutions has he been able to achieve significant turnarounds in their financial performance and public reputation?

That is what happened to Tony Hall, who over the past fifteen years has led major transformations, first at the Royal Opera House at Covent Garden, and more recently at the BBC, one of the world's leading broadcasting organizations. But as with Steve Rattner, there was nothing about Hall's early career that suggested he would become such a transformational leader—or indeed a leader at all.

Tony Hall started his career as a BBC news trainee straight out of university. He rose through the journalistic ranks in a fairly conventional way, primarily as a news producer on television and radio. By the early 1990s he was editing the main evening news broadcast on BBC Television, and he would soon go on to become the overall director of BBC News. Although by now he was very much part of the corporation's senior management team, his entire career to that point had been in television and radio journalism—all of it at the BBC.

In 2000, he applied to succeed the departing John Birt as director-general, the top job at the BBC. A gentle, mild-mannered, cerebral, indeed rather professorial personality, Hall was beaten to the job by his exact opposite in personality, style, and temperament—the colorful, brash, populist, and outspoken Greg Dyke, who had built his career almost exclusively in commercial television, primarily in entertainment rather than news, and who had never previously worked at the BBC. It was a bold, idiosyncratic choice that would ultimately blow up in the BBC's face when Dyke was later forced to resign over the BBC's coverage of the highly contentious Iraq War political environment. But at that point, there seemed to be no future for Tony Hall in BBC leadership, and reluctantly he looked elsewhere.

Up to then, Hall's career had focused on honing his own journalistic skills, then on being an editor, and finally on managing a complex news operation. It wasn't immediately obvious where else those skills might come in handy, except perhaps in another news operation. But his role as director of news had required him to manage the numerous elevated egos in a series of newsrooms, as well as handling the diverse external constituencies who sought to influence the BBC's editorial direction. And it was that experience and skill set that attracted the attention of the Royal Opera House board, which soon appointed him as its executive director.

In 2001, the Royal Opera House, one of Britain's iconic cultural institutions, was still in the throes of an existential crisis that had seemingly persisted for years. As Hall himself recalls, "The whole place was in uproar," referring to the painful aftermath of the Opera House's bungled two-year-long closure at the end of the 1990s to rebuild its new Covent Garden home. As an institution—heavily supported by public funds—it had developed a seemingly well-merited reputation for financial and operational mismanagement.

Over the next few years, Hall would lead the Opera House through an initially tentative and then increasingly confident revival, alongside the respected music director Sir Antonio Pappano. He restored the finances to robust shape, and turned the newly remodeled Covent Garden theater into a bastion of artistic excellence; and in the process he gained experience of what it takes to turn around such a high-profile enterprise in the glare of the public spotlight. He was no longer the journalistic commentator; he was the one being commented upon—and the commentary became increasingly favorable.

It was the reputation he gained at the Royal Opera House for transformational leadership of a cultural institution—married with his unimpeachable BBC credentials—that put Hall atop a very short list to rescue the BBC when it hit its own turbulent waters in 2012. The immediate cause of the disturbance was the scandalous past of one of the BBC's most famous on-screen presenters of bygone years, Jimmy Saville, who it was now confirmed had been a predatory sex offender through most of his time as a broadcaster. This quickly turned into one of those full-blown scandals that periodically roil the BBC—in many ways, Britain's highest-profile and often its most controversial institution—a story of editorial misjudgment and fractious infighting.

In the midst of this particular crisis, the BBC board took the extraordinary step of demanding that the director-general George Entwhistle resign only fifty-four days after taking office because of his perceived mishandling of the unwelcome attention. As the firestorm intensified, BBC chair Lord Patten almost went down publicly on his hands and knees to persuade Tony Hall to come back to the BBC as director-general. And when Hall accepted the offer, one newspaper commentator observed, "Tony Hall must now be the most powerful Director-General since its autocratic founder, Lord Reith in the 1920s and 1930s."

Tony Hall now thinks of himself as having had five main careers—or at least career chapters. He has been a journalist, an editor, a news director, the leader of a performing arts institution, and now the leader of a complex media enterprise. He has learned from each of these roles and transferred whatever he has learned to the next. He reflects upon the approach he has taken: "I have learned to focus on the problem or challenge at hand and develop solutions; to lead through partnership and collaboration; and to try and make things happen, even if sometimes I get it wrong. Those strike me as important things to focus on at any time, but especially when you're in the midst of a crisis and you need to restructure the organization you're leading. I suppose that you could call those my transferrable skills."

WHAT ARE TRANSFERRABLE SKILLS— AND WHY DO THEY HELP?

Steve Rattner and Tony Hall both illustrate the third dimension of the Mosaic Principle—the ability to transfer skills from one context to another with positive effect. Rattner started his career as a political journalist, and the skills and capabilities he gained from covering the policy world, combined with his subsequent careers as a banker, private equity investor, and fund-raiser, enabled him ultimately to become the car czar in 2009 and lead the transformation of the US auto industry. Tony Hall also started his career as a political journalist, and combining that with his experience as an editor, news director, and leader of a performing arts organization, enabled him to come to the BBC's rescue in 2012 and restore its good standing.

At critical points in their lives and careers, both Rattner and Hall were placed in new and potentially uncomfortable leadership roles, and they were required to answer some fundamental questions: What do I know that will be relevant to this challenge? What relevant experience can I draw upon? What skills do I have that will help me be effective? And how can I transfer those skills productively?

Our greatest gift as human beings is our ability to learn from experience and apply what we have learned to future challenges. Whenever we confront a new obstacle or opportunity, our first instinct is to ask, "Where have I seen something like this before, and what did I learn from that experience?" We sometimes call that process of learning from experience *pattern recognition*—and when we are dealing with a familiar environment, it is often instinctive and almost subconscious, enabling Daniel Kahnemann's System 1 thinking.

If we are involved in the same arena for long enough, the number of entirely new situations and challenges will become vanishingly small. We will, as the saying goes, have seen it all before—so we will feel increasingly confident in our understanding of the situation and our ability to deal with it based upon past trial and error, if nothing else. And if we are a deep specialist in that arena, then we will have a very specific set of skills that are directly attuned to the immediate challenge. That, after all, is the whole point of being a specialist.

But when we broaden our horizons, when we step "out of our comfort zone" into a new and unfamiliar arena, then we can no longer rely quite so much on that kind of direct and instinctive pattern recognition. In such a new context, we have not seen it all before—

indeed we may never have seen some of the specific things that we are required to address. We have to think more consciously and reflectively; we have to apply System 2 thinking to identify what we bring to the party. What relevant and transferrable experience might we be able to draw upon; what useful skills can we bring across? The advantage of a broader life is that we will have more and different experiences to draw upon; the disadvantage is that it may be less immediately obvious which are the relevant experiences, which are the most transferrable skills, and what is the best way to apply them.

Steve Rattner and Tony Hall both underwent just such an intuitively reflective process as they took on new and demanding roles. They asked which experiences and which skills would be most relevant. Rattner concluded that his most important skill was his "ability to navigate a sensitive set of issues in the public domain." This was an integrated set of skills gained from years of working in and around the policy world as a journalist and fund-raiser, combined with his experience of financial deal making. In Hall's case, he was able to draw upon his proven "ability to lead a cultural institution full of volatile personalities through a challenging process of transformation"—again an integrated set of skills gained from his leadership of the Royal Opera House's recovery, combined with his earlier experience as the BBC's news director. Each was able to combine the skills that he had developed through a broader range of experiences into something that met the immediate need.

Through a wide variety of educational and professional experiences, you too can develop a multidimensional set of capabilities that can be applied to any manner of situations. This process of skill transfer is greatly enhanced if it is built upon a robust foundation of core skills, relevant to all manner of situations, ideally established early in your academic and professional career. And that is why the choices you make even before you start your professional career make a difference.

In 1828, Yale University published a report on the curriculum in which it articulated the fundamental rationale for a broad liberal education—"not to teach that which is peculiar to any one of the

professions; but to *lay the foundation which is common to them all.*"
The report was quite colorful and evocative about the most desirable
elements of that foundation—it should be "best calculated to teach
the art of fixing the attention, directing the train of thought, analyzing a subject proposed for investigation; following, with appropriate
discrimination, the course of the argument; balancing nicely the evidence presented to the judgment; arranging, with skill, the treasures
which memory gathers; rousing and guiding the powers of genius."

Numerous studies since have sought to isolate the foundational
skills that are most likely to lead to success in any field of endeavor—
especially in the most important endeavor, that of leading others. In
Good to Great Jim Collins found that many of the best leaders are
not flamboyant visionaries, but humble, self-effacing, diligent, and
resolute souls who pursue their goals with grit and determination.
A 2001 academic study surveyed a century's worth of research into
business leadership and agreed that extroversion and big personalities did not correlate well with leadership success. Instead, what
mattered was emotional stability and conscientiousness—being de-
pendable, making plans, and following through. A subsequent study
published in 2009 drew upon detailed personality assessments of 316
CEOs and measured their companies' performance to assess which
CEO characteristics and abilities matter. They found that the leadership traits that correlated most powerfully with corporate success
included attention to detail, persistence, efficiency, analytical thor-
oughness, and the ability to work long hours without losing focus.

These and other studies have coalesced around a series of skills
and capabilities that help to explain success in different walks of
life. Although there are clearly situations that call for the glamor-
ous and charismatic—perhaps especially in politics, media, and
entertainment—there is more evidence of success based upon diffi-
dent but dogged determination, the ability to organize and execute,
and sustained commitment and persistence.

There is also growing awareness that these desirable leadership
attributes are relevant and applicable across multiple different walks
of life. They define what it is that effective leaders need to do, whether

in government, business, or the nonprofit world, whether in the military or academia. The research suggests that these requirements can be most usefully summarized under three main headings—solving problems, leading teams, and driving change. Underpinning these headings, there are typically ten key skills that make the most difference when they are transferred from one walk of life to another:

Solving Problems

1. *Understanding the whole system from end to end*—assessing all its complexity, ambiguity, interconnectedness, and apparent contradictions
2. *Using data to enhance the decision-making process*—collecting and making the most of data, using risk-return analysis, and learning from what works and what doesn't
3. *Thinking independently*—using creative problem-solving techniques and applying technology to enable new models to solve old problems

Leading Individuals and Teams

4. *Leading the team*—bringing diverse people and groups together for a shared purpose and sustaining them through motivation and inspiration
5. *Fostering a culture*—creating an environment that enables and inspires risk taking, honest dialogue, and a focus on the customer, user, or citizen
6. *Managing the power structure*—building productive relationships up and down the power structure, and ensuring a positive authorizing environment for progress

Driving Change

7. *Fostering innovation*—developing new ways of doing things, rather than being constrained by old approaches

8. *Making the case*—creating the story, sharing it, and building movements for change
9. *Making things happen*—crafting strategic, policy, or regulatory frameworks to enable and encourage positive change

And finally, the most important transferrable skill:

10. *Leading yourself*—navigating your own motivation map, charting a professional journey, identifying options, and making clear and timely choices

If you treat this as a self-assessment framework—a kind of checklist for broad, multidimensional, cross-disciplinary leaders, how well do you stack up? If you are skilled on these ten dimensions, or at least a majority of them, then the chances are that you will be able to lead effectively no matter what the circumstances. You will have a tool kit of transferrable leadership skills.

The striking thing is how many different walks of life lend themselves to this process of transferring skills. There are so many "from-to" combinations, where there is both a need and an opportunity to transfer significant skills—between the military and business, between the nonprofit arena and business, between business and government, and—seemingly most difficult of all—between business and politics. There may even be a set of transferrable skills between the religious arena and politics. The stories in this chapter illustrate some of these combinations, and they combine to show why transferrable skills are such an important dimension in building a remarkable life and career.

WHERE FUTURE BUSINESS LEADERS
CAN EARN THEIR STRIPES

After Nate Fick left the Marine Corps, by his own admission he drifted for a while. He recalls, "At twenty-six, I feared I had already lived the best years of my life. Never again would I enjoy the sense of purpose and belonging that I had felt in the Marines." In addition, he observes that "combat had nearly unhinged me. Despite my loving family, supportive friends, and good education, the war flooded into every part of my life, carrying me along towards an unknown fate." His transition back to civilian life was dealt an especially personal blow when his immediate successor as platoon commander, Captain Brent Morel, was killed in an Iraqi ambush, shortly after Fick himself had returned to the United States.

Fick had been an unusual person to go into the Marines—or into the military at all. He had gone to Dartmouth College intending to go to medical school but had ended up majoring in the classics. He had written his senior undergraduate thesis on Thucydides' *History of the Peloponnesian War* and its implications for American foreign policy. But apart from that academic interest in long-ago wars, his only military pedigree was that his grandfather had served as a Navy officer in the South Pacific under Admiral Chester Nimitz.

Nevertheless, inspired by the campus lecture of a distinguished Pentagon correspondent, he chose to attend the Marine Corps' Officer Candidates School, and after graduation he was commissioned as a second lieutenant. He explains, "Dartmouth encouraged deviation from the trampled path, but only to join organizations like the Peace Corps or Teach for America. I wanted something more transformative. Something that might kill me—or leave me better, stronger, more capable. I wanted to be a warrior."

Fick entered the Marines in 1998—during an extended period of relative peace, which he expected to continue throughout his time in the service. But then came 9/11—and over the next three years, Fick fought in two wars, first in Afghanistan, then in Iraq. On his last deployment in 2003, he led Second Platoon of Bravo Company of the First Reconnaissance Battalion during the invasion of Iraq. He was responsible for sixty-five Marines and the related logistics and equipment operations. He led those troops into a series of hostile engagements—many of them unplanned. He was twenty-six years old and responsible for men and women in a life-or-death situation.

But his leadership role was much broader than that. In common with so many young military officers in the Afghan and Iraq Wars, he found himself simultaneously playing the roles of small-time mayor, economic-reconstruction czar, diplomat, tribal negotiator, manager of millions of dollars' worth of assets, and security chief, depending on the specific circumstances. Indeed, all of these roles could combine within a single day to embody an impromptu leadership portfolio. Fick describes how he was trained to fight a "three-block war" in which "Marines could be passing out rice in one city block, doing patrols to keep the peace on another block, and engaged in a full-on firefight on the third block. All in the same neighborhood."

As he was leaving the Marines on his return to the United States, he was able to say, "I took sixty-five men to war and brought sixty-five home. I gave them everything I have. Together, we passed the test. We fought for each other." However, he left the Corps—which he had once considered making his career—because he had become "a reluctant warrior. I couldn't make the conscious choice to put myself in that position [of kill or be killed] again and again throughout my professional life."

Fick didn't drift for long after he left the Marines. Soon he was accepted by both the Harvard Business School and the Kennedy School of Government. After graduating with joint graduate degrees in business administration and public policy, he became first COO and then CEO of the Center for New American Security. And after three years in a think tank, he went into business as the CEO of Endgame Inc., a leading venture-backed provider of advanced cybersecurity solutions, providing software and support to the US intelligence community and Department of Defense. He was soon transferring the skills and insights that he had gained in the Marines.

How do you build a strong foundation of transferrable skills early in your life and career? Well, as Nate Fick illustrates, the answer may be to go into military service. Adam Grant, the Wharton School professor of management and psychology, has made a special study of the relevance of military experience to business leadership. In a 2014 paper he notes that the US military is where Fred Smith, the founder and CEO of Federal Express, and Sam Walton, the founder of Walmart, learned to lead—as did the then-CEOs of Johnson & Johnson, General Motors, Procter & Gamble, and Verizon.

A landmark study by economists Efraim Benmelech and Carola Frydman analyzed the role of military experience in corporate leadership. They found that between 1980 and 2006, roughly 30 percent of all CEOs of large public US firms had military experience—often a consequence of military conscription for World War II and the Korean and Vietnam Wars. But over time, people with military backgrounds have begun to vanish from the CEO ranks. One evident reason is the return to a voluntary military—even after two recent wars, today only 1 in 221 Americans is in active-duty service, compared to the end of the Second World War when 1 in 10 Americans was serving. That has certainly affected the transfer of military leadership skills into business. In 1980, 59 percent of CEOs had military experience, but this number plummeted to 8 percent by 2006. Grant believes that "the decline of veterans in leadership roles is a tremendous loss to companies and the economy."

Another plausible reason military experience became a less fertile pedigree for business leaders is that it ceased to be viewed as a relevant leadership model. As Albert Chandler laid out forty years ago in his landmark book about business leadership, *The Visible Hand,* the military used to provide the predominant organizational and cultural model for the American corporation. Many companies borrowed the military's hierarchical delineation between executives tasked with strategy, the corporate equivalents of colonels and generals; midlevel managers, who played the role of captains, majors, and lieutenant colonels; and operational or tactical staff, the equivalent of enlisted soldiers. In the everyday slang of business, the operational staff in many companies are often still referred to as "the troops" in a semiconscious and usually respectful reference to the military world.

In the first half of the twentieth century, this military-style hierarchy implied a top-down "command and control" environment, which seemed well suited to the steady, highly institutional business environment of that time. But it has seemingly proved much less attractive or relevant in the modern era of globalization, computers, and the Internet, with information flowing far more quickly around the world and decisions needing to be made with greater haste. Today it would be unusual to find any business school professor or corporate executive who espoused the blessings of hierarchical command-and-control leadership structures. There is much more interest in "flat" corporate structures like those in Silicon Valley that narrow the divide between managers and managed, strategy and tactics.

And yet, the military still plays a critical role in building a skilled workforce—and there is even more that it could do, if enabled. For much of the twentieth century, companies employed young people with a mixed set of intrinsic skills and invested in them, knowing that they would most likely secure a return over the employees' long career. It's very rare to see that in business anymore—and some argue that the result is a hollowing out of middle management and the middle class. Today, only one group in our society consciously makes that kind of investment: the military may be the only large employer that is still committed to developing a demographically broad group of people as future leaders. Adam Davidson, founder of Planet Money, places this observation in a socioeconomic and political context: "If we wanted to find a 21st century form of organization that can help rebuild the middle class, we would need it to retain at least a little something from the institution most responsible for building the American middle class in the first place—the U.S. military."

In March 2016, Harvard University president Drew Faust gave a remarkable speech at West Point—the US military academy 50 miles north of New York City. That she gave the speech at all was notable enough, because for several decades from the late 1960s until as recently as 2011 the Reserve Officers' Training Corps (ROTC) was effectively banned from the Harvard campus. The prohibition, initially enacted at the height of the Vietnam War and related campus protests, was lifted only after the repeal of the Don't Ask Don't Tell law on homosexuality in the military, and after President Obama in his 2011 State of the Union address explicitly called on all universities to open their doors to ROTC.

In her speech Faust observes that "over the past 50 years, West Point has transformed its curriculum into a general liberal arts education, graduating leaders with broad-based knowledge of both the sciences and the humanities, and the ability to apply that knowledge in a fluid and uncertain world." She commends the West Point system for leadership development, which focuses on the need for perspective and on "the expansion of a person's capacity to know oneself and to view the world through multiple lenses"—citing what the novelist Zadie Smith calls "the gift of the many-colored voice, the multiple sensibility."

Beyond perspective, Faust argues that leaders need the capacity to improvise—especially, but not exclusively, in the military. She points out that "education is not the same as training for a job. Jobs change. Circumstances evolve. If perspective opens eyes, its multiple lenses give us the ability to act creatively, to improvise in the face of the unexpected." Improvisation, flexibility, contingency, the art of the possible underpin the importance of the liberal arts. "Where there is no rulebook, turn to philosophy, turn to history, to anthropology, poetry and literature. Take the wisdom and inspiration of the great leaders and thinkers who came before you, and then create your own."

Faust ends her speech by noting that according to a recent Gallup poll, the military is the last institution in which Americans still have high confidence. To the future graduates of the military academy she concludes, "We need you now more than ever—as thoughtful, disciplined improvisers, educated broadly in the arts and sciences, as leaders who include and create space for the humanities. I wish there were more of you. The world's best force for the humanities—and thus for human possibility."

There is at least one other country that has shown the power of this model of leadership development: Israel. In their book *Start-up Nation,* Dan Senor and Saul Singer describe the pivotal role that the Israeli military has played in developing and transferring skills to the private sector and fostering an entrepreneurial, technology-oriented culture. In their eyes, it is this culture that has turned Israel from "a besieged backwater to a high-tech powerhouse that has achieved fiftyfold economic growth in sixty years."

One example of this approach to leadership development is the elite Talpiot unit, which started as a one-year experiment and has now been running continuously for more than thirty years. The so-called Talpions who graduate from this program are deliberately given a unique breadth of experience across all the major Israeli Defense Force branches so that they understand all the technology and military needs of the moment—and the connections among them. They are also required to find cross-disciplinary solutions to specific military problems, and many of them take that experience into the private sector. Several of the Israeli technology companies traded on the NASDAQ were either founded by a Talpion or have alumni in key management roles.

Talpions represent the elite of the Israel military; but as Senor and Singer confirm, "The underlying strategy behind the program's development—to provide broad and deep training in order to produce innovative, adaptive problem solving—is evident throughout much of the military and seems to be part of the driving Israeli ethos: to teach people how to be very good at a lot of things, rather than excellent at one thing." In Israel, you get broad experience, perspective, and maturity at a much younger age than you do in most societies, because the system creates so many transformative experiences for young Israelis when they are barely in their twenties.

This is obviously a military system custom designed to meet the unique needs of Israel—a small country facing a constant existential threat. But the transfer of military skills to the Israeli private sector has proved especially successful—and there is growing evidence that some aspects of this skill-transfer program can happen in other countries, including the United States. That's because the US military no longer exhibits the rigidly hierarchical model that the late twentieth-century business world rejected. This reflects the changing nature of modern warfare, most recently in Iraq and Afghanistan. These post-9/11 wars have primarily become counterinsurgencies, where critical decisions have been made by junior commanders on the ground seeking to engage constructively and build mutually productive relationships with local communities.

The US military is no longer the single-speed, one-dimensional force of the past. In my own career, I have hired more than a few people with recent military experience gained early in their careers—especially in Washington. I have been amazed by the amount of authority that had been afforded to an Army captain or Marine lieutenant in his or her midtwenties. Especially at the height of the Iraq and Afghanistan Wars, young military officers had almost total command over whole geographic regions—not to mention over their own units. They handled multimillion-dollar budgets, often transacted in cash—while dealing with everyday dangers and occasionally unspeakable tragedy.

Furthermore, military officers manage "business-critical operations" every day. Given the often acute circumstances, they have to do everything with a sense of urgency, and they have to prioritize. They have to deploy people to key activities and coordinate complex activities through quick and effective communication. And their role often encompasses training, procurement, logistics management, and succession planning. These are all skills that are directly relevant to the challenge of building a business. Nowadays people in the military, particularly those who have deployed, have been through a kind of leadership accelerator.

In 2015, the US Department of Defense announced a program called Force of the Future, its most drastic plan for self-transformation since World War II. The aim is to create a new and more contemporary model for the development of skills and careers. Military officers will get a retirement plan even if they don't stay for twenty years, reducing the need to just serve time. Some will be offered the chance to leave active duty for a year or two to go work and learn at Google or some other private company and then return. And the military hopes to design something a lot like LinkedIn, so that officers can apply for their jobs and be selected on the basis of their interests and abilities, not just their ranks.

The evidence is growing that military experience and skills are once again eminently transferrable to other environments—notably the business world. For instance, Benmelech and Frydman found that between 1994 and 2004, firms led by CEOs with military experience had significantly lower levels of fraud, and they also demonstrated that military experience predicted better leadership in tough times. In addition, a study by the executive search firm Korn/Ferry shows that CEOs with military experience averaged 7.2 years in the top seat—versus an average of 4.6 years for CEOs without military experience. And the CEOs who served in the military consistently outperformed the S&P 500 Index. Between 1995 and 2005, ex-military CEOs led their companies to average returns of 12.2 percent, compared with average returns of 9.4 percent for the S&P Index.

Perhaps the most compelling evidence comes from Adam Grant's own Wharton MBA class. For the past few years, he has asked his students to name the single most impressive of their eight-hundred-plus classmates. Although less than 10 percent of the class has military experience, in each year the overwhelming winner has been a military veteran—a Navy SEAL, an Army helicopter pilot, an Air Force sergeant, and a Navy nuclear submarine engineer. Grant observes, "Although these students are only in their twenties, their experiences leading under fire, exercising willpower, and giving to a cause had made them—in my humble opinion—better hires than many of the senior executives at the world's most respected companies." To his pleasure, *Fortune* magazine reports that "a large and growing group of companies have begun to discover—or rediscover—the benefits of recruiting military talent."

HOW BUSINESS SKILLS ARE TRANSFORMING THE MILITARY—AND VICE VERSA

How can somebody who spent much of his career in public finance and investment banking get to reinvent the US military's whole approach to housing its staff and their families? And how can a Silicon Valley executive lead the effort to re-create jobs and a self-sustaining economy in war-torn Iraq? The answer lies in remarkable people who developed skills that they could transfer and found the opportunity to do so.

Josh Gotbaum grew up mostly in New York, the son of a high-profile public-sector union leader, Victor Gotbaum. He recalls, "My father was on the labor side of a public employees' union, so to work in government or business was basically selling out." Nevertheless, that's what he determined to do. "I didn't plan a cross-sector career—I planned on a public service career. When I did move from government into business, it was in order that I would be better equipped to improve government policy."

What actually happened is that Gotbaum embarked upon an almost unbroken run of working for Democratic administrations in Washington—first under President Carter, then under Presidents Clinton and Obama. Starting in the Carter administration, he took on a series of economic policy and regulatory roles. "Regulatory economics was sufficiently complicated that it was interesting; and some of the largest issues of the day I conceived of as regulatory issues. At graduate school, I talked my way into business courses at the law school without taking any of the prerequisites, which outraged them a little."

Of course, in between there were twenty years of Republican administrations—Reagan, Bush 41, and Bush 43—during which Gotbaum was in mutually agreed exile from government, and he had little choice but to build a business or nonprofit career. Politically, he was always the optimist: "When Reagan was elected in 1980, I knew for certain that he was going to be a one-term president, so I went looking for the opportunity to learn as much about business as I could in four years, so that I could go back and work for President Mondale!" Even when the 1984 election resulted in another Republican term, "I avoided making commitments that would have complicated my life if and when the Democrats came back to power."

The business he chose—investment banking—turned out to be his primary occupation for roughly half of his career. He joined Lazard Frères, initially as a speechwriter for the legendary Felix Rohatyn, who was deeply involved in public policy. He recalls, "The fit was not very good because I didn't know anything. I said to him I don't know finance and accounting, and he said, 'Don't worry. We do politics and psychotherapy, and we don't know how to teach those.' The fact is that that the nuts and bolts of the work was financial analysis of businesses, and it turned out I could learn that on the job."

While working for Rohatyn, he was assigned to work on the project that defined his primary set of transferrable skills for the remainder of his career—corporate restructuring and turnarounds. The transaction involved a steel mill in Weirton, West Virginia. In the course of it, he learned accounting, credit, and corporate organization, and he raised $150 million for a steel company in the middle of a recession. As a result of this success—and a miscalculated contingency fee that turned out to be the sixth-largest in the firm's history—Gotbaum became the firm's go-to guy for this kind of restructuring transaction. "Every time I said 'enough is enough,' something interesting would come along—after Weirton there was Eastern Airlines, then PanAm, then Revlon, then RJR Nabisco, then Avis Europe—and then they sent me to London to drum up more business like that."

Of course, when you are talking about restructuring, airlines and steel have typically been a large part of the market—so in addition to his functional expertise, Gotbaum was becoming something of an industry expert as well. In one form or another, he has worked with airlines for the past twenty-five years. Perhaps most personally enjoyable and fulfilling was the two years that he and his family spent in Honolulu while he worked as the bankruptcy trustee for Hawaiian Airlines in the early 2000s. And much later, when he came to run the Pension Benefits Guaranty Corporation—the arm of government that backstops the pensions of potentially bankrupt companies—several of the companies at risk were airlines.

In between, Gotbaum worked in a series of government roles during the Clinton administration—deploying wherever possible the analytical and financial restructuring skills he had learned as an investment banker. He recalls, in particular, his time at the Department of Defense—the "biggest industrial enterprise in the world outside of China's Red Army"! He worked on property disposals, base closings and openings, housing privatization, and partnerships with the private sector.

It was in that guise that he was able to transfer his restructuring skills directly to the military housing operation. One day, Bill Perry, President Clinton's secretary of defense, called him into his office and said, "Our military family housing is in very bad shape. I don't have the budgets to fix it. You know something about capital markets. Can you figure out a way to use private capital to refurbish our family housing stock?" Gotbaum soon discovered that base commanders were so desperate to improve family housing that they would be willing to give up operational control over the real estate to do so. So he set up an experimental authority that allowed the Pentagon to lease out land on bases and then lease back the use of houses on a rental basis—which after false starts, occasional scandals, and multiple organizations, turned out to work quite effectively.

"Years later in 2009," as he recalls, "I was contacted by a colonel in the Air Force who was writing a history of the program. I asked him what had happened. He said, 'You don't know? Your program has been used to refurbish all family housing in the US including Alaska and Hawaii, and the technique is being tried on barracks and other facilities to see if it can be used there.'"

———

Josh Gotbaum always sought to build his career around government service and used his time in the private sector—primarily in investment banking—to develop new skills that he could transfer back into government. That's how he ended up transforming the military's housing program. Paul Brinkley, in contrast, always wanted to work in business; so when he found himself in Iraq in 2006 as the US government's deputy undersecretary of defense, just shy of his fortieth birthday, he was bound to wonder how he got there and what he could achieve.

His early career was as an industrial engineer, a graduate of Texas A&M University who worked first with Nortel Networks—where he secured four patents—and then with JDS Uniphase Corporation, an optical-technology manufacturer near San Jose. There he ran the logistics, customer service, and information technology departments. It was his logistics skills and experience that attracted the attention of the Pentagon, which was on the lookout for people with relevant experience. In 2004 the Department of Defense recruited him to help modernize the military supply chain. Soon he was starting to consolidate the more than 2,000 business systems for processing financial transactions alone, transferring in some of the problem-solving and change-management skills he had learned in Silicon Valley.

It was this mission—to consolidate and modernize finance and logistics systems—that first took him to Iraq in 2006. In the midst of ferocious fighting, he and a small team sought to simplify contracting processes so that Iraqi firms would have a better chance of providing goods and services to the US military. He recalls, "I was probably a typical American businessperson in that I expected to see deserts, camels, palm trees, oil. I never went to Iraq expecting to find a skilled workforce and an industrial economy. That was completely surprising to me." But Iraq's once-modern industrial economy had essentially shut down as the war took hold—partly a function of US policy.

While Brinkley was in Baghdad, Lt. Gen. Peter Chiarelli, then a top US commander in Iraq, asked him to inspect the bus factory in Iskandariya. Chiarelli said that his troops kept catching former factory workers setting roadside bombs. "So we put our team in a convoy and drove through some extremely rough neighborhoods," Brinkley recalls. When he saw that the factory was shut down, he asked why everybody was out of work. "Those are state-owned industries," he was told later. "If you re-start them, you're going to be employing insurgents."

When he got back to Washington, Brinkley sought to convince his superiors that by restarting Iraq's industrial base he could make a dent in Iraq's unemployment rate and cut off the flow of potential insurgents against the US forces. He thought of it as turning around a company. He was given the go-ahead to establish the Task Force for Business and Stability Operations, charged with restoring something like "normal economic activity in Iraq." The objective was to make business development a component of the broader military counterinsurgency.

By late 2006, he had put together a team of turnaround experts, manufacturing consultants, forensic accountants, and individuals with other loosely related skills. His deputy director for strategic operations, Barney Gimbel, was a former New York–based journalist, who had gotten to know Brinkley when he wrote an article about him for *Fortune* magazine—which helped inform this account of Brinkley's mission. Gimbel's article was fairly skeptical about the mission's chances of success, but Brinkley challenged him to "not just write about it, but try to make it work." An adventurer by nature, Gimbel accepted the challenge and worked alongside Brinkley for the next four years—in government and then in the private sector.

At its peak in Iraq, the business and stability task force had more than 350 professionals deployed in every province of Iraq, including large numbers of civilian business leaders and agriculture experts from the American private sector and academia. For example, faculty and staff from American universities worked on farms all over Iraq, helping farmers increase production levels and learn modern farming techniques. More than two hundred international companies visited Iraq as part of the task force initiative—resulting in more than $8 billion of foreign direct investment. By 2010, the task force had helped restart production at more than sixty Iraqi factories, facilitated contracts worth more than $1 billion between foreign private investors and Iraq's state-owned enterprises, and helped provide jobs for 250,000 Iraqis.

Although there were plenty of skeptics—including from within his own government—Brinkley was convinced that it made perfect sense to transfer American business leadership and change-management skills to the Iraqi private sector. He would say, "We've seen in places like Iraq and Afghanistan a synchronous linkage of violence and economic deprivation. We need to look proactively for ways to uplift the economic prospects of a society to help stabilize it. We don't have that institutionally in the government; the U.S. government is not designed to assist in that capacity. That's why we need to transfer skills from the private sector and from academia."

That said, he would add that his new colleagues in the Department of Defense did have relevant skills of their own when it came to managing large industrial enterprises: "The DoD itself is a huge business operation. It is the world's largest industrial enterprise by a factor of about three, much larger than the world's largest corporation, so it has people who understand business. It can draw on its own business management skills and expertise. That's how we initially engaged in Iraq."

In 2009, the task force's mission was extended to the other principal war zone in Afghanistan, with a particular focus on the development of mining resources, a key industry for the country. In both Iraq and Afghanistan, the work continued to be risky and dangerous. In 2010, Brinkley and four members of his team were meeting with a hotel manager in downtown Baghdad when a powerful car bomb detonated thirty meters from their conference room. The blast destroyed much of the building, and Brinkley and his team were all injured. But they returned almost immediately to work, and sometime later they received the Defense of Freedom Medal, the civilian equivalent of the Purple Heart.

In the midst of trying to restart two war-torn economies, Brinkley was asked what had been the hardest part of his job. He replied, "We've grown so accustomed to the success of our free-market model that we've lost sight of the fact that, for a country coming out of violence, or engaged in violence, this alchemy isn't natural. So the hardest part of my job has been to confront the deeply embedded belief among people in our own government that what we're doing in Iraq and Afghanistan isn't necessary, or even that what we're doing is wrong. This has led to tremendous bureaucratic barriers being thrown up at every stage of the process. That's been our most difficult hurdle. But I think we've overcome it."

In May 2010, after four years of work in war-torn Iraq and Afghanistan, the work of the task force was ruled to be outside of the normal role of the Department of Defense and was moved to the Agency for International Development. Brinkley left the government and cofounded a private investment vehicle to fund infrastructure projects in the regions where he had done so much work for the government.

One of the first projects was a $14 million agreement with the Iraqi government to modernize the Port of Maqal in the city of Basra, which had been largely inoperable since the Iran-Iraq War. Within a year, the port established a modern container terminal in the city center of Basra and provided a gateway for commercial goods into the Iraqi economy. Once again, Paul Brinkley was transferring important skills—but this time they were skills that he had learned in government and he was now applying in the private sector.

HOW SILICON VALLEY CAN BRING
TECH SKILLS TO GOVERNMENT

Aneesh Chopra and Todd Park have shared a specific mission—to transfer Silicon Valley technical and entrepreneurial skills to government. That was the objective that President Obama gave them when he appointed them successively to the role of chief technology officer of the United States.

Born in New Jersey, the eldest son of Indian immigrants, Aneesh Chopra developed his early career in public health before becoming secretary of technology for the government of Virginia and then for the federal government. Todd Park is also the son of immigrant parents—in his case from South Korea—who raised him in Salt Lake City, Utah. His father, a chemical engineer, reportedly had "more patents in Dow Chemical's history than anybody, except for Dr. Dow himself." Park started his career in consulting at Booz Allen Hamilton—and then founded two health technology companies, Athenahealth and Castlight Health, as well as advising on the establishment of Healthpoint Services, which brings affordable clean water, drugs, diagnostics, and telehealth services to rural villages in India. He came into government initially as chief technologist at the Department of Health and Human Services, before moving to the White House.

Both Chopra and Park have sought to bring a sort of Silicon Valley technology start-up ethos to government. In a conversation with me on his last day as chief technology officer in 2012—before he left to run for lieutenant governor of Virginia—Chopra described the aspiration that he and Park have shared, to bring into government the operational model that drives the technology industry—especially the open-source innovation approach that has enabled entrepreneurs to find new and creative solutions to almost every aspect of modern society. As he argues, "If we're designing a leadership development model for the twenty-first century, let's use twenty-first-century technology and innovation models. Let's not keep fighting the last war."

For instance, they developed an Open Innovators tool kit, as well as an entrepreneurs-in-residence program at key government agencies like the Food and Drug Administration. In a separate initiative, they worked with LinkedIn to devote a hackathon to the problem of getting military veterans trained and employed in the civilian economy. Their whole objective has been to open up government and lower the barriers for talented people with big ambitions.

They call this concept *frictionless participation in government*—comparing it to the ease with which even young amateur developers create apps for iPhones and iPads. In a later echo of this aspiration, President Obama told an audience at the 2016 South by Southwest festival in Austin, Texas, "The technologies behind today's entertainment and communications apps should also be directed at solving the problems of voter turnout, access to political leaders and civic engagement."

Obama added that this wasn't just about the application of modern technologies to meeting government challenges—it was also a talent strategy aimed at attracting more technology executives into government, in order to make federal agencies more responsive to their customers. "We want to create a pipeline where there is a continuous flow of talent that is helping to shape government."

Back in 2012 Chopra outlined the early contours of just such a vision: "I want government to be a place that invites and attracts business and social entrepreneurs. They don't necessarily have to work for government in the formal employment sense. But they can help solve our biggest problems, and we should encourage that. We need to create digital health-care, education, and energy systems. To enable that, I think we should create rules of the road that allow the equivalent of *app store economics* to come to bear. We should establish the data foundations for an innovation economy, upon which entrepreneurs can build."

The initial trials and tribulations of the Obamacare website in 2013 illustrated the scale of the challenge facing people like Chopra and Park (on whose watch as government chief technology officer it happened). But it also gave a glimpse of how their preferred model might work to solve big government and social problems.

In his book dissecting the health-care crisis, *America's Bitter Pill*, Steven Brill recounts how what he calls the "geeks in a van" came to the rescue when all else seemed lost with the initial Obamacare website in October 2013: "The now-energized Todd Park was riding in a White House van around D.C., Maryland and Virginia with the beginnings of a hastily assembled team trying to assess the damage." Among the people in the van was Ryan Panchadsaram, recently appointed as a presidential innovation fellow, part of a scheme launched by Park to bring high-tech achievers into government to work on specific projects that they design.

This team quickly established a classic "war room" approach, along with an open phone line to all the affected locations, so that everyone could instantly talk to the others if an issue suddenly came up. They didn't come up with an instant fix, and there were more than a few operational problems before the system stabilized. But eventually it did—and on Sunday, December 1, Todd Park issued a public report, which as Brill writes, "impressively detailed the website's rescue." The numbers kept on improving through December, "helped by a group of recruits from Silicon Valley who parachuted in for a stay of a few weeks or, in some cases, vowed to stay until the close of enrollment in March." It seemed that the new model of frictionless participation was starting to work—none too soon.

As a consequence of experiences like this, the Obama administration has created the US Digital Service as a kind of troubleshooting team to upgrade the technology involved in the delivery of government services—staffed with people from Silicon Valley and the wider tech community. Jason Goldman, chief digital officer for the White

House, believes that it may be President Obama's most important accomplishment, calling him "the first tech president: establishing a lasting legacy of service that will carry on long after he leaves office." He adds, "The work they are doing is impactful, and it's hard to see how they don't become a permanent feature of government."

SERVING GOD, MAMMON AND THE PUBLIC

Is it possible to build a career—and develop a set of skills—that straddle the worlds of business, religion and public service? It may seem implausible, but a few have tried with some success in building a foundation common to each of these arenas—although they have certainly met obstacles along the way.

Mitt Romney—perhaps more than anybody else in American political history—seemed to construct his career with the intent of running for the post of "*CEO President*". Inspired by the example of his father George Romney who had been CEO of American Motors before becoming governor of Michigan (and who had run unsuccessfully for president in 1968), Romney put together a broad, cross-sector resume—starting as a management consultant with Bain & Company; then building Bain Capital into a leader in the private equity industry; then leading a turnaround of the 1992 Winter Olympics in Salt Lake City; culminating in his election as a Republican governor in the normally Democratic state of Massachusetts. Along the way, he made no secret of his political ambition—indeed he would confide to colleagues: "I need to be careful about this; I might run for public office one day."

Romney's objective—both as governor and then as a presidential candidate—was unquestionably to transfer a clearly defined set of skills from business to government. One former lawmaker recalls him saying: "My usual approach has been to set the strategic vision for the enterprise and then work with the vice presidents to implement the strategy." He followed a trusted formula: "pursue data aggressively, analyze rigorously, test constantly, and observe always." Although the reaction among seasoned government officials and legislators was often skeptical, he had at least partial success with this approach in the Massachusetts state government, for instance in enacting a novel universal health-care program (the de facto precursor of "Obamacare").

And yet Romney's political career—like his father's—ended in failure, at least measured against his own singular objective. Romney has lost more political races than he has won—and the ultimate prize, the presidency, proved elusive twice. His prolonged experience—more than that of anybody else—seems to illustrate why it has typically proven so difficult to adapt a successful business leadership approach to politics.

For one thing Romney's analytical approach to strategy was based on the premise that almost any policy issue or problem could be taken apart, studied, and re-engineered—"everything could always be tweaked, reshaped, fixed, and addressed," observed one of his aides. But in politics, that could look too much like opportunism—or worse, insincerity. Coming from the world of analysis, finance, and corporate strategy, Romney struggled in the world of "conviction politics"—the world in which two of his political heroes, Ronald Reagan and Margaret Thatcher, had been so comfortable. It was foreign to him that core enduring principles mattered on policy issues—that somebody would go back and say, "Well, three years ago you said this, and now you've changed your position. That smacks of flip-flopping."

There is no secret why some successful business leaders choose to go into politics: to amplify their influence and impact and, frankly, to hold greater power on a bigger stage. Max Weber, the sociologist, describes holding that wider power as one of the "inner enjoyments" of political leadership: "The knowledge of influencing men, of participating in power over them, and above all, the feeling of holding in one's hands a nerve fiber of historically important events can elevate the politician above everyday routine"—including, one presumes, everyday business.

But, at least when it comes to presidential politics, there is scant evidence that business leadership has been systematically accepted by the electorate as a transferrable skill. Indeed, the last president to win office largely on the basis of business experience was Herbert

Hoover in 1929, and he presided over the Great Depression. Since then thirteen presidents have served (Roosevelt, Truman, Eisenhower, Kennedy, Johnson, Nixon, Ford, Carter, Reagan, Bush 41, Clinton, Bush 43, and Obama)—with minimal combined business experience among them.

There are numerous theories as to why this is empirically the case. The most common hypothesis was expressed by Hank Paulson in a 2011 lecture at Northwestern University: "One reason why private sector leaders often fail to transition effectively to public service roles is that they are used to 'being king' within their organizations. This attitude can be a liability when working to design and advance complex legislation on Capitol Hill."

There is some risk in exaggerating this observation. As I observed earlier in this chapter, few businesses these days—least of all the kind of consulting and private equity partnerships in which Mitt Romney had succeeded—are run on the kind of hierarchical "command-and-control" principles in which the CEO is really seen as "king." Most CEOs—even high-profile entrepreneurs—spend a lot of their time negotiating with internal and external stakeholders to secure their aspirations. And, on the other side of the equation, even experienced political leaders, schooled for a lifetime in the requirements of government, struggle to secure their desired outcome in a polarized legislative process.

Nevertheless, there clearly are differences in the leadership challenge in politics and the nonprofit world that constrain the process of transferring skills from business. The political scientist Nannerl O. Keohane—who served on several corporate boards, while also leading successively Wellesley College and Duke University—recalls an IBM board meeting early in the tenure of Lou Gerstner, "an aggressive and very successful CEO," when he reported on his decision to close one of the US plants that manufactured components for IBM computers. She says, "He consulted with his trusty lieutenants, but the decision was basically his own. It was a bold decision . . . but Gerstner simply told the board about the closing and shared the timetable for rolling out the announcement. I mused how differently the same kind of action would be regarded on any university campus."

Nannerl Keohane adds wistfully, "Because I had no interest in being tarred and feathered and ridden out of town . . . I never saw the IBM example as relevant for Duke University. But I did think wistfully about how much easier it is for a leader in a corporate setting who just wants to get something done." Roderick Kramer's essay "The Great Intimidators" describes this model of contemporary business leaders "who are not averse to causing a ruckus, nor are they above using a few public whippings and ceremonial hangings to cause attention."

But a more convincing explanation of the challenge of transferring business skills to politics is that offered by Mark Philp, who notes in his book *Political Conduct* that "politics is a much more internally complex, human and grubby domain of activity than most political theory recognizes. It is a domain in which human passions, ambitions, loyalties and treacheries have a major impact on who gets to exercise political power and how it is exercised."

The irony is that Romney had another set of experiences and skills upon which he could have drawn—if he had been prepared to do so openly—his leadership in the Mormon Church. His lifelong commitment as a volunteer started when he went on a two-year mission to France before college graduation (during which he was almost killed in an automobile accident). At various stages of his life and career, Mitt Romney served as a bishop and then as a "stake president" of the Church of the Latter Day Saints in Massachusetts.

In the latter role, he oversaw about a dozen congregations with close to 4,000 members. Positions like this in the church amounted to a significant leadership test, exposing him to personal and institutional crises, human tragedies, immigrant cultures, social forces, and organizational challenges that he had never before encountered. As one of Romney's local church leaders observed to his biographers, "It really is quite a tremendous amount of trust that's placed in the leadership."

As bishop of Belmont Ward, Romney was intimately involved in families' lives, counseling and guiding them through marital problems, illness, unemployment, and other struggles. But the biggest challenge for Romney was the destruction by fire of the Mormon

church in Belmont, which required him first to find alternative facilities in the area and then to raise funds for reconstruction of the
church. That kind of early leadership experience—especially for a
man who otherwise operated in the somewhat rarefied air of private
equity—was in many respects his most meaningful credential for
political office. Yet, when it came to running for political office, he
rarely mentioned it. He was seemingly concerned that voters would
think the Mormon Church "weird" and too awkward to talk about.

Roger Sant, a fellow Mormon, would later observe: "You know
there is an element of truth in the belief that business leadership
skills can be transferred to political office—but it's probably best not
to exaggerate it. Probably the most humanistic experience comes
from the issues you deal with as a pastor. That may be the best leadership credential of all."

Mitt Romney is not alone in blending leadership credentials from
business, government and religion. Stephen Green, formerly Executive Group Chairman of the global banking giant HSBC, wrote a
book entitled *Serving God? Serving Mammon?* which drew upon his
experience as a business leader who, in the midst of a highly successful banking career, also became an ordained priest in the Church
of England. If his commitment to the church seemed unusual in a
business leader, it was perhaps more consistent with someone who
had spent his first year after college volunteering at a hostel in the
East End of London for recovering alcoholics, and who had started
his professional career as a civil servant in the British government
working on overseas development assignments.

In a subsequent book *Good Value: Reflections on Money, Morality
and an Uncertain World*, Green would observe: "To live a complete
human life we must . . . accept that our end is in our beginning, that
we will find our purpose in our roots, and that our beginning is in
our end, that we will find our roots in our purpose." He adds: "A
large part of our quest as humans is to explore what can come to accept as our 'home' in the profoundest sense, for that is where we will
discover our true spiritual purpose."

And then there is the remarkable, and still unfolding story, of Justin Welby, who in 2013 became Archbishop of Canterbury, the most

senior bishop in the Church of England, 105th in a line that began with St. Augustine. Before committing himself fully to the church, Welby spent the first eleven years of his career as an executive in the oil industry—first with the French oil giant Elf Aquitaine in Paris, and then as treasurer of the fast-growing exploration group Enterprise Oil, focused on West Africa and North Sea oil projects.

In 1989, he quit the oil industry to train for the priesthood, was ordained in 1992, and served in a series of provincial parishes before taking increasingly senior positions first at Coventry and then Liverpool and Durham cathedrals—culminating with his election as Archbishop of Canterbury just twenty-one years after he first entered the priesthood. He was clearly on a fast track—despite having originally been rejected for ordination with these discouraging words from the presiding bishop: "There is no place for you in the Church of England!" A religious commentator would note: "His energy, intelligence and experience marked him out for promotion even in an organization as sclerotic and short-sighted as the Church of England."

Welby's transition from business to religion might seem unusual—but the foundations had been built earlier. He had actually committed himself to the church in 1975 while at Cambridge University, where he had "suddenly felt a clear sense of something changing, the presence of something that had not been there before in my life." He would also say of the tragic death of the first of his six children at the age of seven months in a 1983 car crash: "It was a very dark time for my wife Caroline and myself, but in a strange way it actually brought us closer to God". And throughout his business career, he and his wife were active members of Holy Trinity, Brompton—one of the more contemporary and evangelical of London churches. In their summer holidays, the couple would go "bible smuggling" behind the Iron Curtain in then-communist Eastern Europe.

Once Welby did commit himself fully to a career in the church, there's no doubt that he applied the skills and experience he had acquired in business. He observes, for instance, that he had acquired decisiveness—"markets don't allow you to hang about"—as well as teamwork and an understanding of balance sheets. He also developed more intangible skills, as one commentator would describe: "He's tough, street-wise and might turn out to be a real nettle-grasper". Another suggests that he could "combine the cunning of Machiavelli with the majesty of the archangel Gabriel".

"He's definitely an executive type", says one senior colleague, "he thinks in those terms". For instance, as dean of Liverpool Cathedral, he had a business plan to double the congregation in five years—which he did. Others observe that he exhibits in private a "remarkably hard-nosed realism, no matter how uplifting he has been in public. He doesn't build systems, he looks for what works". At Canterbury, he consults with groups of six or seven, and debates decisions thoroughly before they are taken.

His time in the oil business also gave him a sense of adventure, even of derring-do. In 2005, for instance, while a canon at Coventry Cathedral, he also became co-director for international ministry at the International Centre for Reconciliation. In that role, he embarked upon one especially dangerous mission to negotiate between the Shell oil company and the Ogoni people of south-east Nigeria—a region he knew from his own time in the industry. "Don't worry," he told a colleague, "I'll leave my phone on so I can be traced". And indeed at one point, he was arrested by militants at gunpoint, although subsequently released.

As an experienced businessman—a man who understood money and could chastise bankers in their own language—Welby was distinctively qualified to comment on business ethics and related public policy issues. His original theology dissertation had led to a book entitled *Can Companies Sin?: "Whether", "How" and "Who" in Company Accountability.* And many years later, he would observe of the 2008 global financial crisis: "A society which has built its life on the material will sooner or later be deceived by the gods in whose hands it has put itself. That's what we did. It's not that prosperity and growth are not good things. It's a matter of what you put your ultimate security in."

And the man who early in his religious career had written a book entitled *Managing the Church?: Order and Organization in a Secular*

Age would later observe of his leadership challenge: "The longer I go on with this, the more I realize that the Church of England is not an organization in any recognizable sense. Because bishops are dressed up in funny hats and special sticks, it's assumed if they say to a bunch of parish clergy 'Do something', they will do it. But that's not how it works and never has been."

HOW EARLY VOLUNTARY ROLES CAN BUILD TRANSFERRABLE SKILLS

Fighting in foreign wars, leading in business, serving in government, or even leading a religious order—these are excellent ways to accelerate the development of a broad set of transferrable skills. But they are not the only options. As Mitt Romney illustrated, another way is to take a position of responsibility in the nonprofit world, something that is much more likely to happen early than in a conventional business or government career.

Take Irfhan Rawji, who in the first decade or so of his career in Canada built up an impressive resume of business leadership roles— at McKinsey, Accenture, a private equity firm called Onex, and most recently as vice president of strategy and operations at Parkland Fuel Corporation. But what makes Rawji truly distinctive is his role in the nonprofit Heart & Stroke Foundation.

He initially got involved in the foundation as an ordinary volunteer—motivated by the impact that heart disease and strokes had had on his immediate family: "My family taught me that I should do something for the community—and I was happy to do it." It was a simple volunteer job. He was a canvasser, going door to door asking for money. From that early experience, he became really interested and asked to do more—and the organization was happy to comply. It asked him to do more routes, more programs, and eventually to join the board. He didn't really seek to be a leader of the organization; it was more a matter of interest, because it had become important to him.

Rawji's contributions to the Heart & Stroke Foundation became more and more significant—and while he was still in his early thirties, he was asked to become chairman. He reflects, "If you're a person who's willing to volunteer and give their time, you may be asked to play a role that is more 'senior' in status than you would in your full-time work. I found myself in senior roles in the nonprofit world that I would never get in business, because there was nobody else who was equally passionate and willing to give their time."

When he took over the chairmanship of Heart & Stroke, it was generating about $120 million in cash flow each year. A publicly traded business that generated that kind of revenue could have a market capitalization of upwards of $1 billion. As he observes, "Would any such company ask somebody to be the chair of the board at this young of an age? Definitely not."

In this part-time leadership role, Rawji has learned how nonprofits set strategy, compete for and raise funding, develop programming, and partner with other enterprises to complete their mission. He's also learned about the challenge of leading and motivating people in this kind of an environment. He started to understand how an organization's mission can be a real driver of individual actions.

There is one catch to all this. As Rawji discovered, it can be difficult to reconcile this kind of commitment to a part-time role with your full-time job. Once he became chairman of Heart & Stroke, he left management consulting for a role that he believed he could manage better.

He recalls his sense of irony about this: "The funny thing is that many of the most attractive, selective firms deliberately seek out candidates with diverse experience and interests. One of the things they look for in the interview process is leadership experience outside of the work setting—or in a different sector. But then, once you've entered they don't let you do anything outside of client demands. Before I left and became chairman of Heart & Stroke, I missed 50 percent of board meetings because I couldn't get out of commitments with my firm. Eventually, it got to the point where I couldn't find any role models who were pursuing things outside of immediate demands, and so I left to find that balance in my life that I felt was at risk."

THESE STORIES ILLUSTRATE why transferrable skills represent an important dimension of the Mosaic Principle—a critical challenge as you seek to build a broader life and career. They help people to solve significant problems, and they help people to broaden the range and diversity of their experiences. They also show that there are transferrable skills in every walk of life—not just, as is often assumed, in the business world. There are skills to be transferred from and to government and politics, as well as the military, academic, nonprofit, and volunteer arenas—even religious orders.

The actual process of transferring skills between different walks of life is rarely straightforward. There are often barriers—sometimes as high as the barrier between business and politics. Nobody wants to fall flat on his or her face by trying to transfer skills that are not welcomed or even accepted. For that reason, it makes sense to be strategic about skill transfer—to ask, "In what other arenas would my skills and experience be useful?"

That's what Josh Gotbaum did when he transferred his airline restructuring skills to government. And when it comes to making a transition, build upon the skills you already have—while seeking to acquire the skills you lack. Part of your objective in making such a transition should be to plug gaps in your own skills and experience—just as Steve Rattner and Josh Gotbaum did when they went into investment banking.

A broader life and career will certainly expand your range of skills to transfer—skills that enable you to solve problems, lead individuals and teams, and drive change. But that's not all it will take to succeed in new and different environments nor to benefit from the experience of doing so. You will also have to understand the differences and similarities between different contexts. That's why contextual intelligence is the next dimension of the Mosaic Principle.

6

LISTEN, LEARN, ADAPT
Investing in Contextual Intelligence

Everything that is new or uncommon raises a pleasure in the imagination, because it fills the soul with agreeable surprise, gratifies its curiosity, and gives it an idea of which it was not before possessed.

—Joseph Addison, the *Spectator*, 1854

Oxford Union Society, Oxford—April 1994
The speaker has been in full flow now for more than an hour and a half, but nobody looks bored and nobody is moving from their seat. This typically restless and impatient crowd seems transfixed, almost as if under a spell. There is indeed something hypnotic about his style of speaking—a slow, steady, and rhythmic cadence with occasional lengthy, theatrical pauses in which he seems genuinely to be unsure of what to say next. He conveys the impression that he is giving this talk for the first time ever, although it is probably the third time this week. He has one PowerPoint slide with eight numbered points to which he refers occasionally when he wants to move on to the next theme—but mostly he just talks and we listen.

He has just told a slightly risqué joke about Princess Diana, currently going through a tortuous divorce from Prince Charles—and after a moment's hesitation, the audience laughs knowingly. It's well past time for lunch, so the speaker pauses and says, "I'm not done yet; do you guys mind if we carry on with this after lunch?" The audience—the entire London Office of McKinsey—applauds in approval, casting aside by popular acclaim the carefully planned agenda for the afternoon. Who knew that a lecture on *adaptive leadership* could be so mesmerizing?

The speaker who has so captured our attention describes himself as a physician, psychiatrist, musician, and university lecturer. He is, by all accounts, an accomplished cellist who has studied under the great Gregor Piatigorsky. He is also a former clinical instructor in psychiatry at Harvard Medical School. But his main occupation— and the reason that he is the guest speaker at this off-site meeting in Oxford—is that he is a lecturer in public leadership at Harvard University, and specifically at the Kennedy School of Government.

By any measure, Ronald Heifetz has already built a remarkably broad career—and he clearly believes that we need that breadth of perspective to address what he calls our "crisis of leadership in many areas of public and private life." In his view, we need breadth because the nature of our problems demands it: "Pinning the blame on authority provides us with a simple accounting for our predicaments," he says. "'Throw out the rascals! They're the reason we're in this mess!' Yet our current crises may have more to do with the scale, interdependence, and perceived uncontrollability of modern economic and political life." In circumstances like these, we cannot afford what Heifetz calls "work avoidance mechanisms" like blaming other people for general government dysfunction.

He carries with him several self-declared "biases," born first of his training and practical experience as a physician. He believes that many of society's problems are embedded in complicated and interactive systems, just like the human body's response to illness. He also believes that much of our behavior reflects a kind of biological and social adaptation to these changing circumstances—for instance, to changes in climate, competition, resource supply—helping us to meet problems successfully according to our values and purposes. And above all, he believes that leadership roles (or what he calls "authority relationships") are best characterized in terms of service. "My job as a physician consists of helping people solve the problems for which I have some expertise. That is why they authorize me; authority is a trust. If in some problem situations my latitude for action—my authorization—must expand, then the bases of my trust may have to change."

This change in "authorization," in the trust accorded to leaders, is the essence of what he calls "adaptive leadership." It matters because fewer and fewer of our problems are purely technical in nature—problems that can be solved by the knowledge of technical experts or deep specialists. Narrow technical expertise can only be pre-eminent when the problem definition, solution, and implementation path are specific, clear, and well understood. But more and more of our problems are adaptive—they are complex and ambiguous in nature, and they require new learning, experimentation, and collective engagement to solve.

We have many such problems: uncompetitive industries, drug abuse, ethnic strife, budget deficits, economic dislocation, and national security. Problems such as these require leadership that mobilizes people from different walks of life and perspectives. They cannot be solved by a single wise person with deep specialist knowledge in a position of declared authority—"I'm the expert, do what I say." As he points out, "The concept of adaptation arises from efforts to understand biological evolution. In our world, in our politics and business, we face adaptive challenges all the time. Every time we face a conflict between competing values, or encounter a gap between our shared values and the way we live, we need to learn new ways."

In addition to his medical training, Heifetz draws upon his experience as a musician to define the key features of adaptive leadership. Music teaches that dissonance is an integral part of harmony. Without conflict and tension, music lacks dynamism and movement. He quotes Plato: "If there is no contradictory impression, there is nothing to awaken reflection." Music teaches what it means to think and learn with the heart. In part, it means having access to emotions and viewing them as a resource rather than as a liability. It also means having the patience to find meanings left implicit.

Adaptive leadership requires a learning strategy. A leader has to engage in facing the challenge, adjusting her values, changing perspectives, and developing new habits of behavior. The adaptive demands of our society require leadership that takes responsibility, without waiting for revelation or request. As he observes, "One may perhaps lead with no more than a question in hand."

It's clear that this kind of adaptive leadership depends upon breadth of experience and perspective—as illustrated by Heifetz's own mix of medical, psychological, musical, and behavioral insights. The first and most important of Heifetz's prescriptions for adaptive leadership is to "get on the balcony"—so that you can see the whole arena and gain a holistic perspective. Leadership, he argues, is both active and reflective. One has to alternate between participating and observing. Walt Whitman described it as being "both in and out of the game." For example, Magic Johnson's greatness in leading his basketball team came from his ability to play hard on the court while keeping in mind the whole game situation, as if he were watching from the stands.

What the balcony allows you to do is to understand the full context in which you are operating. This is especially important when you are dealing with a new and unfamiliar situation. You need to take a whole-system view—to see the full picture and gain a multidimensional perspective of the context. If you are figuratively on the balcony, then you can see all the individual pieces of a complex puzzle and how they are interconnected. President Lyndon Johnson was able to manage the Selma crisis and the battle to secure the Voting Rights Act successfully because of his ability to get on the balcony and see the full context. He understood ultimately what the crisis was all about and consequently was able to respond productively. But with the issue of the Vietnam War, Johnson got caught up in the unfamiliar routines and confusing rhythms of wartime foreign policy and never got to the balcony. "He engaged in the nation's conflict without ever leading it," suggests Heifetz.

We are all familiar with the metaphor of the elephant that is so large that if you come up close you can only see a part of it—just the trunk, or just the mammoth legs, or just the tail. If you are standing too close, you can't see the whole context. Another related metaphor is the Pando forest of aspen trees that spread over more than one hundred acres in Utah. These trees rise as high as one hundred feet, and each has its own branches, bark, and leaves.

To the untrained eye, each appears to be an independent, stand-alone tree. But in fact, every tree in the area shoots upward from a single organism, sharing a giant underground root system. Estimates suggest that the Pando tree system has a collective weight of 6,615 tons, making it the heaviest living organism in the world.

Like a botanist who studies the root system of an aspen and appreciates the interconnection of aspen trees in the Pando system, adaptive leaders see relationships among seemingly disparate problems, events, or actors as different elements of the same issue. This allows them to tie together sectors, intellectual disciplines, cultures, functions, and industries in a manner that others cannot. They have contextual intelligence.

FIGURE 6.1. The Pando appears as separate trees, but are actually connected to a single organism. Reprinted with permission of Alamy Limited, Abingdon, Oxon, England.

CONTEXT MATTERS

Contextual intelligence is born of broad and diverse experience that enables you to understand and adapt to different contexts, and to operate effectively in all manner of situations and environments. It is rooted in the simple empirical observations that context differs and context matters—and that is why contextual intelligence is the fourth dimension of the Mosaic Principle.

In 1884, the social theorist Herbert Spencer suggested that the times produce the person and not the other way around. Through that lens, the more or less contemporaneous coexistence of the United States' first generation of great leaders—Washington, Jefferson, Adams, Madison, Hamilton, Monroe, Franklin—could be seen not simply as a fortuitous demographic fluke that helped forge a nation but as a function of the extraordinary times in which they all lived. Indeed, historians have noted that several of the founders performed superbly in some roles but were relatively undistinguished in others.

The historian Jack Rakove declares that "the men who took commanding roles in the American Revolution were as unlikely a gang of revolutionaries as one can imagine. They became revolutionaries despite themselves." For instance, John Adams, fearing British retaliation against the revolution, hesitated to give up his law career and only threw in his hat once elected as a delegate to the First Continental Congress. In turn, George Washington was happily focused on managing his agricultural and horse-breeding business until Adams nominated him as commander in chief of the Army. "I have used every endeavor in my power to avoid it," he wrote. Stimulated by examples of adaptive leadership like this, Herbert Spencer argued that "what an individual actually does when acting as a leader is in large part dependent upon characteristics of the situation in which he functions."

At the start of the twenty-first century, two Harvard Business School professors, Anthony Mayo and Nitin Nohria (who later became dean of the school), set out to fill a void in the field of management thinking: the lack of a canon of history's greatest business leaders. Students of literature read the classics of Shakespeare, Milton, and Joyce; the Harvard professors believed that students of business should understand the history and critical biographies of Sloan, Procter, Disney, and the other business leaders from the past century who profoundly shaped American life. So Mayo and Nohria identified 1,000 great chief executives and company founders of the twentieth century; they then surveyed 7,000 of today's business executives, asking them to evaluate and rank the original list of 1,000. Out of this they produced a ranking of the top 100 business leaders of the last century.

The resulting book, published in 2005 and entitled *In Their Time: The Greatest Business Leaders of the 20th Century*, seeks to isolate the most important lessons learned from the experience of these great men and women. Although their focus is on individual leaders, they argue that we should move beyond the "great man theory." Long-term success is not derived from the sheer force of an all-powerful individual's personality and character, triumphing over everybody and everything. In reality, long-term success depends much more upon ability to develop a sophisticated understanding of context. Without that, an individual risks being surpassed by competitors or falling victim to hubris. They suggest the following equation of success: "Great leadership is a function of context plus personal characteristics plus adaptive capacity." So they share with Ronald Heifetz a belief in the importance of adaptation.

Context comes first in this equation, and Mayo and Nohria conclude that the most important attribute for a business leader to develop is contextual intelligence, which they define as "the ability to understand an evolving environment and capitalize on trends." They recommend that the same sensing capacity that has brought success to the greatest CEOs and founders should be developed by individuals as they build their lives and careers. They call this being a "first class noticer."

In a more recent *Harvard Business Review* article, another Harvard professor, Tarun Khanna, offers a slightly different and fuller definition of contextual intelligence. He calls it "the ability to understand the limits of knowledge and to adapt that knowledge to an environment different from the one in which it was developed." Khanna is particularly focused on the enormous differences that exist in geographic context—between different countries and regions of the world.

Much of his own research is focused on emerging markets, especially in South Asia—and he has observed the key contextual differences within that region and between South Asia and the rest of the world. Conditions differ enormously from one place to another, he observes—conditions not just of economic development but of institutional character, physical geography, educational norms, language, and culture. These are supplemented by differences in legal and political norms and expectations—on issues as diverse as intellectual property rights, aesthetic preferences, attitudes toward power, beliefs about the free market, and even religious traditions and cultures. Khanna concludes, "Trying to apply management practices uniformly across geographies is a fool's errand, much as we'd like to think otherwise. To use the language of business strategists, the logic of how value is created and divided among industry participants is unchanged, but its application is constrained by contextual variables."

These business school professors have reached their conclusion about the importance of context by looking at the leaders of large business enterprises. But if contextual intelligence is a key to success within business, how much more important must it be for those of us who seek to build a broader life and career across sectors, industries, functions, disciplines, or cultures? As we navigate this wide-ranging landscape, there are many fewer common assumptions that we can take as givens and many more things that we need to glean from a full understanding of the specific context in which we operate.

Some people seem hardwired to succeed in one context and fail in another. When asked why that is, we turn to the oft-used expression "horses for courses." The implication is that these people have a fixed repertoire of skills, which limits and conditions their responses to new situations. Changes in context require leaders to adjust their values, change perspectives, and develop new habits of behavior. As you might expect, this is very hard to do, and Ronald Heifetz observes that "many leaders fail to meet adaptive challenges because they cannot make the mental leap of faith to pursue a course that does not have a guaranteed outcome." They are unwilling or unable to change their approach to fit the needs of the new context—or they simply don't take the time to listen and learn what changes are required in the first place.

In contrast, some other people *are* able to transfer their skills across contexts. They seemingly have a wider repertoire and a better idea of which arrows to select under which circumstances. To use a metaphor born of our digital age, they have more bandwidth and are able to tune carefully for different situations. They have an intuitive diagnostic skill that allows them to adapt their leadership style and approach and to achieve alignment with their objectives. They have contextual intelligence.

Writers and philosophers through the centuries have echoed the thought that the way in which you adapt to a new context will go a long way toward determining your success. In the fifteenth century, Machiavelli wrote, "We are successful when our ways are suited to the times and circumstances, and unsuccessful when they are not. Two men may both succeed, although they have different characters, one acting cautiously and the other impetuously. The reason for these different outcomes is whether their ways of acting are in conformity with the conditions in which they operate." In the nineteenth century, the Japanese scholar Okakura Kakuzo wrote, "The art of life is a constant readjustment to our surroundings."

So how do you go about this enormously difficult and important challenge of developing contextual intelligence? The answer is that you need to listen, learn, and adapt to each new context and to adopt a professional mind-set in everything you do.

LEARNING THE NEW CONTEXT

The noted psychologist and chronicler of emotional intelligence Daniel Goleman observes in an article entitled "What Makes a Leader?" that "every businessperson knows a story about a highly intelligent, highly skilled executive who was promoted into a leadership position, only to fail at the job. And they also know a story about someone with solid—but not extraordinary—intellectual abilities and technical skills who was promoted into a similar position and then soared." The reason these stories are so well-known is that they exemplify the right way and the wrong way to approach new challenges—which is a prerequisite to building a broader life.

For the first six years of the Obama administration, Jonathan McBride worked in and ultimately led the White House Office of Presidential Personnel, responsible for the 3,000 presidential appointments that any administration has to make. Prior to the White House, he had built a broad career for himself. He was a congressional staffer on Capitol Hill, then an associate at Goldman Sachs, followed by leading an entrepreneurial venture—Jungle Media Group, focused on "career lifestyle" issues and career options for MBAs, JDs, college students, and African American and Hispanic young professionals. He came to the White House from Universum, a global employer-branding company, where he had served as chief strategy officer. Since he left the White House in 2014, he has served as senior vice president of talent at BlackRock, the massive investment management firm.

This eclectic background has given McBride plenty of experience of changing contexts—and he has seen many others take up leadership roles in the government as a result of his selection process. He has one overriding piece of advice for people joining a new organization—including when that organization is the government: don't assume that the people who came before you were idiots and that the way things are currently done is stupid! Assume that things are done for a reason.

Roger Sant, who made a similar transition more than thirty years before when he joined the Carter administration, agrees: "You have to start from the understanding that the culture and thinking processes of government and business are fundamentally different. If you can believe that there is a benefit from cross-fertilization between these sectors, you can also respect that each sector has reasons for the way it operates—and learn how to work in that new context." You should try first to understand how things currently work and why, before shaking them up or dismissing them altogether. In other words, learn the pre-existing context first—the history, the people, the aspirations and expectations—before you try to change it.

How do you learn a new context? The experience of McBride, Sant, and others who have made this kind of transition suggests a checklist:

1. *Understand the organization's purpose and mission.* These may be explicitly stated and easy to divine, or they may be implicit and embedded within the unspoken culture and values. Either way, they will likely provide the raison d'être for you and your new colleagues. When Jeff Seabright left government service and moved into the private sector—first with Texaco and then with Coca-Cola—he knew that he had to modify the approach that had become second nature to him in government and understand the "company DNA." He asked himself, "What is the beating heart of the organization that defines its dominant character?"

"At Texaco," he recalls, "I learned quickly that this was a company built on an engineering culture. I had to align the engineering processes with the approach I was recommending on environmental and sustainability issues, or they wouldn't have held. On the other hand, Coca-Cola is primarily a marketing organization. It's the owner of the brand—so marketing and brand management really constitute the company's DNA."

So when Seabright spoke about the south India crisis to a meeting of global senior Coca-Cola leaders, he used language and graphics that centered on the risk to the brand and marketing strategy if the company didn't deal with the crisis immediately: "I remember honing my pitch. This is a marketing company, and it expects you to convey your ideas powerfully. I told them, 'We can have all the caps, crowns, and concentrates in the world, but without water we will have no business.'"

2. *Map the leadership hierarchy and approach.* This is easy to do in command-and-control hierarchies like the military, much harder in consensus-oriented professional service partnerships and even in the government. In his popular guides to the first ninety days in a leadership role, Michael Watkins observes that people typically focus too much on technical skills and not enough on the company's

politics—on who is responsible for what, and how they get things done.

3. *Learn the language (and acronyms).* Most organizations have a distinct language—almost a "secret code," replete with obscure acronyms—that underpins the culture and conveys a sense of being an insider. The sooner you can speak this language with fluency, the sooner you will look and feel like you're at home.

4. *Understand the key performance metrics and incentive structures.* You will quickly want to gain a sense of who and what are adding value to the organization through the activities they undertake and the way they do so. Understand what success will look like, how it will be measured, and how it will be rewarded—both for you and your counterparts. Diana Farrell recalls from her time as deputy director of the National Economic Council how important it was—especially in the teeth of an unfolding crisis—to "understand the structural and temporary elements of value creation. There are enormous differences, which are only exacerbated by a crisis, and they give rise to some skills and capabilities being more appropriate than others."

5. *Assess the competitors, partners, and stakeholders.* It will be tempting initially to focus all your attention internally, as you seek to figure out "what goes on around here." But it's equally important to understand the external environment, and you may never see it as clearly as you will in the early stages.

6. *Understand financial and funding models.* The old adage "follow the money" holds true, even—perhaps especially—in government and nonprofit institutions. You will want to understand where the money comes from, how it is raised, and how it is allocated—especially how financial resources are deployed against strategic goals.

7. *Learn the expectations for transparency and accountability.* One of the biggest differences among organizations is often the expectation for transparency and accountability—sometimes highest in government, where so much is required to be in the public domain and formal accountability is to the people through their elected representatives. You will need to understand how open, clear, and accountable you need to be.

Jonathan McBride reflects upon his experience of running the presidential appointments process for President Obama: "If I could reduce the entire process down to one defining characteristic, it is the candidate's temperament. People who are in control of their own emotions and impulses, who demonstrate consistency and reliability, are typically better able to adapt to a new context. They attract the support and encouragement of their new colleagues, and they stay calm and controlled in the face of change and uncertainty—even when placed under extreme pressure."

LEARNING BY LISTENING

Having broader experience cultivates imagination and a spirit of inquiry, teaching you above all to ask questions and listen to the answers. Bernie Ferrari is one of the best people I know at asking and listening—as I observed firsthand when he joined McKinsey as a partner, having already distinguished himself in other professional arenas.

McKinsey was, in fact, the fourth of Ferrari's five professional life chapters (so far)—he has been a surgeon, a lawyer, a businessman, a consultant, and is now a university professor and dean of the Carey Business School at Johns Hopkins University. By the time Ferrari became my colleague, he had operated on patients with gunshot wounds in South Central Los Angeles, performed cardiothoracic surgery on numerous people with heart and lung conditions, and run a substantial medical clinic in New Orleans.

From all those experiences Ferrari has concluded that listening is the most important skill that enables success in life. "Though each career had its own unique domain knowledge," he reflects, "they all had something in common. The leaders in each field—those most respected, accomplished, and able to inspire others—outdistanced their peers by practicing better listening skills."

Bernie Ferrari is not by any means a passive personality who just asks questions and nods his head. His approach to listening is active and purposeful, drawing directly upon his unusual range of experiences. His questions are direct and specific—he calls them "pesky."

His direct inquisitive approach reflects his belief that listening is no more a passive, innate ability than is speaking. He also believes that listening is a learnable skill. If we can teach people to write and speak more clearly or more persuasively, if we can break down the process of imparting information into discrete and learnable steps, then we can do the same with the process of receiving information.

Like Atul Gawande and Ronald Heifetz, Bernie Ferrari has taken a lot from his earlier experience as a medical doctor. Think about what happens when you are unwell and go to see the doctor. First—usually even before the doctor "lays hands" on you—he or she asks a lot of questions. Some are general like "How are you feeling?" and some are quite specific like "Does it hurt here?" or "How long have you been experiencing shortness of breath?" Others relate to your so-called patient history, like "What other medical conditions have you had in the past?" or "Has your mother or father had comparable health issues?" And some are explicitly contextual, like "Have you been under a lot of stress lately?" or in the case of a communicable disease, "Have you visited a place where this kind of condition is common?"

This is the environment in which Bernie Ferrari first learned how to ask questions and understand context: "I began my career as a surgeon, which may explain why . . . I have a more clinical method of listening than most. One broadly applicable thing I learned in medicine is that you have to ask a lot of direct questions to really understand what is being said and why it's being said. Since every patient is unique, and each illness or injury manifests itself differently from patient to patient, asking the right questions and listening carefully to the answers were the keys not only to making a good diagnosis, but also to managing treatment."

Ferrari also draws upon the teaching of George Engel, one of his professors in medical school, who developed a distinctive model of medicine that he called *biopsychosocial*—and it depended almost entirely on active listening. He believes that a doctor could diagnose people most accurately by using gentle questioning to tease out a deep and broad array of information—about their lives, their habits, their families, their jobs, anything that might (or might not) be relevant. "The patient is your teacher," he says. "The clinical triad is observation, introspection, and dialogue . . . it's a negotiation."

Ferrari also recalls the most profound lesson of medicine, enshrined in the Hippocratic Oath, sworn by every graduating physician: "Do no harm." He observes, "As I went on in my medical career, I learned that the surest path to violating that oath, despite my best intentions, was to proceed with a treatment under a misdiagnosis." As a former surgical mentor said to him, "You can't fix it if you don't know what's wrong"—and he might have added, if you haven't secured the patient's help in understanding what's wrong with him or her.

Ferrari now believes that the direct, pesky questions that he instinctively asks are crucial in helping his clients and colleagues to challenge their assumptions and open their minds to new aspects of an issue. They are especially important in testing and challenging some of the pre-existing biases that we all tend to have. You know the kind of thing—"business is fast-moving, cut-throat, and all about making money," or "government is slow-moving, bureaucratic, and lazy," or "nonprofits are idealistic, underresourced, and impractical."

In a recent study entitled "The Chameleon Effect," two professors, Tanya Chartrand and John Bargh, surveyed the social interactions of a sample of their students. They observed that those who had previously been assessed to have greater social functioning and compassion for others would also engage in what they call "behavioral mimicry." In lay terms, they would copy their audience. They were, metaphorically, social chameleons who "anticipated the behavior and actions of others, thereby facilitating smoother and more rewarding interpersonal relationships."

Bernie Ferrari also believes that empathy and adaptability are crucial to operating effectively in different contexts: "Not everyone is going to adapt to you, so the best listeners learn how to adapt to others. In this sense, the best listeners are chameleons. They recognize early on the particular paces and cadences of their conversation partner and adjust their listening accordingly."

For some, this kind of adaptability is a natural act—it's just what they do instinctively to fit in, like kids adapting to a new school, or my kids quickly developing American accents when we moved to the United States. For others, it is more of a learnable skill—figuring out by trial and error what it takes to adapt socially, culturally, and emotionally to a new context. And for many of us it's a mixture of instinctive and learned adaptation.

ADAPTING TO A NEW CONTEXT

How does a man who has spent his life directing plays lead a transformation in the financial condition and public reputation of a major national theater company? And how does a highly analytical management consultant become the charismatic and inspirational leader of a large grocery retail company? In both cases, the answer lies in their ability to adapt to a new context, by adjusting critical aspects of their mind-set and approach.

Royal Shakespeare Theatre,
Stratford-upon-Avon, England—May 2007

So, as you can see, our theater company is in pretty good shape. The Complete Works of Shakespeare Festival last year was a great success—we performed every Shakespeare play in one calendar year with a variety of theater partners, and we reached more than 1.5 million people. Next up is the Shakespeare's Histories program in which thirty-four actors will play more than 260 parts as the eight plays unfold. We are very excited about our planned production of Roald Dahl's *Mathilda,* which if all goes well, should be a great commercial success. And we are ready for the long-awaited physical transformation of the Royal Shakespeare Theatre here in Stratford, which should give us a wonderful new—or rather, modified—home for our performances. Oh, and our finances are in good shape—we are even on schedule to make a small surplus this year.

The speaker is Michael Boyd, artistic director of the Royal Shakespeare Company. He is sitting alongside his executive director, Vikki Heywood—and both are under the benign gaze of Sir Christopher

Bland, chair of the board. Assembled around them is the board of directors of the RSC, of which I have been a member for the past six years. This is my final board meeting before I move to the United States, and it is the culmination of one of the most remarkable and emotionally rewarding experiences of my professional career.

It is almost impossible to exaggerate how different things were just five years earlier when Michael Boyd took over as artistic director. A retrospective in the *Guardian* newspaper recalls, "It was July 2002. The RSC was flailing: Boyd's predecessor, Adrian Noble, had been torn apart for simultaneously abandoning its London base at the Barbican, pushing through a costly internal shake-up, and announcing that he would demolish the Royal Shakespeare Theatre—something that the *Guardian*'s Michael Billington likened to a man deciding to 'leave his job, his wife and his home all on the same day.'"

I had lived through those dark days as a board member, and it was quite as awful as the *Guardian* portrayed. I recall one all-day board off-site at Eton College, the elite private school where we hid away under the watchful eye of the headmaster, an RSC patron. In theory we were there to plan the future of the theater company, but in practice we were waiting to see whether there would actually be a future—which largely depended upon a "stabilization grant" from the Arts Council to subsidize our recovery plan. If the government had decided to abandon us, then we would have been forced to close the company or merge it with the Royal National Theatre—the country's other leading theatrical institution. Either way a wonderful cultural institution would have been wrecked—and on our watch. There didn't seem to be any good options.

Late that day came news that the government would indeed agree to the subsidy—my first experience of a government "bailout." But it was clear that we would need to make some changes—the most significant being to hire Michael Boyd as the artistic leader of the company. That turned out to be the single most transformative appointment in which I have participated—even though headline writers reached immediately for that hoary Shakespearean cliché, "poisoned chalice," to describe the legacy being handed to Boyd on his arrival.

There was little in Boyd's background to give great confidence that he would so manifestly succeed as the leader of the company. Up to that point, his principal accomplishments had been as a director with a long resume of successful productions. But we had learned the hard way that theater company leadership is susceptible to the so-called *Peter Principle*—the whimsical management theory that states that the selection of a candidate for a position is all too often based on the candidate's performance in previous roles, which may have little or nothing to do with the required abilities for the intended role. Think of doctors running hospitals, lawyers running law firms, athletes running sports franchises—and of course, actors or directors running theater companies.

The Peter Principle derives from the ubiquitous observation: anything that works will be used in progressively more challenging applications until it fails. According to Lawrence J. Peter and Raymond Hull, the inventors of the principle, this explains "why things always go wrong." They observe that "in time, every post tends to be occupied by an employee who is incompetent to carry out its duties." This is because "in a hierarchy every employee tends to rise to his level of incompetence."

But in this case the worst fears of the Peter Principle have clearly not applied—rather the contrary. It has become clear to everybody on the board that Michael Boyd was an inspired choice—and the reason is also becoming obvious: Boyd exhibits an almost exceptional level of contextual intelligence, an ability to understand and adapt to a new role and a new setting. It is not that Boyd has ceased to be a theatrical director—indeed he has continued to direct wonderful plays throughout his tenure. But it is that he has developed an extended range of other talents and insights that have enabled him to succeed in this quite different context.

Michael Boyd's father—a doctor of public health in Scotland—fought hard to prevent his only son from studying literature at university, insisting that he should do something more worthwhile. But he did it anyway—a theoretical education at Edinburgh University and a practical education at the Edinburgh Festival: "Swiss mime-clowns, French puppet companies, avant-garde mixed-media artists, all a walk away. It was astonishing." He won a British Council fellowship to spend a year at the Malaya Bronnaya theater in Moscow, then run by the legendary director Anatoly Efros. This was 1978, and "it was like going to the moon. These huge building-sized portraits of Marx, Engels, and Lenin." The experience left him with two overriding beliefs that he would eventually bring to the RSC: first, that theater mattered and could change society; second, that the best way of working was to collaborate as an ensemble, a close-knit group of actors and technicians pulling together to create theatrical magic. He would always acknowledge that Russian theater—its unswerving dedication, its tradition of lifelong acting ensembles—laid the foundations of his approach to the theater.

Boyd went through a lengthy apprenticeship in the British theater—including time as an associate director at the RSC itself. He also played an entrepreneurial role in setting up the Tron Theatre in the east end of Glasgow—which did give him some limited experience of running a small theater company. But when he arrived at the RSC, he was largely an unknown quantity—at least in a role of this scale and significance. So why has he so palpably succeeded?

In part, it's because he is a purposeful, energetic, and totally committed leader of a theater ensemble—who understands the challenge he has been set. Those who have worked with him emphasize his inclusiveness, the way everyone in the building feels part of the company, and his democratic methods in, and beyond, the rehearsal room. Although the RSC has had its commercial successes—and *Mathilda* will be another one—entertainment for its own sake isn't really Michael Boyd's thing. He forswears a "bland, sentimental, acceptable, handsome sort of approach. There's a vanity about that kind of work," he says, "a self-preening quality. The RSC has been as guilty of that as anyone. But I like to think not often in my time."

As importantly—at least from the board's perspective—he has proven a skilled manager of the company's finances and operations. The days of significant financial losses are seemingly behind us, demonstrating a heretofore unprecedented level of budgetary discipline. And the physical reconstruction of the company's aging physical plant has been turned into a triumphant march into a bright new future. The Transformation of Our Theatres project will yield an Elizabethan-style space within the shell of the old one, and in the meantime it involves a unique prefabricated temporary theater literally dropped into a local parking lot like a gigantic cargo container. He is delivering on his early commitment—made at his first press conference—"to create a space where there will be no excuses not to aspire to great art."

Early in his tenure as artistic director, Boyd spoke to the whole company of actors, directors, and theater hands. In a long and eloquent description of his philosophy of theater management, he made a rather blunt statement that I'm sure struck others, as it did me: "If we can balance the books, the bastards will leave us alone." Of course, as a member of the board, I was one of the "bastards," but I didn't mind the characterization because he was right and I was glad he knew it. He had understood the context in which he had been placed—and I knew he would have the contextual intelligence to succeed.

————

THOUGH WE DIDN'T HAVE bosses in the traditional sense at McKinsey, Archie Norman was effectively my first boss—the partner who took me under his wing at the start of my career and guided my early steps toward professional competence. He was a "tough love" kind of boss—although not the loud, profane *Master Chef* stereotype that people like Gordon Ramsay personify. He was calm, quiet, thoughtful, confident, smoothly assured but austere—and never, ever satisfied.

Years later I heard a story that reminded me of Archie Norman—although the person featured in the story was Henry Kissinger. The story went that when Kissinger was national security adviser in the Nixon White House, a staffer sent him a memo with recommendations for executive action. The next day the memo came back with a scribbled note from Kissinger: "This is not good enough—do it again." The chagrined staffer did exactly that—rewrote the memo, submitted it again to Kissinger, and a day later received a similar response: "This needs to be better, have another go." Without any more detailed guidance, the staffer had a third try, and this time decided to take it in person to Kissinger, rather than send it through the internal mail. As he handed over the third draft of the memo, Kissinger asked, "So, is this really your very best work?" to which the staffer responded, "Yes, it really is." Kissinger paused for a moment, and then said: "Good, then this time I'll read it."

That was what it was like to work for Norman, although I'm sure he read all my drafts—and he genuinely thought that none of them were remotely good enough. But I persevered, because I was learning a lot and he seemed to think it was worth his while to teach me. In addition to being tough to please, he was extremely analytical, dry, and almost unemotional. He loved spreadsheets, numbers, and quantitative analysis—just the way he had been taught at Harvard Business School. In the words of the American TV series of the time, his motto might have been, "just the facts, Jack." He was an interesting person to be around, but charismatic he was not.

Sometime later, Archie Norman left McKinsey—and in 1991 was appointed as the chief executive of ASDA, the UK's third-largest grocery retailer, which was in desperate trouble, almost on its last legs. He subsequently led one of the most remarkable turnarounds in British corporate history—so much so that eight years later Walmart acquired ASDA as the best means of establishing itself with a high-performing business in the UK. In the process, he and his team reinvented the layout and makeup of the stores, reoriented the strategy to focus on "everyday low prices," and re-energized a previously demoralized workforce.

But even more remarkable than the performance turnaround was the way in which he led it. Out went the dry, analytical, slightly dour Archie Norman I had known, and in his place emerged a warm, high-energy, charismatic "man of the people"—who built a relationship of rapport and even affection with his "colleagues" (the term he decided to adopt for every ASDA employee). He also transformed the office space in ASDA's Leeds headquarters, creating a primarily open-plan layout in which he would sit without grace or favor.

And he built what can be described only as a personality cult around himself, creating a Tell Archie program—so that colleagues felt that they worked for Archie, not just for a faceless CEO. Like everybody else in the company, he had on his desk an ASDA baseball cap, to be donned as a signal that you needed two hours of uninterrupted thinking time. But he never wore his, preferring to be accessible to his colleagues at work. The ASDA Way of Working, the name given to the new approach, was intended to transform the old culture, which had grown autocratic and slow moving, to one where all members of ASDA felt involved in improving the business—the equivalent, within the context of a corporation, of market stallholders, who run their own show and who engage actively with their customers.

How did he do it—this transformation of the ASDA culture, and seemingly of his own personality? Looking back more than twenty years later, it's evident that this was what Archie thought it would take to succeed in this new and challenging context. He learned what that context was, and then he adapted—he changed who he was, or at least how he presented himself, just as he figured out how to change the company.

Reflecting on the experience, he recalls, "A failing company needs new direction and a firm hand on the tiller. But as the new leader, you probably don't know exactly what to do on day one. So you have to set a degree of direction and a broad sense of purpose, because the defeated army needs to know which way to march. At the same time, give yourself time to listen. Listen to the front line. If it's a retail company, wander around the stores. Talk to the people who run the stores. Talk to the checkout operators. Understand the DNA of the company and what—culturally—led it to be in a failed situation. Behind all financial failures is organizational failure."

Archie Norman's transformation of ASDA's performance and culture was later the focus of a *Harvard Business Review* article co-authored by the same Nitin Nohria who had literally written the book on great twentieth-century leaders. The article praises Norman for exemplifying the "hard and soft approaches" to business management. It goes on, "Norman laid off employees, flattened the organization, and sold off losing businesses—acts that usually spawn distrust among employees and distance executives from their people. Yet during Norman's eight-year term as CEO, ASDA also became famous for its atmosphere of trust and openness. It has been described by executives at Wal-Mart—itself famous for its corporate culture—as being 'more like Wal-Mart than we are.'"

The *Harvard Business Review* article also notes that Archie didn't have a complete "personality transplant." He knew his own limitations as an "energizer"—so he hired Allan Leighton, a former Mars executive who has since become a famous business leader in his own right. "As one employee told us: 'People respect Archie, but they love Allan.'" Norman was always quick to credit Leighton with having helped to create stronger emotional commitment to the new ASDA. Although it might be possible for a single individual to embrace a completely different leadership style, accepting an equal partner with a contrasting personality makes it easier to achieve a more sustainable transformation.

Archie Norman succeeded in adapting to the different business context at ASDA. But rather like Mitt Romney, he later struggled to adapt to politics. While still the chair of ASDA, he was elected as a Conservative member of Parliament for Tunbridge Wells in the 1997 election with a large majority. He is to this day the only person to have been the chair of one of Britain's one hundred most valuable companies and an MP at the same time.

This was a low point for the Conservative Party, which had just been handed a landslide defeat at the hands of Tony Blair's Labour Party. When William Hague became party leader, he appointed Archie Norman as the first-ever "chief executive" of the Conservative Party, a role for which his background seemingly equipped him perfectly. His role was to "bang the modernization drum"—to recruit more female and ethnic minority candidates, to tell the "old guard" that they needed to turn away from their unfashionable obsessions with Europe and immigration, and of course to get the party's finances in order. For all intents and purposes, he was asked to "turn around" the Conservative Party.

But it did not go well—at least in the eyes of the media and the change-resistant backbenchers, who made merciless fun of his attempt to run the party like a business with strategic plans and off-site retreats. It was clear to everybody that it wasn't working, and when the Conservatives suffered a second successive landslide election defeat in 2001, and William Hague was replaced as leader by Michael Howard, Archie Norman was quietly dropped from the party leadership, not to return. The "experiment" in having an elite businessman in a senior political role had seemingly failed. Nobody was surprised when he gave up his safe Tunbridge constituency in 2005 and stood down as an MP. By the time the Conservatives came back into power in 2010, Norman was once again a full-time businessman, becoming the chair of ITV, the UK's most prominent commercial television company.

He recalls the conditions that eventually drove him out of politics: "It was like a different world. What struck me most was the insularity of Westminster. The way that parliamentary process, everything from the buildings, the atmosphere, the voting late at night, the eccentric lifestyle comes to absorb people and becomes their world. So that events that are miniscule in the national political theatre are extremely important to them, some adjournment debate or late night vote." He concludes, "I think that I probably did upset people with my views on the party, where it had to go, which is no bad thing, somebody had to be the messenger. The pioneer is not necessarily the most rewarding occupation in life."

ADOPTING A PROFESSIONAL MIND-SET

Richard "Dick" Cavanaugh was a partner in McKinsey's Washington, DC, Office long before I showed up there—working as he recalls on "public issues involving private enterprise"—having previously served in the federal government with the intriguing title "director of cash management" in the Office of Management and Budget. As a consultant, he worked on the rehabilitation of America's railroads after most of them went bankrupt in the 1970s; the reorganization of New York City's municipal finances, also in the 1970s, after the city nearly went belly up; and the rebuilding of the country's federal air traffic control system after President Reagan fired the controllers who went on an illegal strike. Since then he has been executive dean of the Kennedy School, CEO of the Conference Board, and chair of the Educational Testing Service.

It was in the early days of the Reagan administration in 1981 that he wrote a *Wall Street Journal* article under the title "Why the Government's Business Isn't Businesslike." The article cites four reasons why proven business leaders have found it so difficult to transition into government: line management has often been captured by special interests, so only immediate staff can be relied upon; there is more of a focus on process than on substance, so that government becomes overcontrolled and undermanaged; in any case, managers don't have enough time to manage because of all the press briefings, congressional hearings, and largely ceremonial functions of government; and there is no such thing as a politically neutral decision, not least because of the 535-person "board" called Congress.

Notwithstanding this skepticism, Cavanaugh's own list of personal heroes includes several who have successfully made the transition from government to business—people like George Shultz, a titan of commerce and diplomacy; Bill Donaldson, a pioneer in Wall Street, government, and academia; John Whitehead, Robert Rubin, Jon Corzine, and Hank Paulson, who all transitioned from Goldman Sachs into government and later into philanthropy; Pete Peterson and David Rubenstein, both pioneers in private equity and philanthropy; and Michael Bloomberg, who built an extraordinarily successful financial information business, then became a three-term mayor of New York City, and is now back running the company that bears his name, while also operating as a corporate philanthropist and social activist.

These are all people who have built remarkable lives and careers—and in the process left enduring legacies. What are the common bonds among them—what enabled them to shape such broad lives and to be successful in multiple walks of life? First, says Cavanaugh, they were the *brightest and the best* in the fullest sense of that term. They had what he called *cognitive blessing*—they were in the top 5 percent of all business executives, much smarter than the average

CEO. Second, they were enormously skilled socially—people like John Whitehead, Bill Donaldson, George Shultz, and Bob Rubin. They didn't necessarily flourish in big groups (or they would have been politicians). But they could establish relationships quickly and easily, no matter what the setting.

Third and most important, "They were professionals—they had a professional mindset. Most of them started their careers on Wall Street or other professional firms. They had their first jobs with *academy organizations,* which had robust training programs that taught more than just how to do this or that task. They taught them how to understand culture and values." And he adds, "Dealing with the ambiguous situation of many professional firms, and learning to adapt to the culture and values of their clients—that's a pretty good training for business, for government, for the non-profit world. It's a pretty good training for life."

What is a professional mind-set? And why does time spent in a professional setting enhance your contextual intelligence? Why does it strengthen your ability to build a broader life?

First, in a professional firm you are required to learn a lot of new contexts. I recall early in my career at McKinsey when one of my colleagues left to become head of strategy for a beverages company. A little while later I bumped into him, and I asked him how it was going. "Fine, it's been pretty smooth," he said. And he added, "If there's one thing you learn as a consultant, it's how to join a company." By a quick count, I reckon that I have had more than a hundred significant institutional clients during my three and a half decades as a professional adviser. Some I just advised for a few months, even a few weeks. But some I advised for many years. Either way, my first task in each case was to learn the new context—to understand the enterprise that had sought my advice and that of my colleagues. Understanding a new context was like a muscle that I got to exercise regularly and that gained strength as a consequence.

Don Baer, now the worldwide chief executive of Burson-Marsteller, had a similar kind of early experience—first as a lawyer, and then as a journalist. That stood him in good stead when in 1994 he went to the White House initially as one of the president's speechwriters. "I had never written a speech before the first one I did for the president; there's nothing like on-the-job training!" He had to learn immediately the nature of this new context, and when he later became director of strategic planning and communications, he needed to do the same for the federal government as a whole. "I had to coordinate across all sorts of people around the government, all of whom reported to somebody else, and none of whom reported to me. I had to learn and adapt to a whole range of unfamiliar needs and expectations."

Second, you learn as a professional how to adapt to different contexts. You do that because the client always comes first. Don Baer notes that "in a profession, the bottom line isn't king, the client is king or queen, and you're motivated by his or her interests, and by a set of disciplines and values. Professions lack some of the clarity of the financial bottom line; but they do focus you on a meaningful measure of success—client satisfaction. That's a value and a discipline that you can transfer from job to job, from sector to sector."

Third, you have a kind of client orientation that sticks with you whatever the context. When David McCormick went into the US Treasury, he took the client orientation that he had learned from his early professional experience. If someone from Congress or someone from a nonprofit pressure group called—even if they were opposed to the government's position—he would always try to be responsive and respectful. For example, he recalls, "I dealt with climate change issues. You can imagine how much criticism there was about climate change policy when you're in the Bush administration. But when it came to the Sierra Club, or groups like that, I would call the senior person and I would try to deal with them in a forthright way. Where we were, why we were there, what questions could I answer?"

He was also close at hand to see Hank Paulson draw upon his thirty years of professional experience at Goldman Sachs. "When Hank was trying to make the case for TARP (the Troubled Asset Relief Program), he would meet with the House and Senate leadership. He basically viewed them as his 'client' with whom he was going to build the case, establish the trust." McCormick adds, "This kind of professional background helps you to see the problem at multiple levels, trying to be fact-based and logical, so that you can sort through the choices and manage all the key stakeholders."

In a professional environment—in an academy organization—the need to listen, learn, and adapt is married with a culture of rigor, discipline, and self-criticism. Don Baer notes, "As a professional, you have to be constant in asking yourself—given what I was tasked to do, did I do it? If not, where do I have to go back to? Where did I go off track, so that I can get back on track and make this happen?" He recalls that as a trainee lawyer there was a sense of analytical discipline and thoughtfulness. He learned how to do things the right way, even how to deliver a document to a partner or make sure that a submission was filed without error.

As a young journalist, he had similarly felt accountable for delivering something that had an internal logic to it and that was reported, researched, and delivered in a way that stood up to critical scrutiny. Like Steve Rattner, he found that his early experience in journalism shaped much of his subsequent career philosophy: "I think that journalists see themselves as in a form of public service—that's why they're willing to take less money for it. One of the reasons why there's tension between them and a lot of the people they cover is because they tend to bring a certain amount of self-righteousness to what they're doing. I never thought of myself as a government creature, but I did think of myself as a person involved in public affairs and politics in that respect."

Taking a professional mind-set requires you to listen and learn a new context, to adapt and evolve how you operate—and in the process, it helps you to build a remarkable life and career, rich with experience and insight. It also enables you to build an extended network of relationships and connections that would be impossible if you were to live a narrower life.

STRUCTURED SERENDIPITY
Building an Extended Network

The answer is to make change our friend. The answer is to
have broad access to information and information technology,
to have broad-based systems of education and healthcare and
family supports in every country, and to try to shape the global
economy.

—President Bill Clinton, 1999

Potomac, Maryland—Saturday, December 12, 2015
The cars begin to arrive in the early evening, lights piercing the
mid-December gloom. A small army of valets springs into action,
shepherding cars toward their appointed destinations in neighboring
fields and yards. A couple of police cars stand watch at the end of the
road, although it's unclear whether they are there to provide security,
to act as a deterrent against excess revelry, or simply because they are
curious to see what's going on. Despite everybody's best efforts, by
7:30 p.m. there is a substantial traffic jam along this quiet, prosperous
neighborhood street in the Maryland suburbs of Washington, DC—
the more remarkable because it is a Saturday evening.

Inside, the already substantial and beautifully appointed house has
been extended by a huge marquee that envelops most of the backyard.
It's a cold night, but the rented marquee seems to come with more
than adequate built-in heating. So guests are able to shed their heavy

winter coats and mingle in search of people they know. This is no trivial task, because at last count the guest list has risen above 750 people.

And not just any old 750. I turn to my right and there is John Roberts, chief justice of the Supreme Court—and nearby are a couple of his associate justices. Around the corner, I almost bump into Wolf Blitzer, CNN's redoubtable anchor—then various other journalists heave into view. In the corner, several members of Congress are huddled together, deep in discussion. Some of them are instantly recognizable, some of them not. And then clustered in the kitchen is a group of teenagers—children of our hosts and their friends.

It is easy to parody this event as a scene out of *This Town,* Mark Leibovitch's satirical take on the insularity and chumminess of political Washington—which he calls "America's gilded capital." That is, until you ask the obvious question, "How do you know John and April?"—referring to our hosts for the evening. Then you get a sense of the breadth and range of their networks. John Roberts is there because he and Delaney met through their respective kids' school; others because they have worked on nonprofit initiatives with April; several because they are business partners and counterparts; almost all because they have known both of their hosts as friends, neighbors, and colleagues for a long time in a variety of settings.

John and April Delaney are almost embarrassed that their annual holiday party has grown to this size. "This just started as a few of our close friends fifteen years ago—and now look at it," says April. "It seems like we add a hundred people to the guest list every year." But they acknowledge that as their professional context has changed in recent years, the scale and scope of their networks have come in more than handy. And their guests are equally happy to be there—and would be worried if the annual invitation failed somehow to arrive.

John Delaney trained as a lawyer, but he has spent most of his career as a businessman, founding two companies listed on the New York Stock Exchange before he was forty years old. He has shown a flair for finding underserved segments of the financial services market. In 1993, he cofounded Health Care Financial Partners, to make loans available to smaller health-care service providers ignored by larger banks. Then in 2000 he cofounded CapitalSource, a commercial lender aimed at funding small and medium-size enterprises. In addition to his companies, he founded Blueprint Maryland, a nonprofit group that aims to create jobs in the state.

Delaney had always been involved in politics—most recently as a Democratic fund-raiser and supporter. But in 2012, he decided to take a step further and run for Congress—specifically for the Sixth District of Maryland whose southernmost boundaries almost, but not quite, coincide with this street in Potomac. Although the previously Republican district had recently been redrawn by the state senate to give the Democrats a better chance of winning, the overwhelming favorite was incumbent state senator Robert J. Garagiola. That's when Delaney drew upon his by now prodigious network—for fund-raising, endorsements, and on-the-ground volunteers.

His campaign proposition had strong echoes of Mitt Romney's pitch for the presidency, albeit from the other side of the political aisle: "I understand how to create jobs and the needs of small businesses—and small businesses are the job creation engine." And in another echo of the presidential campaign that year, his opponent accused him of "loaning money to unscrupulous companies and gouging businesses with exorbitant interest rates."

In April 2012 Delaney pulled off a stunningly large victory in the Democratic primary, beating Garagiola by 54 to 29 percent; and in November he beat ten-term Republican congressional incumbent Roscoe Bartlett by 59 to 38 percent. When he took the congressional oath in January 2013, he became the only former CEO of a publicly traded company to serve in the 113th US Congress.

Delaney is adamant that he did not assemble his network for political purposes. "I really never thought that I would run for office until 2011. When I made the decision, it was great to be able to draw upon such a wide circle of friends—not least because so many of them have experiences and insights upon which I could draw. But in many respects, it was just a coincidence—these are just the people I have gotten to know during 25 years of living and working around here."

As IT HAPPENS, John Delaney was one of the few people I knew when I moved to Washington in 2007. It wasn't that Delaney's network extended to London—although it probably did. It was just that my wife and I had met them on vacation in the Northern Rocky Mountains many years before. We were also brought together by our children, who were roughly the same age. We had kept loosely in touch; but it was completely coincidental that when we moved to the Washington area, we bought a house just around the corner from theirs, that our younger children attended the same high school across the river in Virginia, and that our older children both ultimately chose to go to Northwestern University— where April had also graduated. Networks can sometimes get like that—a kind of "mutual stalking."

I moved to Washington in my late forties—which some might think of as the "peak of a career," the time when you really start to "cash in" on your network. That was certainly the prevailing model at McKinsey, where senior partners sought to build enduring client relationships out of networks that they had built up over the preceding two or three decades. That's just what you did as a senior professional in a client service firm. But my own networks were primarily in London; so having made the decision to move to a new city and country, I had little option but to build a new set of networks— essentially from scratch.

There was a sort of liberation in being new in town. I could turn up to events—fund-raisers, benefits, think tank seminars, political meetings—without feeling self-conscious that I didn't know anybody. My English accent immediately revealed that I wasn't from these parts. I am far from a natural extrovert, but I can usually persuade myself to walk into a crowded room full of unfamiliar faces and make some kind of a connection.

My wife, Alyssa, had it tougher, because she didn't have the same built-in support system I had at McKinsey. But she is a natural entrepreneur and network builder, and before long she was well entrenched in the local business and nonprofit communities, and soon after that she started work as a program director at Georgetown University McDonough School of Business, drawing upon her own professional experience as an entrepreneur. And while we were primarily focused on building new and eclectic networks in Washington, we did our best to stay connected to London—and our McKinsey network around the world.

BROAD NETWORK BENEFITS

When you ask people about the secrets of their success, it's remarkable how often they talk about other people—about mentors who helped them on their way or steered them at a critical juncture, about partners and collaborators who helped them tackle a complex problem or resolve a difficult challenge, even about competitors who kept them on their toes, and above all about friends and family who helped them through difficult times or who celebrated their victories—large or small. Each of us has a network; it's just that some are broader and more eclectic than others.

That's why developing an extended network is the fifth dimension of the Mosaic Principle. It is both a route to building a broader life and one of the most significant consequences and benefits of doing so.

When you meet people who have built a broader life, it is quickly apparent that they know a lot of people from a variety of different arenas. This is not just in the name-dropping sense, although some are not averse to the occasional name-drop. But it's much more that networks have a self-reinforcing quality—more begets more, better begets better, broader begets even broader—and because extended networks are a source of pleasure and pride, not just of career-building utility. In his appropriately titled book *The Social Animal,* David Brooks describes the motivation that drives most people to build networks: "If the outer mind highlights the power of the individual, the inner mind highlights the power of relationships and the invisible bonds between people."

The early stages of building a professional network can be as simple as having lunch with colleagues, clients, former classmates, and casual friends and then keeping in contact by, for example, sending congratulatory notes for personal or professional landmarks or articles on topics of mutual interest. Most of us do something like this—a kind of natural, easygoing approach to networking. But some people take a much more conscious and deliberate approach to extending their networks—like Brian Grazer, the Hollywood producer. For decades now Grazer has collaborated with other producers, and especially with Ron Howard, on a series of film and TV projects—several of which, like *Apollo 13* and *Parenthood,* have become contemporary classics.

While he has been doing all that, he has made a habit of arranging what he calls *curiosity conversations.* At first, these conversations were just inside the entertainment business. He recalls, "For a long time, I had a rule for myself: I had to meet one new person in the entertainment business every day." But pretty quickly he realized that he could actually reach out and talk to anyone in any walk of life about whom he was curious. He realized that "it's not just showbiz people who are willing to talk about themselves and their work—everyone is." And he realized that one of the chief benefits of his curiosity was to see the world through other people's eyes, to see the world in ways that he might otherwise miss.

So Grazer started broadening the range of people with whom he had these curiosity conversations. As a film and television producer, he believed that almost any such conversation could be useful to his work—and if it wasn't, then he would gain something from it personally. He wanted to be "plugged in to what's going on in science, in music, in popular culture"—not just what's happening, but "the attitude, the mood that surrounds what's happening." He also sought out people from "other communities"—physics, medicine, modeling, business, literature, law—and tried to learn something about the skill and the personality that it takes to perform in those worlds. These conversations have enabled him to build what he calls "a reservoir of experiences and points of view."

Grazer believes that this kind of curiosity is crucial to the process of innovation and experimentation. He cites medicine as an example—an arena that steadily, sometimes radically, advances primarily because of curiosity, from hand washing and sanitation to laparoscopic and robotic surgery. So "you need a doctor willing to step outside her comfortable point of view in order to benefit from those improvements yourself." He draws upon Procter & Gamble's approach to innovation and creativity to argue that what broad networks enable you to do is to "systematize serendipity"—finding ways to uncover great ideas. As he observes, "Curiosity is the tool that sparks creativity. Curiosity is the technique that gets to innovation."

Sheryl Sandberg, COO of Facebook, echoes this thought in her foreword to Adam Grant's book on originality and creativity: "Great creators," she says, "don't necessarily have the deepest expertise but rather seek out the broadest perspective." This is for the very evident reason that creativity depends upon generating a concept that is both novel and useful—and that is most likely to happen if you invoke curiosity and broaden your network.

Grazer also came to define curiosity—about people and about things—as the means of building a network and of enhancing his own capacity and courage as a network builder: "I use curiosity as a management tool. I use it to help me be outgoing. I use curiosity to power my self-confidence. I use it to avoid getting in a rut, and I use it to manage my own worries." He believes that these conversations help him create a network of information and contacts and relationships—not unlike the networks of information that intelligence officers develop over time. He also believes it helps him to be more creative and innovative—but he realizes that these can seem like rather abstract concepts. People often need something more tangible—and unlike creativity and innovation, curiosity is by its nature more accessible, more democratic, easier to see, and easier to do.

Brian Grazer may not know it, but he exhibits an advanced form of what scientists call *anthropocentricity*. Edward O. Wilson defines this as "fascination about ourselves and our fellow human beings." Anthropocentricity comes naturally to most of us because "we are an insatiably curious species—provided the subjects are our personal selves and people we know or would like to know." And this very human phenomenon plays a crucial role in "sharpening our social intelligence, a skill in which human beings are the geniuses among all earth's species." We naturally turn our curiosity about ourselves and our fellow human beings into a mosaic of stories "because that is how the mind works—a never-ending wandering through past scenarios and through alternative scenarios of the future."

Other people take a more relaxed, even casual, approach to network building than does Brian Grazer—although it is probably best to be more alert than the young lawyer whom I met recently. He had found himself sitting next to Supreme Court justice Ruth Bader Ginsburg at a benefit dinner for a legal charity—but did not recognize her. After telling her all about his recent cases at great length, he finally turned to the ageing but whip-smart judge, and asked, "So, what do you do?" Without a moment's hesitation, she responded: "Oh, I'm a lawyer too!"

Reid Hoffman, the Silicon Valley entrepreneur who founded and runs LinkedIn—the world's largest professional online network—has every reason to believe in the power of professional and personal networks. He notes that the practice of network building, which has enabled him to build such an iconic business, is rooted in the American experience—in the coffeehouse tradition that Benjamin Franklin established, in Alexis de Tocqueville's 1835 observation that nothing was as distinctive about America as its people's proclivity to form associations around interests, causes, and values.

Hoffman believes that that tradition is alive and well—and that "small, informal networks" are highly efficient at circulating ideas and connections. He advises, "If you want to increase your opportunity flow, join and participate in as many of these groups and associations as possible." For many people, these groups naturally include alumni associations that connect you to your former classmates, as well as groups of current and former professional colleagues. These are networks with a healthy blend of shared interests and diverse experience. For instance, Hoffman outlines the distinctive characteristics of what he calls the "PayPal mafia" of which he is a founding member: "high-quality people, a common bond, an ethos of sharing and cooperation, concentrated in a region and industry. These make it rich in opportunity flow, and the same factors make any network and association worth your while."

SOCIAL TRADING TO
SOLVE COMPLEX PROBLEMS

Once you have built broader networks, you will have access to genuine reciprocal relationships with others across a diverse range of intellectual disciplines, cultures, functions, and industries. Because of those relationships, you will be able to see trends that may affect your work and life long before they might be apparent to others. You will have what Reid Hoffman calls "network literacy"—that is, you will know how to perceive, access, and benefit from the information flowing through your professional and social networks.

Above all, you will strengthen your ability to solve complex problems, either by your own devices or in collaboration with others. You will naturally approach problems in a broader and more collaborative way, drawing upon diverse sources of insight and perspective. And you won't be on your own—you will be able to build broader and more diverse problem-solving teams, rather than simply trying to find people who look and sound like you.

Israel is one place where these kinds of broad, integrated networks have become especially effective. As Dan Senor and Saul Singer describe in *Start-up Nation,* Israeli entrepreneurs benefit from the country's nonhierarchical culture, where everyone in business belongs to overlapping networks enabled by small communities, common army service, geographic proximity, and informality. Israel's distinctive approach to network development starts in the military, a unique environment within Israeli society where young men and women work closely and intensely with people of different cultural, socioeconomic, and religious backgrounds. And because of the unusual nature of the Israeli model, it continues for years if not decades through participation in the military reserves.

In the Israeli military, a young Jew from Russia, another from Ethiopia, a secular native-born Israeli from Tel Aviv, a yeshiva student from Jerusalem, and a kibbutznik from a farming family might all be in the same unit. They'll spend two or three years serving together full-time and then spend another twenty-plus years of annual service in the reserves. The Israeli Defense Forces were always intended to rely heavily on reserve forces—so for a few weeks a year, Israelis depart from their professional and personal lives to train with their military unit. A lot of future business networks are constructed during the long hours of operations, guard duty, and training.

Back in the United States, a team of researchers at MIT's Human Dynamics Laboratory led by Sandy Pentland coined the term "social explorers" to characterize people who actively search for hidden knowledge within their extended networks. In one research project, they observed the relative success of 1.6 million day traders on the on-line platform eToro during 2011. The eToro platform allows individual traders to observe one another's moves, portfolios, and past performance. Information on the site is extremely transparent, so it's easy to see and precisely measure how interactions affect decisions and results.

On eToro, investors can do two main types of trades—a "single trade" is a normal stock transaction that a user makes on his or her own; a "social trade" is when a user places a trade that exactly copies another user's single trade. Users can also "follow" all of another user's trades automatically and review all real-time trades, choosing which ones to copy.

What the MIT researchers witnessed was that one group of investors worked in almost total isolation—they would follow few other traders and generate their investment strategies and tactics entirely on their own. At the other end of the spectrum, another group of "hyper-connected traders" would follow—and be followed by—many other traders and would draw upon "social learning" to guide much of their investment strategy. And of course, there was a group in the middle that exhibited a blend of "single" and "social" trading.

The researchers' analysis of the comparative rate of return from these alternative investment approaches showed that the effect of social learning is considerable—although it should not replace independent judgment. Those who employed a judicious blend of single and social trading consistently achieved a return on investment that was 30 percent higher than the returns achieved by either the isolated traders or those who simply followed the herd.

Sandy Pentland draws a wider lesson from this research into network-based "social trading." He thinks of social explorers as people who spend enormous amounts of time searching for new people and ideas. They seek to form connections with many kinds of people and to gain exposure to a broad variety of thinking. Explorers then winnow down the ideas they've gathered by bouncing them off other people to see which ones resonate. They hope that this will yield the very best ideas, although of course there's no guarantee of that.

Generally, the ideas that emerge from this process are discrete microstrategies—examples of actions that might be taken in the prevailing circumstances. Then, by assembling a great set of microstrategies, social explorers hope to make good overall decisions. He argues that the most effective way to leverage a broad network is to seek out diverse points of view but then to cross-reference them against what you already know, what you would have done without the broader range of perspectives. This social trading concept is not intended to replace your own intuitive problem-solving approach but rather to pressure test and strengthen it.

Social trading can be a highly valuable attribute of a broader life. You will gain most from social trading if you build professional and personal connections with people from completely different intellectual disciplines; if you associate with policymakers, businesspeople, and nonprofit social entrepreneurs; if you befriend people from Asia, Africa, South America, and Europe. If you apply the "curious state of mind" that Brian Grazer has spoken about, you will learn a lot and "invest" more wisely in your own life and that of others.

Social trading will also enable you to act as a bridge or a switch between seemingly disconnected communities. The need for people who can play that kind of bridging role is evident. In his landmark book *Bowling Alone,* Robert Putnam addresses the eroding effectiveness of the civic institutions and practices that we have inherited. He argues that we need to fortify our resolve as individuals to reconnect with each other, in order to overcome a familiar paradox of collective action, which goes as follows: "Even if I privately would prefer a more vibrant community, I cannot accomplish that goal on my own. Actions by individuals are not sufficient to restore community, but they are necessary."

In today's society, there are two particularly important opportunities to provide a bridge between disconnected communities. The first lies in what Harvard Kennedy School professors Jack Donahue and Richard Zeckhauser call *collaborative governance*. They suggest that there would be a "force multiplier" effect if people from different governance groups—notably in government, business, and the nonprofit world—could collaborate more systematically to solve shared problems.

The reason why collaborative governance is currently underemployed is that social networks are narrow and weak and we have not built up a foundation of trust and respect among different communities. Particularly in the public policy arena, the onus is on government leaders to orchestrate collaboration, rather than just define policy and manage agencies. The scientific philosopher Edward O. Wilson observes that "the most complex forms of social organization are made from high levels of collaboration. They are furthered with altruistic acts performed by at least some colony members."

Wilson leads us to the other principal area of opportunity for advanced social trading. This lies in *consilience* among intellectual disciplines. You will recall that consilience is the principle that evidence from independent, unrelated sources can "converge" to strong conclusions. When multiple sources of evidence are in agreement, the conclusion can be compelling even when none of the individual sources of evidence are sufficiently robust on their own. And although collaborative governance seems to be getting harder, consilience seems to be getting intrinsically easier and more natural—as evidenced by all the interdisciplinary institutes on academic campuses and task forces in leading think tanks.

Wilson argues that the disciplinary boundaries within the natural sciences are indeed fast disappearing, to be replaced by what he beguilingly calls "shifting hybrid domains in which consilience is implicit." And this is not just a matter of consilience among the sciences. There is both need and opportunity for increased consilience across a wider set of disciplines. "There has never been a better time for collaboration between scientists and philosophers, especially when they meet in the borderlands between biology, the social sciences, and the humanities."

So by building extended networks, by increased amounts of social trading, you can play a role in solving large and complex issues, whether acute crises or chronic problems. You can initiate and foster collaborative governance across and between the often disconnected elements of our society. And you can strengthen the bonds of community that we need to reinforce by collective action between people who are well inclined toward each other.

Leading a major university puts you at the heart of both areas of opportunity—collaborative governance and consilience. Nannerl O. Keohane, who has twice been a university dean, as well as a professor of political science and a member of several corporate boards, notes that "leadership in a complex institution such as a university allows one to encounter many aspects of human life from a new perspective, to know and work with people from all kinds of backgrounds—philanthropists and housekeepers, groundsmen and post-docs, librarians and state legislators." She adds, "One attraction of leadership is expanding one's horizons, satisfying one's curiosity about what it is like 'on the other side of the fence' between leadership and followership."

She adds that good leadership often stems from a "capacious appreciation of the varied features of a situation. This can be achieved through imagination—enlarging one's mentality, or listening to good counselors." It can also come from gathering multiple perspectives, bringing interested parties together. That process, enabled by broad and diverse networks, enables "peripheral vision": the habit of looking around to gauge the tone of your environment and note where the next opportunity or threat is coming from.

FORMING BROADER TEAMS

In the late 1950s, the West End of Boston was a tight-knit community of recent immigrants, primarily but not exclusively from Italy—and living conditions were poor. The bonds among families and neighbors seemed strong, forged by a common experience of the "hard knock" life experienced by most lower-middle-class Bostonians. This seemed like a very robust social "network"—knowing your neighbors, standing up for each other, looking out for the community.

Those bonds were tested when the city government initiated plans to redevelop the West End. Rumors circulated of an urban renewal process that would result in modern new skyscrapers but would displace the existing communities. The West End, as people knew it then, was at risk—and everybody expected the community to fight for a way of life they held dear.

At that time, the sociologist Herbert Gans embedded himself in the West End community. Gans was an immigrant himself—from Germany—and would later become president of the American Sociological Association. What he observed was that, rather than coalesce to try to save their cherished community, the West Enders quickly fragmented and dissolved as a "fighting force." Suspicious of outsiders and of the unknown—and especially of government, which they glibly dismissed as a "bunch of crooks"—they showed little interest in engaging with the powers that be. With little money or influence at City Hall, they couldn't properly voice their grievances, even if they had wanted to. They couldn't effectively organize under an accredited leader. And, constrained by the narrowness of their network, they couldn't influence Bostonians outside of their immediate community.

Gans concludes that the deep but narrow insularity of the West Enders' network was their undoing—putting aside the rights and wrongs of the urban renewal scheme. He observes that "it was only outsiders who could have saved the West End from the bulldozers, though it was the natives who felt it most painfully." Had the community been able to connect with other communities, they would have been better able to communicate their concerns about the neighborhood's impending fate to other prospective advocates. And if they had been able to relate their own interests with those of others with comparable beliefs and agendas, then they might have been able to organize more effectively to preserve at least the most treasured aspects of their neighborhood.

Deep but narrow networks act as a terrible constraint on effective team building in all walks of life. They confine people to narrowly defined "echo chambers." Nannerl O. Keohane observes this as a common failure of imagination among leaders: "Many leaders recruit people they already know and trust to join them in their endeavors, from the Oval Office to local community organizations. This makes detachment especially difficult. Even where friendship is not an issue, having power threatens to destroy what one might call the 'authenticity of relationships.'"

As an individual, you are much more likely to have a positive impact if you work well in teams—and especially if you help those teams to form. And you will amplify that impact if the teams you construct are broad and diverse.

Stan Litow built broad and diverse teams throughout his career. In 2010, Litow was running IBM's corporate citizenship programs when he started to wrestle with what he came to describe as the "skills mismatch" in the technology industry. How could it be that IBM and companies like it were having difficulty filling open positions?

Litow's response was to create a cross-sector, multidisciplinary program that he called P-TECH—Pathways in Technology Early College High School—a program for grades 9–14 designed to equip students with the specific skills required for high-growth technology jobs, while still taking core courses in English, the arts, science, and mathematics. There had been similar schemes before, but it was the way that Litow was able to draw upon his broad and integrated networks that gave this one a better chance of success.

He recalls, "I had a long-standing relationship with the City of New York University chancellor, and I was able to get him onboard. Our CEO, Ginny Rometty, had worked closely with former New York City mayor Michael Bloomberg. Both were essential to getting us over difficult challenges. And because I myself had been deputy chancellor of the New York school system, I had credibility with the current chancellor and his team."

The P-TECH program has gotten off to a strong start, in part because of the network that Litow was able to deploy. In its third year it engaged more than three hundred students; and over half have exceeded state-wide high school graduation requirements in three years or less. It is now getting reinforcement from the federal and state governments—a $100 million grant from the federal government, announced by President Obama on a visit to a P-TECH facility, and state awards announced by New York governor Andrew Cuomo to the sixteen winners of a competition to execute key components of the P-TECH program.

Mark Zuckerberg and Sheryl Sandberg, respectively the CEO and COO, wanted to build broad and integrated networks at Facebook. But they realized that they had a looming problem when the number of computer engineers they employed passed the threshold number of 150. This is known as *Dunbar's number*—based upon the theory developed by British evolutionary psychologist-cum-anthropologist Robin Dunbar. His research, initially among primates and subsequently among human beings, suggested that the optimal size for a social group among humans is 150—because the human brain has the capacity to maintain only that many close ties via what is called "social grooming." Using examples like how many Christmas cards the average British person typically sent (answer: 153), Dunbar concluded that "this limit is a direct function of relative neocortex size, and this in turn limits group size. The limit imposed by neocortical processing capacity is simply on the number of individuals with whom a stable interpersonal relationship can be maintained."

For a fast-growing company like Facebook, this would typically be the point at which it would start to splinter into a silo organization structure of divisions and subdivisions. As told by Gillian Tett in her book *The Silo Effect*, that is exactly what had happened at other technology companies like Sony and Microsoft with damaging consequences—a warning sign that Facebook took very seriously. So Facebook declared that all of its new employees—no matter how junior or senior—would undergo the same six-week induction process when they joined. Although these groups of trainees would not stay together as a unit—and would soon be scattered across the company—the joint experience would create lasting ties among them.

These induction programs were—and are—called "bootcamps," and the man who originated them, Andrew Bosworth (or "Boz") was named "Bootcamp Drill Sergeant." Boz observes about his social innovation, "Bootcampers tend to form bonds with their classmates who joined nearer the time and those bonds persist even after each has joined different teams. Bootcamp [can foster] cross-team communication and prevent the silos that so commonly spring up in growing engineering organizations."

Tett notes that as Facebook continued to expand, the company was naturally being organized into discrete project teams, dedicated to performing specific tasks. But the bootcamp concept helped to overlay those project teams with another set of informal social ties not defined by the formal departmental boundaries. This prevented the project teams from hardening into rigid, inward-looking groups and ensured that employees felt a sense of affiliation with the entire company, not just their tiny group.

From there, Facebook went further down the road of social experiments. The chief technical officer Mike Schroepfer observes, "There is all this research out there which shows that if you can keep people moving and colliding with each other, you get much more interaction." Facebook managers conceptualized the company as a single, open mass, where everybody could collide with each other on a random basis. That led to the architectural design of the Silicon Valley campus they took over from the former Sun Microsystems, and it stimulated cross-company "hackathon nights" at which people had to work together with people from different teams from their normal projects and work on something outside their day job.

Stories like these illustrate how important network breadth can be to the delivery of core business and governmental programs— both between institutions and even within the same organization like Facebook. Mike Schroepfer says, "I never used to think about this social stuff. It didn't seem that important. But then when I came to Facebook, I realized how much it matters. That's a real change! And now I cannot stop thinking about it."

BROADENING YOUR CAREER OPTIONS

John Berry reflects upon the path that took him to Congress as a staffer, to the Maryland state government, to leadership of the

National Zoo in Washington, DC, to the senior personnel leadership job in the US federal government, and then to his current role as US ambassador to Australia. "You see, the only job I actually applied for was the first one. After that, there's been a kind of *structured serendipity* to my career. People have asked me to do things—people who had a challenge, who knew me, who trusted me, who worked with me on some issue before."

When you ask people how they got their current job—or the one before that—the answer is typically a lot like John Berry's. An acquaintance, colleague, mentor, or a friend suggested it and in some cases made it happen. That's especially true for people who are crossing sector or other professional boundaries. There's no surprise here—the US Bureau of Labor Statistics estimates that 70 percent of professional jobs are filled through networking, and that only includes jobs that are posted publicly in the first place.

In her book *Lean In,* Sheryl Sandberg, who herself has already had a notably broad professional career in government and business— observes that "the most common metaphor for careers is a ladder; but this concept no longer applies to most workers." As of 2010, the average American had eleven jobs between the ages of eighteen and forty-six alone—although some of these may be various forms of internships or part-time roles. She suggests that "the days of joining an organization or corporation and staying there to climb the ladder are gone" and that a more appropriate metaphor for career management in today's world might be the jungle gym. Of course, every one of those job changes provides an opportunity for greater breadth and provides a test of gymnastic ability.

The seminal work on the importance of networks in career development was developed by Mark Granovetter, an American sociologist and professor at Stanford University. In his 1974 book entitled *Getting a Job: A Study of Contacts and Career,* he explores how the diversity and quality of network relationships influence professional opportunities. His research focuses on a Boston suburb, analyzing how 282 men identified job opportunities and were then hired or not.

What he found from this research provides academic reinforcement for the old adage "It's not what you know, it's who you know"—but it also helps to clarify what that really means: what really makes the difference to success in finding an attractive job is having a higher volume of work-related contacts in different domains, rather than leveraging strong personal ties with family and friends. He also demonstrates that people are much more likely to make a significant change in their career direction if they have contacts in other walks of life than their own. In other words, when it comes to finding a job and changing the focus of your career, the breadth of your network really makes all the difference.

By the way, professional networks sometimes (perhaps often) operate at one or two removes. John Berry did not know Barack Obama very well before he received a call from the newly elected president asking him to run the government's personnel operation. He had been recommended by people who had admired his work in state government and in running the National Zoo. It turns out that most presidential appointees (of which there are more than 3,000) don't know the president at all. They are typically suggested by someone who knows someone who knows there's an opening that needs filling.

If you're going to build a broader life and career, you are going to need to take a broader approach to building your network. The primary reason is that hiring managers rarely look outside established and familiar pools of talent—so you will need to help them do so. Small organizations typically operate through referrals and word of mouth, and larger enterprises apply a kind of "weak-network" approach to sourcing their people.

The segregation of communities that has become such a persistent feature of our society applies in the professional world as well. One of the biggest structural impediments to improved collaboration between sectors—and one of the outcomes of an increasing preference for depth—is that we cluster together in tightly defined professional communities, creating barriers to entry for "outsiders." This kind of professional concentration can be inadvertently exacerbated by professional networking services like LinkedIn, which operate in part on a labeling system. It's worth asking the question—if each member of your own LinkedIn network is labeled by the same sector or industry, how diverse can that list be? For many of us, there is a high concentration in a single walk of life.

The tendency of individuals to associate primarily—or even exclusively—with others who are similar to them is readily understood as "love of the same." It is self-evidently easier to establish a connection with someone who can relate to your own life experience—where you grew up, the school you attended, or the industry in which you work. The consequence is that most of us operate within "closed networks," using shared "love of the same" as a filter and a guarantor of conformity. Similarity breeds connection—that's the reason why there are relatively few interracial marriages, why teenagers choose friends who smoke and drink as much as they do, and why communities isolate themselves. It also helps to explain why the electorate in most countries is polarized into a small number of equally self-regarding and self-reinforcing political communities—sometimes, as in the United States, just two dominant party affiliations.

For the same reason, as Geoffrey Miller notes in *The Mating Mind,* people tend to choose spouses of similar intelligence, and the easiest way to measure someone else's intelligence is through their vocabulary. One specific by-product of this pattern is that people tend unwittingly to pick partners who have lived near them for at least parts of their lives. Numerous studies show that most men and women fall in love with individuals of the same ethnic, social, religious, educational, and economic background, those of similar physical attractiveness, comparable intelligence, similar attitudes, expectations, values, interests, and those with similar social and communication skills.

This tendency is also evident in the hiring process. Many firms implicitly or explicitly practice the "airport test." The governing question is, "Would I want to be stuck in an airport with this person, if we were on a business trip and our flight was delayed for a few hours?" It's a reasonable question—I have used it many times myself! The effect is to create a cordial but generally homogeneous cultural environment.

In her study entitled *Pedigree: How Elite Students Get Elite Jobs,* Northwestern University professor Lauren Rivera demonstrates the "closed circle" bias of modern recruiting programs for elite firms and shows that the inherent bias can be disturbed only by targeted intervention. Her research chronicles how—starting in the 1980s—many large enterprises moved to tightly structured recruiting programs that prioritize candidates from prequalified sources such as professional schools, strong "academy organizations," and other proven talent pools. As she observes, "What ends up happening is that firms create lists. So there's a school list, and on the list there are cores and there are targets. Cores are generally the most prestigious schools; targets are quite prestigious schools. Cores receive the most love. But basically if you're not from one of these cores or target schools, it's extremely hard to get into one of these firms."

A comparably narrow approach often applies at more senior levels, where executive search firms are employed to identify people who are pretested and who clearly "fit the bill." The measure of "cultural fit" is that the candidate should closely match the qualifications of people already in the organization or of peers in similar roles across the industry or sector. I have even come across this in discussions with joint MBA and public policy students at Harvard and the University of Pennsylvania—two demonstrably elite universities. Students there have told me that they struggle to attract the interest of potential employers in either the business or government sector because employers distrust their reasons to study the "other sector's discipline."

This is what you're sometimes up against when you're seeking to build a broader life—a narrow and reductionist approach to talent identification reinforced by implicit or explicit bias. But there are some reasons to be optimistic as you seek to expand and explore your options and build an extended and mutually supportive network.

First, building a career-enabling network is no longer just a matter of public or private sector, government or business. Nowadays, there is a legitimate and substantial *third option,* given the increasing professionalism of the nonprofit sector. More than a few people—especially new graduates—are placing a lot of reliance and hope on this third sector. They have good reason to do so, because institutions in the nonprofit sector are certainly growing in scale and significance.

In one sense, the nonprofit sector often presents like a kind of "quasi-government sector." But it can also act as a genuine bridge between the government and business sectors. In multiple business schools around the world, some of the most popular academic programs focus on "social entrepreneurship" and the "management of nonprofits"—programs like the one that Bill Novelli leads at Georgetown University's McDonough School of Business. These kinds of programs are attracting a great deal of funding support. For instance, Wharton now has a high-profile Social Impact Initiative, and Georgetown University has launched the Beeck Center for Social Entrepreneurship and Innovation led by Sonal Shah, a former White House director of social innovation, supported by an initial $10 million grant.

David Rubenstein, cofounder of the Carlyle Group and a significant benefactor of the Kennedy School, is a strong supporter and funder of this movement. He notes, "When I went into government in the 1970s, if you wanted to serve your country, typically you did it in government. You might be in the military, the Peace Corps, or in federal government service. Now there are many NGOs that are providing extensive services to our country, so that you can serve in one of those NGOs and do a very good job, or create your own NGO as a social entrepreneur. And I think many people who want to go into public service today don't feel they have to go into government."

The largest and most sophisticated example of this phenomenon is the Bill and Melinda Gates Foundation, which would be conventionally classified as a social-sector nonprofit but somehow seems like much more than that with ambitious and well-funded programs to strengthen public health care, education, and skill development around the world. It is arguably acting today with more "soft power" than many governments and with more financial and organizational sophistication than many businesses. When Arne Duncan became

US secretary of education in 2009 with an ambitious reform agenda, he quickly turned to the Gates Foundation for several members of his top team, who in turn developed his signature initiative—the Race to the Top competition.

From his experience at the World Wildlife Fund and the Smithsonian, Roger Sant has observed the growing scale and sophistication of nonprofits in the environmental arena: "Before it was just a cause; now it's a cause backed up by data and a professional argument machine, and it operates at a wholly different level of impact." And of course the boards of these nonprofits are often replete with business and government experience—drawn together in self-reinforcing networks. For instance, ClimateWorks is a nonprofit that "supports public policies that prevent dangerous climate change and catalyze global prosperity." It takes on this challenge "with a strong executive team and a board of directors that includes some of the world's top scientific, regulatory, business, environmental, and academic institutions." Enterprises like this, typically chaired or led by former government or business leaders, are animated by what Roger Sant calls "the driving concept of any business—the ability to go back to funders and have things they want to invest in."

A second reason to be optimistic is the growing scale and range of *academy organizations,* which set high aspirations for the early development and social consciousness of talented people. You'll recall Dick Cavanaugh's observation that many of the most successful cross-sector leaders of his generation had started their careers in academy organizations. Well, that is true—but the range of options for that approach has expanded. It is no longer just the universities and graduate schools leading to professional service firms—lawyers, accountants, management consultants, and others. It is also Microsoft, Google, Facebook, Apple, IBM, and Cisco—which hire huge numbers of graduates each year—and certainly the Gates Foundation and Ford Foundation.

These academy organizations share a similar goal of attracting and retaining exceptional people. More and more, they seek to create networks of professionals across the public, private, and nonprofit sectors—and to encourage their people to get involved and engage on important issues. There is certainly more that they can do—but it seems apparent that they are keen to be part of the solution, rather than part of the problem.

So there is some comfort in the rebalancing of institutional structures and relationships in our society—more options for collaboration and professional development, more benefits from building strong networks. There is also comfort in the research on how networks help people advance their careers. What the research shows is that "weak ties" matter. You don't always have to have the inside track or even come straight from "central casting." But you do have to be on the "radar screen," and that depends to a large degree on the breadth and diversity of the network that you have built.

PUTTING YOUR NETWORK TO WORK

When I decided to leave McKinsey in 2012 after more than thirty years, I knew that I wanted to do something different, but I didn't know what. In the short term, I sought to broaden my horizons by building a miniportfolio of diverse activities—working with the Albright Stonebridge Group under the guidance of Madeleine Albright and Sandy Berger (which certainly taught me a lot about geopolitics very quickly), teaching and researching at the Kennedy School—initiating the work that has led to this book—and advising the Shakespeare Theatre Company in Washington, which reconnected me to the theatrical arts. I thought that that would give me some options and insights—and so it did. Meanwhile, I applied some of what I have learned about how to put broader networks to work.

First, I established a kind of informal *board of personal mentors*. These were mostly people who had known me a long time and who understood my interests and aspirations. The key lesson I have learned about putting together this kind of a board is to ensure that it is drawn from different walks of life and that it brings diverse perspectives. In *Ask . . . How to Get What You Want and Need at Work*, Priscilla Coleman advises that "the people on your board should know more than you about something, be better than you at something, or offer different points of view. Putting only buddies on your board won't help you grow and develop."

My board included some colleagues whom I had known a long time and whom I already thought of as my professional mentors—people like Ian Davis, the former worldwide managing director of McKinsey, and Larry Kanarek, a close friend and McKinsey colleague in Washington. But I also sought the counsel of people like Rachel Kyte, my favorite client at the World Bank; Jack Donahue and John Haigh at the Kennedy School; and Ngaire Woods, dean of the new Blavatnik School of Government at Oxford. I made quite a long list and organized a series of conversations with as many of them as I could track down. Some of these conversations would ultimately prove very useful when it came to writing this book—they turned into the kind of "curiosity conversations" that Brian Grazer would recognize and applaud.

As it happens, one of the most valuable pieces of advice came from somebody whom I had known a very long time and with whom I shared a lot in common. Pat Butler—a former McKinsey partner in London whom I consider a "peer mentor"—encouraged me to find a smaller professional services firm to which I could apply some of what I had learned at McKinsey. He said, in a phrase that has stuck with me since, "If there's one thing people like us know how to do, it's how to build a really good professional partnership."

Second, I reached out to some people in my network with whom I had relatively *weak ties*. We would typically think of strong ties as our close friends and colleagues, the people with whom we have grown up and really trust—in my case, people like Ian Davis and Pat Butler. Weak ties, in contrast, would be our wider acquaintances, people we have known for a shorter time or in a less significant way.

I had heard of a classic study by the Stanford sociologist Mark Granovetter, whom I mentioned earlier in this chapter. He set out to test the intuitive assumption that we get the most help in life from our strong ties. He surveyed people in professional, technical, and managerial professions who had recently changed jobs. Nearly 17 percent heard about their new job from a strong tie. It seemed like their close friends and trusted colleagues had really come through for them.

But surprisingly, almost 28 percent had heard about their new job from a weak tie. In practice, it seemed that people were significantly more likely to benefit from a weak tie. Granovetter's explanation is that "strong ties provide bonds, but weak ties serve as bridges"; they provide more efficient access to new information. Our strong ties tend to travel in the same social circles and to be familiar with the same opportunities as we are. They tend not to add much to what we already know. In contrast, weak ties are more likely to open up access to a different network and a different flow of opportunities.

The weak tie that was most directly valuable to me in this situation was with Harry Clark. By the time he helped me find my current job, I had only known him for a year or so, and we had probably only had half a dozen meaningful conversations. A veteran of the public relations and government affairs arena, he had cofounded his own firm (Clark Weinstock), sold it to a large marketing services group, and was now a senior adviser to several firms and individuals, including the Brunswick Group. "Well," he said, "Brunswick is looking for a US managing partner, and you might be able to do that."

Harry is what Wharton professor Adam Grant would call an "otherish giver." Grant's research shows that many of the most successful people across a wide range of sectors, industries, and roles are those who focus on contributing to others. A key reason they are successful is that they become the "go-to person" whenever you need help. We all know somebody who is our "first call" whenever we or somebody we care about is in trouble. That person may not be able to help directly, but he or she will know somebody who can. People like that naturally and instinctively build integrated networks—indeed they become the "network bridge" or "switch."

But in Adam Grant's analysis "otherish givers" are often more successful than totally altruistic "selfless givers." He explains, "Those who burn out consistently put the interests of others ahead of their own, sacrificing their energy and time and undermining their ability to give in the long run. Those who maintain success are careful to balance concern for others with their own interests." These "otherish givers" have both the interests of others and of themselves in mind at more or less the same time. They are not looking for a quid pro quo in the traditional sense of "give and take." But they are looking to gain a return on the investment they have made in building their network.

With Harry Clark's help, I was able to take the third step in my process—to revive some previously *dormant ties*. Dormant ties can be thought of as a particular variant of weak ties. They are typically people whom you used to see often and knew well, but with whom you have since fallen out of touch. There aren't many advantages of age, but one of them is that the older you get, the more dormant ties you have—and, studies suggest, the more valuable they become.

The management professors Daniel Levin, Jorge Walter, and Keith Murnighan have been studying the whole subject of dormant ties. They observe that "adults accumulate thousands of relationships over their lifetimes, but prior to the Internet, they actively maintained no more than 100 or 200 at any given time." The professors have been studying what happens when people do something they often find difficult, which is to reactivate dormant ties.

For instance, in one study they asked more than two hundred executives to reactivate ties that had been dormant for at least three years. Each executive reached out to two former colleagues and sought advice on a work project, and at the same time they asked for advice on the same project from two current colleagues. Afterward, they evaluated the advice they had been given, and they concluded that the advice from the dormant ties had contributed more value than the advice from current ties.

The reason seems to be that dormant ties provide more original insights than current and stronger ties. While they have been out of touch, they have had new and different experiences, gathering fresh ideas and perspectives—or they have made additional contacts of their own. There is one other benefit of reactivating dormant ties— it's not as uncomfortable as trying to activate weak ties or create new ones altogether. As Levin and colleagues observe, "Reconnecting a dormant relationship is not like starting a relationship from scratch. When people reconnect, they still have feelings of trust."

The other advantage of dormant ties is that we tend to have quite a lot of them. When we need help, advice, or new information, we may run out of weak ties quickly, but we are likely to have a large pool of dormant ties that prove to be helpful. The professors found that people in their forties and fifties received more value from reactivating dormant ties than did people in their thirties, who in turn benefited more than did people in their twenties. As Adam Grant observes, "Dormant ties are the neglected value in our networks."

By the time I was considering my post-McKinsey options, I was well into my fifties—so I had a whole lot of dormant relationships, in my case on both sides of the Atlantic. I reactivated quite a few of them, some of whom you have read about in this book—people like Tony Hall at the BBC and Bernie Ferrari, who told me about his work on listening skills.

But the dormant relationships that were ultimately most propitious were those with the founders of the Brunswick Group. I had known Alan Parker (now Sir Alan) off and on for fifteen years. We had served together on the Royal Shakespeare Company board in 2000; and it was Alan who, alongside his colleague Nick Claydon, had been our principal media adviser when McKinsey was under such feverish attack from the British media in 2005. And his co-founders Louise Charlton and Andrew Fenwick had subsequently reached out to me for advice when they were first exploring the establishment of a Washington office for Brunswick.

Alan and his senior colleagues concluded that I was indeed the right person for the US managing partner role, which I have played ever since. And I have been able to reflect with pleasure and gratitude upon the benefits of my own broad network—my board of mentors, my weak ties, and my dormant ties—some of them no longer dormant.

Meanwhile, I had been pursuing a similar path toward my objective of publishing this book. Rik Kirkland, McKinsey's director of publishing and a former editor of *Fortune* magazine, had become a de facto member of my board of mentors, especially after he had helped to edit and submit my original article on trisector leadership to the *Harvard Business Review*. Jack Donahue, John Haigh, and Richard Zeckhauser—all professors at the Kennedy School, the first two of them former classmates of mine—were dormant ties, who guided some of my initial research. And two Wharton professors, Adam Grant and Witold Henisz, whom I had not known before the *Harvard Business Review* article, and whom I met almost by chance, helped guide me in the early stages of writing the book. Indeed, it was through Adam Grant that I met my (and not coincidentally, his) literary agent, Richard Pine, who set the whole process in motion. These were weak ties in action.

So I have learned from experience the critical role that a network can play in building a broader life. But I could probably have learned that lesson earlier, if I had had more of a prepared mind.

8

CARPE DIEM

Having a Prepared Mind

> In spite of illness, in spite even of the archenemy sorrow, one
> can remain alive long past the usual date of disintegration if one
> is unafraid of change, insatiable in intellectual curiosity, inter-
> ested in big things, and happy in small ways.
>
> —Edith Wharton, *A Backward Glance*

US Department of State, Washington, DC—October 2012
Sitting in his mahogany-lined office on the sixth floor of the State
Department, Robert "Bob" Hormats is polite and attentive but
clearly in a bit of a hurry. As soon as our conversation is over, he
will leave for a G20 foreign affairs and finance ministers' meeting in
Mexico City—seeking to tackle the still-lingering effects of the global
financial crisis. He has been doing this sort of thing for quite a while,
as he casually observes: "I have been working on international economics and financial systems across all three sectors of the economy
for more than forty years."

The breadth and durability of his experience are beyond question.
Now approaching his seventieth birthday, he has served under President Obama and Secretary of State Hillary Clinton since 2009. His
current title is undersecretary of state for economic growth, energy,
and the environment—in a nutshell he is the State Department's senior point person on anything to do with the financial crisis.

This is not, as they say, Hormats's "first rodeo." More than forty years ago, he first came to official Washington in 1969 as a staff member of the National Security Council—just as he completed a PhD in international economics at Tufts University. He stayed in Washington for the next thirteen years, serving under three presidents (Nixon, Carter, and Reagan), playing a variety of international policy roles. In his early years, he worked for Henry Kissinger on—among other things—the Nixon administration's transformational opening of diplomatic relations with China's Communist government. He then held a series of diplomatic roles—including ambassador and deputy US trade representative from 1979 to 1981.

In 1982, he left the government and joined Goldman Sachs in New York, thus beginning a twenty-five-year career in investment banking. His focus—perhaps we can call it his "intellectual thread"— was international economics, and he became Goldman's vice chair (international). Along the way, he wrote several books on economic history; held part-time academic posts at Princeton, Tufts, and Harvard Universities; and maintained an active portfolio of nonprofit interests. Then when his career might otherwise have seemed to be winding down, he came back to government and this most demanding of roles.

So I ask him, "How much of this was planned? When you were in government before, did you anticipate that you would have such a substantial career in the private sector? And when you were an investment banker, did you think that you would go back into government?" He smiles and says, "None of it was planned, or even foreseeable. It just happened."

But then he pauses and adds a crucial closing sentence: "Mind you, I am a believer in Louis Pasteur's famous saying—'In the fields of observation, chance favors only the prepared mind.' You don't know what's going to happen, but you should be prepared to take advantage of any opportunity that might occur—to seize the day. I always thought that that was a useful way of looking at the world."

HOW MUCH IS CHANCE;
HOW MUCH IS PREPARED MIND?

Louis Pasteur used this phrase in a lecture at the University of Lille on December 7, 1854—"dans les champs de l'observation le hazard ne favorise que les esprits préparés." It has been otherwise translated as "chance favors the prepared mind" and "fortune favors the prepared mind." A website called Pasteurbrewing.com, dedicated to the iconic French chemist and microbiologist whose discoveries resulted in the germ theory of disease, reveals the context. Pasteur was speaking of the Danish physicist Hans Christian Oersted, and the almost "accidental" way in which he discovered the basic principles of electromagnetism.

In his Lille lecture Pasteur noted that much scientific experimentation occurs in the realm of the "half-knowns." The scientist conducts physical experiments in an attempt to prove a hypothesis. It is at the point when none of the experiments provide a definitive proof that the hypothesis is true that the chance of making an accidental discovery is amplified. However, it is not during this accidental moment that an actual discovery occurs. That only happens if the scientist is able, if she has a prepared mind, to interpret the accidental observation and situate the new phenomenon within her existing work. That's when the breakthrough happens. Random events occur in the laboratory or in another observational arena, but only a mind alive with relevant facts and experience will recognize the truly original insight.

Pasteur used the phrase to describe another scientist, and indeed he might have used it to describe many other scientific discoveries— for instance, those of Archimedes, Newton, or Mestral. It also came to define much of his own pioneering work. His initial research involved collaborating with a beetroot alcohol manufacturer on observations about the fermentation process. That led him to identify the process that has since been dubbed "pasteurization" and to develop the whole new science of microbiology.

So chance favors a prepared mind. What does that mean for those of us who are trying to build a broader life? First, it means that we have to be aware of, and alert to, the *importance of chance.* Things will happen in our lives that we could not or did not predict and over which we have little or no control. It, therefore, makes sense to anticipate that there will be unpredictable elements in life, even if we can't know in advance precisely what they will be.

Writing more than five centuries ago about the challenges of leadership, Machiavelli highlighted the critical role of Fortuna, the inscrutable goddess whose whims play a large part in determining whether a leader succeeds. He suggested that "Fortuna is the arbiter of half our actions, but that it lets us control roughly the other half." He compared fortune to a dangerous river that sweeps everything before it when it is in flood. Cicero also marveled at "the great power of fortune, which impels one in either direction, towards success or towards adversity. Whenever we enjoy her prospering breezes we are carried to the haven for which we long; when she blows in our face we are wrecked."

In general, we tend to feel more directly in control of our own fate than this implies. But this feeling of being in control can be a consequence of self-delusion. Dan Ariely writes in *Predictably Irrational,* "If I had to distill one lesson from my research . . . it is that we are pawns in a game whose forces we largely fail to comprehend. We usually like to think of ourselves as sitting in the driver's seat, with ultimate control over the decisions we make and the direction our life takes; but, alas, this perception has more to do with our desires— with how we want to view ourselves—than with reality." David Brooks adds, "The human mind is an overconfidence machine. The conscious level gives itself credit for things it really didn't do and confabulates tales to create the illusion it controls things it really doesn't determine."

The second implication of "chance favors only the prepared mind" is that our primary task is to *put ourselves in the way of chance, of good fortune.* That is the part of life's progress that we can control—which Machiavelli generously estimated as "the other half." We can and must have a prepared mind, able to anticipate, interpret, and navigate the aspects of life over which we have some control, or at least influence. And unless we have a surefire way of predicting what chance will deliver, we would be well advised to create some options, lest we become too dependent on a single throw of the dice.

HOW DO YOU PREPARE YOUR MIND?

A prepared mind is the sixth dimension of the Mosaic Principle. We can recognize the crucial role of chance but still do something to shape and respond to events as they transpire. It need not, and probably should not, imply a predetermined life plan—"I will do this in my twenties, this in my thirties, this in my forties," and so on. But we can structure and give shape to our lives—a sense of purpose and direction that enables us to make informed choices. What's the best way to do that?

From his experience in founding LinkedIn with more than 100 million members worldwide, Reid Hoffman believes that the business strategies employed by highly successful start-ups and the career strategies employed by comparably successful individuals are strikingly similar. He essentially thinks that you should apply the Silicon Valley model—the entrepreneurial mind-set—to professional development.

Hoffman believes that you can and should create a "career plan"— even if you then put it in a locked drawer and rarely look at it, and even if you then adjust it every time something unexpected happens. He suggests that a good career plan accounts for the interplay of three key elements—your assets, your aspirations, and the market realities. These pieces need to fit together, otherwise the best-laid plan will come to nothing. "Just because you're good at something (assets) that you're really passionate about (aspirations) doesn't necessarily mean someone will pay you for it (market realities)." But by a careful assessment of market realities—which, of course, change over time—you are likely to identify opportunities that meet your aspirations and make full and productive use of your assets.

Even if you are reluctant to follow Hoffman's advice, it might be helpful to have some decision rules or guiding principles. Recall Josh

Gotbaum, who transferred his investment banking skills to the Department of Defense and restructured the whole military housing stock. Gotbaum had a decision rule that he would always make himself available to serve in a Democratic administration, whenever one gained power in Washington. He couldn't have known this in advance, but it turned out that this simple decision rule has served him pretty well—he has spent roughly half his professional life working in government and the other half working in business or in nonprofits. By following this rule or guiding principle, he is probably having pretty much the life he would have chosen if he could have predetermined the outcome in more precise terms from the outset.

Patty Stonesifer has a different kind of prepared mind, which she has applied in building a distinctively broad career. I first met Stonesifer in 2010, when she had just been appointed to a three-year term as chair of the Smithsonian Board of Regents. At just fifty-four, Patty was one of the youngest regents—and considerably younger than Wayne Clough, the secretary of the Smithsonian over whom she presided. But she already had both a pedigree and stature that afforded her natural authority.

The sixth of nine children, a graduate of Indiana University, Stonesifer found an early route into the technology industry in the 1980s—and stayed. She describes her big break: "This was back when Microsoft was really small. They had an annual managers' retreat, each vice president picked a new leader to bring along, and I was chosen. There were only two women." She recalls further, "When we were discussing an issue, I started questioning where the group was heading. The executive team, especially Bill [Gates], decided after that I was somebody they should move around so that I had the opportunities to use those skills. I literally was packing my bags within a few weeks of the retreat to run our operations in Canada."

From that start, she played a series of increasingly senior roles as Microsoft grew toward industry pre-eminence in the 1990s. And then in 1997, Bill Gates asked her to launch what would soon become the Bill and Melinda Gates Foundation. By the time she left that role ten years later, the Gates Foundation was far and away the biggest and most influential philanthropic enterprise in the world, donating more than $1 billion a year in pursuit of its mission "to improve access to advances in global health and learning."

Stonesifer's career focus is now exclusively on nonprofit initiatives. Since she completed her term at the Smithsonian, she has become president and CEO of Martha's Table, a much smaller Washington, DC–based nonprofit that develops sustainable solutions to local poverty. And she maintains a portfolio of other nonprofit initiatives—not least as an organizer of the Giving Pledge, which coordinates the commitments of many of the world's wealthiest people to donate much of their fortunes to good causes during their lifetimes.

She has a very distinctive way to describe her mind-set in building a broad life. "I think *zigzagging* is a better approach than pursuing the idea of a fixed career ladder. Some of the roles I've taken looked like they were significantly less important than other roles, but they all led me to new knowledge and new skills that allowed me to keep zigzagging more or less on an upward trajectory. Don't look to take a job just because it's up the ladder. Maybe go for a lateral move to learn a whole other area."

She adds, "A lot of young people will ask, 'Do I go broad or do I go deep?' I think it's often great to go broad before you go deep. It's like going to school. You get a broad view of the world, but then you have to own something. You have to know what the quality of your work is and get feedback on it and understand it."

Zigzagging might be a good way to describe the approach that Steve Jobs took—although he used a different phrase: "connecting the dots." In his 2005 Stanford commencement address, he recounted how he dropped out of Reed College after six months but stayed around as a "drop-in" for another eighteen months before he "really quit." He added, "The minute I dropped out I could stop taking the required classes that didn't interest me, and begin dropping in on the ones that looked interesting. . . . And much of what I stumbled into by following my curiosity and intuition turned out to be priceless later on."

One of those classes was in calligraphy. He realized that Reed College at the time offered perhaps the best calligraphy instruction in the country. Throughout the campus, every poster, every label on every drawer, was beautifully hand-calligraphed. He decided to take a calligraphy class to learn how to do this. He learned about sans serif typefaces, about the varying amount of space between different letter combinations. "It was beautiful, historical, artistically subtle in a way that science can't capture, and I found it fascinating."

He didn't think that any of this would have practical application—until ten years later, when he and Steve Wozniak were designing the first Macintosh computer. "We designed it all into the Mac. It was the first computer with beautiful typography." He reflected, "If I had never dropped in on that calligraphy class, the Mac would never have had multiple typefaces or proportionally spaced fonts. And since Windows just copied the Mac, it's likely that no personal computer would have them."

Jobs never used the phrase "prepared mind" in this or any other address. But it was implied in what he said next: "You can't connect the dots looking forward; you can only connect them going backwards. So you have to trust that the dots will somehow connect in your future. You have to trust in something—your gut, destiny, life, kharma, whatever."

And you will also need to be willing to take the road less traveled. It is hard, perhaps impossible, to live a broader life without taking some professional and personal risk—so you will need to assess your tolerance for risk. You will want above all to avoid feeling trapped or diverted down a blind alley. As the novelist Paulo Coelho observes, "If you think adventure is dangerous, try routine—it's lethal."

TO LIVE A BROADER LIFE, you will need a mind prepared to make professional and personal choices—to be ready emotionally, intellectually, and financially. You will need to give some thought to the kinds of contributions you will make, the impact you will have, the capacity and character that you will develop. And, just to be practical for a moment, you will need to do some basic personal financial planning, so that you are able to say yes when an opportunity arises that involves some financial sacrifice. Just ask anybody who has gone from the business world to government or the nonprofit sector. It certainly helps to have your financial house in order when an opportunity comes out of the blue.

Fifteen years ago, I had an opportunity to come out of the blue—and I didn't take it. To my surprise, I was offered the chance to become the next director-general of the Confederation of British Industry—colloquially known in the UK as the CBI, the leading employers' organization. When I was growing up, the person who held this role was a household name—largely because he represented business in the ferocious and seemingly endless tug-of-war between employers and the trade unions that characterized much of the 1970s and 1980s. In the post-Thatcher era when unions were much less powerful, the CBI also declined in public prominence—but it was still a significant organization, actively engaged in the major public policy issues of the day. And its leader was still a prominent and prestigious figure.

I said that this opportunity came "out of the blue," as if by complete chance, which is the way it seemed at the time. But honestly, I should have been prepared. The three previous directors-general all had very similar backgrounds to mine. Adair Turner, the incumbent at the time, whose term was coming to an end and whom I would be replacing, had gone to the CBI straight from McKinsey, where he had been a good friend and mentor to me. As the interview process proceeded, it became apparent that it was Adair who had recommended me and that the board was pretty much acting upon his proposal.

When I was offered the job, I thought that I was going to accept—and thus draw my McKinsey career to a close after "only" eighteen years. But as I reflected upon it some more, I realized that I wasn't prepared—above all, financially, practically, and to some degree emotionally. My wife and I had just had our fourth child—all under the age of six. We had arranged our lives to make this practical, while we both worked—but at a considerable financial cost and with quite a lot of debt. It was all fine but depended on the compensation that I was getting from McKinsey—with more on the horizon as I became more senior. In contrast, the CBI role was pretty much a "government salary," which would have required considerable sacrifice not just for me but for my family. I recalled Adair saying that when he took the CBI job, he was in healthy financial condition— and I thought, "Well, I'm not." It would also require a lot of time on the road, meeting CBI members and giving speeches—which would have been time away from my young and growing family.

Over a fairly agonizing weekend, I concluded that our life as a whole worked pretty well and that now was not the time to disrupt it. On the Monday morning, I called the CBI to turn down the job. A few weeks later, they appointed somebody else—somebody completely different in background and style. I felt a tinge of regret, which I have continued to feel over the years—although my life has turned out pretty well. But I have always felt bad that I had not prepared myself better for this kind of opportunity—that I had not had a *prepared mind*.

As a sequel to this story, in 2015 the CBI appointed Carolyn Fairbairn as director-general, the first woman to have the job. Carolyn and I were colleagues and friends—indeed at one point office mates—at McKinsey in the 1980s and had stayed in touch as she built a broad and full life, with spells at the BBC, ITV, and the Prime Minister's Office. It's become obvious to me that she had a much more prepared mind than I did!

As I have reflected upon my own experience and that of others, it has become apparent to me that the need for a prepared mind starts early and finishes late—assuming that you're trying to build a broader life. You need a prepared mind as you build the early foundations of your life, you need a prepared mind to assess the foreseeable and unforeseeable opportunities in the middle period of your life, and you need a prepared mind to assess and capture the many opportunities that now arise in the later stages of your life. Preparing your mind for a breadth of opportunities is a lifelong pastime.

PREPARING YOUR MIND
FOR EARLY OPPORTUNITY

Seth Siegel, now in his early sixties, has been an advertising copy-writer, an assistant district attorney, a Broadway producer, a branding agent, an entrepreneur, and an activist. Today, he makes his living as a writer and public speaker. By his own count, he has had careers in seven industries or professions, each unrelated to the others. On the surface, this sounds pretty random and unplanned—the career trajectory of somebody who doesn't know what he wants out of his professional life. But on the contrary, Siegel insists, this is exactly what he had in mind—he insists that it all matches a plan he developed while still in his late teens.

Like many people, in his college years, Siegel was interested in lots of potential career options—especially politics, academia, the military, and journalism—but reluctant to commit to any one of them. Every time he came close to choosing a single career option, he'd start to feel claustrophobic. So he prepared his mind for a very particular kind of life, making himself a two-part promise. First, he would go into a field only if he could easily exit; and second, he would stay in that field for only as long as it brought him joy.

Although Siegel's college promise sounds somewhat antiestablishment, he didn't really think of himself then as a countercultural type, nor has he since. He was a conventional undergraduate and then law school student at Cornell University. But if not a laid-back hippie, he did internalize the carpe diem ethos of that time of life. He believed then, and he believes now, that the largest part of who we are is what we do. As he observes of his unorthodox approach to shaping his life, "I've always felt that major new challenges and exposure to new ideas are among the greatest things life has to offer."

The career that Siegel's prepared mind enabled has been far from mediocre or dull. In 1990, after fifteen years in various aspects of advertising, marketing, and the law, he cofounded the Beanstalk Group, a trademark licensing and brand extension agency. Beanstalk advised companies like Coca-Cola, Harley-Davidson, and Hormel;

and Siegel personally served as an adviser and licensing agent to Hanna-Barbera Productions for its many characters, including the Flintstones, the Jetsons, Yogi Bear, and Scooby-Doo. The company grew to be the largest of its kind and was sold to Ford Motor Company in 2001—although Siegel stayed on as co-CEO until 2005 when Omnicom purchased the company.

Since then Siegel's career has become ever more eclectic—the producer of a hit Broadway show, cofounder of a boutique financial services firm, cofounder of the Harley-Davidson restaurant chain, and creator and funder of a public school literacy program in New York. His long-standing involvement in Israel—again, going back to his time as a student when he spent a year at Hebrew University in Jerusalem—recently resulted in a book entitled *Let There Be Water: Israel's Solution for a Water-Starved World.*

Siegel has little doubt that he has paid a price—both financially and psychologically—for what he calls his "staccato career outlook." For instance, starting anew usually means starting with a pay cut, a situation he has prepared for by saving as much as he could before leaving one position for another. And he notes that psychologically, it isn't always easy to be twenty years older than others at a company meeting.

But as he observes, "The scariness of repeatedly walking that metaphorical career high wire without a net has been balanced by the opportunities each move gave me to acquire a new professional vocabulary, new skills and new relationships. For those of us who wish we could clone ourselves to experience different aspects of life and to grow from it, my career pattern has permitted that, even if sequentially and not simultaneously."

And as he reflects now upon this career pattern, it no longer seems as "scattershot" as perhaps it did at first. He now sees that each move has built on the others and that the time needed to master each new field grows shorter and shorter. Because, as he has learned, all business has some common DNA, he is not really starting from scratch with each move; and as he changes careers, he is able to draw upon different experiences, perspectives, and insights that others with longer tenure in the specific field may not have—although he is always intent on maintaining professional relationships from his previous careers.

He has never had that feeling of being trapped in a job, which allows him to remain enthusiastic about what he does, while being open to doing something else. "Plus," as he notes, "always being on the lookout for my next career helps me stay current with changes in business, society and technology. Who knows what career might come next?"

———

THE SOCIAL CRITIC MICHAEL BARONE argues that the United States produces moderately impressive twenty-year-olds but very impressive thirty-year-olds. He says that the hard pressures and choices that hit people during their wide-open, relatively unsupervised twenties forge a new and much better kind of person. Increasingly, those choices are made during what are now often called the "odyssey" years. We used to think in terms of four life phases—childhood, adolescence, adulthood, and old age. Now we can recognize at least six—childhood, adolescence, *odyssey*, adulthood, *active retirement*, and old age.

Odyssey is sometimes described as the decade or so of wandering that occurs between adolescence and adulthood. This decade of wandering is becoming increasingly foundational for many people— and sometimes it lasts quite a bit longer than a decade. We typically define the onset of adulthood in terms of four accomplishments: moving away from home, getting married, starting a family, and becoming financially independent. In 1960, 70 percent of American thirty-year-olds had done so, but fewer than 40 percent in 2000. In western Europe, the numbers are even lower. The evidence is clear— more and more people are deferring conventionally defined adulthood and making the most of their odyssey years to explore what kind of life they want to build.

Perhaps as a consequence of "deferred adulthood," many people now use their odyssey years to prepare their minds for a variety of possible options and chance events. And by doing so, they sometimes achieve things that they could never have anticipated. For instance, who would have thought that the guy who in his twenties created the Ethos Water brand, which is available in almost every Starbucks, would now be leading the Jewish Anti-Defamation League, after a spell in the White House defining the policy framework for social entrepreneurs across the United States? That's what Jonathan Green-blatt did during his passage into adulthood.

Greenblatt got into politics straight out of college, working in Little Rock, Arkansas, on Bill Clinton's successful presidential campaign in 1992. He went on to join the administration as an aide in the Clinton White House and the Department of Commerce, where he focused on international economic policy in emerging markets and postconflict economies. But it's what happened after he left government, still in his late twenties, that defined his career direction since.

Along with Peter Thum, his roommate at Northwestern University's Kellogg School of Management, he cofounded Ethos Water, which they described as a "premium bottled water social enterprise." The central value proposition of the company was (and still is) that it would help children around the world get access to free water by donating a portion of its profits to finance water programs in developing countries. Remember the issues that Coca-Cola (and indeed PepsiCo) had with water security in emerging markets. Well, that has been the focus of Ethos Water since the beginning—seeking to link cause to consumption.

The reason you can now see bottles of water in most Starbucks outlets is that in 2005, Greenblatt and Thum sold their business to Starbucks, and Greenblatt served for a time as Starbucks' vice president of global consumer products, which enabled him to scale up the distribution of Ethos across the United States. Along with the Starbucks Foundation, he cofounded Ethos International, creating a multimillion-dollar global investment fund to bring clean water to communities in need around the world. And he also founded All for Good, an open-source platform that now stands as the largest aggregator of volunteer opportunities on the web, supported by a coalition of leading companies, nonprofits, and government agencies.

This focus on social entrepreneurship led him back to the White House with the Obama administration as the president's director of social innovation and civic participation. In that role, he championed social impact investing, social entrepreneurship, national service, and civic engagement. He led the expansion of the Americorps national service program, designed a $300 million Pay for Success Fund to advance social impact bonds, expanded the Social Innovation Fund, secured $1.5 billion in private commitments to impact investing, and launched several public-private partnerships such as the My Brother's Keeper initiative and Joining Forces impact pledge.

Now in his early forties, Greenblatt has the demeanor and bearing of a maturing rabbi—and indeed he has recently been appointed as the fifth national director of the Anti-Defamation League, one of the most respected civil rights organizations, which "fights the defamation of the Jewish people and works to secure justice and fair treatment for all." The prepared mind that he developed during his odyssey years has enabled him to launch and lead a socially oriented company, work in a large-scale corporate environment, found high-impact nonprofit ventures, serve at a high level of government, and write and teach on social innovation.

Like Greenblatt, Julius Genachowski had also served in the Clinton administration, but when he returned to government in 2009, he was determined to learn from the experience he had gained from the private sector during the intervening years. Genachowski was actually returning to the same government agency—the Federal Communications Commission—that he had left a decade before. But his prepared mind had enabled him to broaden his experience at a critical time for the communications industry, and that changed his whole approach to being a government regulator.

Julius Genachowski is the son of eastern European Jews who survived the Holocaust. He entered Columbia University as a pre-med student but graduated with a degree in history. From there he spent some time on Capitol Hill and at Harvard Law School, where he was a notes editor on the *Harvard Law Review* when Barack Obama was its president. In the mid-1990s he served as counsel to then–FCC chair Reed Hundt, but it is what he did when he first left the government that changed his philosophy and approach.

He wanted to work for an innovative, risk-taking company, so that he could experience what it was really like on the front lines. So he joined Barry Diller's new company, which became known as InterActiv Corporation (IAC). This company was really exploring what could be done at the interface of cable television and the Internet—still in the fairly early stages.

The other conscious decision he took was not to go into government affairs, but rather to get involved in core business operations. Indeed his initial title at IAC was chief of business operations. As part of the office of the chair, he worked on a string of business deals—sports rights and other properties—and as the company grew he took on more bottom-line responsibility. The company certainly did grow—from two fairly small businesses to a substantial group of media technology properties including Expedia, Ticketmaster, the USA Network, and Match.com. He also cofounded LaunchBox Digital, a technology incubator.

This conscious decision to go into the risk-taking end of the communications arena had direct consequences for Genachowski when he returned to government in 2009. He recalls that "by the time I came back to the FCC, I really knew—I had experienced directly—the transformative effect that new technology can have on so many fields of life. For instance, I had worked with Expedia, which had transformed the travel media marketplace. And I wanted to ensure that what the FCC does is helpful, and especially that it does not hinder that kind of innovation and productivity."

In 2009, *Wired* magazine named the "new FCC" under Julius Genachowski's chairmanship as one of the "top 7 disruptions of the year." This reflected the fact that, soon after his Senate confirmation to the FCC chairmanship, Genachowski announced plans to create the country's first national broadband plan, reallocate the spectrum from over-the-air broadcasters to meet demand for wireless usage, and pursue rules to preserve Internet freedom and openness. For instance, the National Broadband Plan that the FCC released in March 2010, entitled *Connecting America,* included proposals to reallocate airwaves for mobile broadband and to modernize the FCC's $9 billion Universal Service Fund from a program that supports phone service to a program that effectively supports broadband.

Genachowski's agenda centered on making the FCC a business-oriented innovator in government: There had been a tendency in the past to work on yesterday's technologies. He focused instead on unleashing the opportunities of broadband. Early on he signaled to the major potential investors and broadband networks that the FCC and the Obama administration would be friendly and encouraging to private investment, focusing on four key principles: driving private investment, driving innovation, promoting competition, and protecting consumers. As Genachowski observed, "The time I spent at the cutting edge of the digital revolution profoundly affected my approach as an industry regulator. I am glad that I prepared my own mind in that way."

PREPARING YOUR MIND
FOR MIDLIFE ADJUSTMENT

How does a physician and college professor of medicine become the president of the World Bank, the leading global institution for economic development? That happened to Jim Yong Kim as the result of a decision he took a few years earlier to broaden his life. He took that decision in 2003 when he was forty-four years old with a well-established professional platform and reputation.

Along with Paul Farmer and Ophelia Dahl, Jim Kim cofounded Partners in Health while he and Farmer were medical students in the late 1980s. In many respects, he was Farmer's professional twin. He was the doctor with whom Farmer shared the attending physician job at Brigham & Women's Hospital, so that Farmer could spend half the year in Haiti. Kim spent less time himself on the ground in Haiti, focusing more on establishing the organization's base in Boston and doing more of what he calls the "menial chores."

But Kim was much more than the chief of operations at headquarters. He was often the primary spokesperson for the organization and the chief recruiter. As Tracy Kidder describes him in *Mountains*

Beyond Mountains, "What Jim had, above all, was enthusiasm. He weighed facts against possibilities as if the two were equivalent. A lot of students had joined PIH after hearing him talk. Change the world? Of course they could. He really believed this, and he really believed that 'a small group of committed individuals' could do it. He liked to say of PIH, 'People think we're unrealistic. They don't know we're crazy.'"

It was also Jim Kim who extended PIH's focus beyond Haiti into other territories and public health challenges. In particular, he headed the PIH-led initiative to address multidrug-resistant tuberculosis, starting in Peru, and then Russia and parts of Africa. Although Kim was almost as much of a visionary as Farmer—"we know that things change all the time"—he describes himself in more prosaic terms, almost as the pragmatic fixer. "Will things change for the better? Who knows? But these would-be 'Paul Farmers,' they'll drop out, and when they do, we stalwarts will still be here figuring out the best way to spend two dollars and twenty-seven cents per capita for healthcare."

He also discovered from his work on TB in Peru that he liked to work on health policy—it was the big issues surrounding health that excited him. He actually liked sitting for hours in conference rooms talking about the finer points of international TB control. And it was that which persuaded him in his midforties to move decisively in the direction of health policy and economic development. He left PIH and took a senior advisory role at the World Health Organization in Geneva.

There he certainly got the opportunity to work on the big health policy issues—and specifically on AIDS, which was cutting a swathe through sub-Saharan Africa. He helped develop and champion the 3×5 Initiative, designed to put 3 million patients in developing countries on AIDS treatment by 2005. The goal was actually met in 2007—but by now the number on treatment has reached 7 million. It is one of the rare public policy programs whose success is acknowledged by all.

His time at the World Health Organization, combined with three years as president of Dartmouth College, raised his own profile—so that when the Obama administration was looking to make an imaginative American choice for the presidency of the World Bank, it alighted on Jim Kim. He was not an economist or an established international development expert, like his predecessor Robert Zoellick, nor did he have a lot of experience running large institutions, like earlier presidents such as James Wolfensohn and Robert McNamara. But he did have the experience of building a remarkably successful social enterprise at PIH and of driving a major health-policy program in poverty-stricken countries. And that is what motivated him to take the job: "I've seen with 3×5 what can be achieved when large public institutions get behind a bold policy initiative, and that's what I want the World Bank to do. I want it to commit to eradicating poverty by 2030."

Since arriving in 2012, Jim Yong Kim has initiated the bank's first significant reorganization in nearly two decades, committed to cutting $400 million in administrative costs over the next three years, and restructured the organization into fourteen global practices focusing on global policy areas such as energy and agriculture. He knew what he was taking on—although maybe not the ferocity of the resistance:

> Many people told me, "Jim, you can't do that. These types of bureaucracies are huge supertankers and you can't ever really change them. The only thing you can ever do is choose the people who will run the silos." I fundamentally rejected that idea. I understood that if we didn't make some serious changes, the culture would never change.
>
> These are hard things to do, especially when you're coming in through a political process like the selection of the World Bank president. But I have in many ways been preparing for this my whole life. Working in the field in places like Haiti and Peru and the former Soviet Union and Siberia and Africa. I have been thinking about this question, How do you get large groups of people to deliver on promises to the poor? We're trying to end extreme poverty in the world. If we're really going to address this challenge then we're going to have to change, and that's what we're going through now.

BY THE TIME YOU REACH your midforties, goes conventional wisdom, the basic contours of your life are set. You are at or near the peak of your career, with a well-established reputation and network in your community. You are preparing your mind primarily to build upon the platform that you have already developed rather than to change the platform—let alone build a new one. According to the "learn, earn, return" model of career development, these are the "earn" years—the years when you "cash in" on the professional, social, and emotional investments you have already made.

But if you think along these conventional lines, then you may be forgoing game-changing opportunities to broaden your life. That's what I experienced when I was asked to lead McKinsey's Washington Office. I was forty-seven, I had a flourishing career in London, and along with my wife and four children, we were all pretty settled at the time. Nevertheless, we said yes—because we were all excited at the unexpected opportunity to broaden our lives at a time when we thought such opportunities were in the past.

This time, it turned out that I did have a prepared mind. Why was that? Just before I was asked, a couple of my colleagues had accepted overseas assignments, and I remembered feeling a tangible sense of envy at their good fortune. Then one weekend in October 2006, my wife and I went to the wedding of her young cousin, who was marrying a State Department official. Although they were posted to Tel Aviv, the wedding was in Cyprus. It was a lovely location and wedding, but what I mostly remember is how much I enjoyed talking to the other young diplomats, who had come from their various postings around the world. What an interesting, eclectic group of internationalists, I thought. I wished that I was living that broad a life. A couple of days later, I was asked to move to another country—and I was emotionally prepared to say yes.

By the way, when I took my current job at Brunswick I was fifty-five. I went into a new industry, with new people, facing new issues. It turns out—for me at least—that my middle years were just the beginning of a new and broader chapter in a new country, a new profession, and a new way of life.

What persuades people to make these kinds of decisions in the midst of their careers? Typically, it's because by that stage you have a pretty good idea what the future looks like if you just stick to your current path—and you conclude that it's not quite good enough. So you prepare your mind for alternative options, which may or may not come along. You may also have greater confidence that you can make that kind of transition, because—as Seth Siegel pointed out—you have gained a lot of experience that you can bring to any new walk of life, and the core DNA of any business is much the same.

David Bradley was also in his midforties when he took decisive steps to shape a broader life. He had already built two successful businesses, he had an established professional reputation, and he had every reason to settle back and enjoy the fruits of his labor. Instead, he started along a completely new and risky path—motivated as much by personal adversity as by his very evident success.

Bradley became an entrepreneur while he was still at law school. His original venture, which he called the Research Council of Washington, soon morphed into the Advisory Board Company, which offered companies continuous DC-based research capacity for fixed sums—like joining a "research club." By the mid-1990s, the company had thousands of clients paying between $20,000 and $200,000 a year for research services.

Along with Jeff Zients, a highly talented former consultant who ran the business on a day-to-day basis, they decided to split the company into two. The Advisory Board took all of the health-care clients, while the Corporate Executive Board handled research duties for banking and other business clients. When they took the Corporate Executive Board public in 1999, Wall Street responded enthusiastically—and the same thing happened when they floated the Advisory Board in 2000. (By the way, Jeff Zients himself went on to a highly successful career in business and government, culminating in his current role as President Obama's director of the National Economic Council.)

There was no particular moment, no epiphany, he says, but sometime in 1995 Bradley began to explore the idea of buying a political magazine and becoming a media company owner. He had failed in an earlier attempt to build a political career for himself as a putative congressional candidate, and he figured that if he couldn't be in politics, at least he could get "a derivative pleasure" from participating in the political process. He bought the National Journal Group—a portfolio of political and policy media properties that was somewhat akin to the Advisory Board in that it produced high-quality reports for a high price to a select group of subscribers.

Two years later, Bradley would add the *Atlantic* magazine to his media stable. But in the midst of the negotiations, he faced real personal adversity. He woke up one morning to find that he couldn't speak. He had had vocal problems for ten years, but now his voice was gone. His vocal cords hurt when he tried to talk. In the months that followed, he would go through three operations on his vocal cords, none successful. He recalls, "It was the most isolating experience of my life."

He spent much of the time reading biographies of great men—Churchill, FDR—and especially of great media moguls—Luce, Hearst, Disney. Eventually, a new diagnosis and new medication led to the pain receding and his voice coming back. As he recalls, "My whole life returned in a twenty-four-hour period"—and he was able to complete the construction of what is now the Atlantic Media Company. He had a wholly new focus for his life, which started when he was going into his fifties.

JHUMPA LAHIRI ALSO MADE A significant change of direction in the middle of her career. At the age of forty-five, she moved herself and her family from the United States to Italy in 2013. There is nothing especially remarkable about that—I had done the same thing myself, albeit in the opposite geographical direction. The difference is that when she moved to Rome, Lahiri decided to speak, read, and write only in Italian; and that mattered because she is a highly acclaimed author, who had previously written exclusively in English—including her Pulitzer Prize–winning short-story collection *Interpreter of Maladies*.

She tells the story of this transition in her book *In Other Words*—written in Italian and translated into English by an accomplished translator, rather than by Lahiri herself. It is the story of a "passion that verges on obsession: that of a writer for another language," the Italian language, which first captured her affection during a post-college trip to Florence. Although she studied Italian off and on for many years after that, true mastery always eluded her. Italian became "an infatuation"—a "strange devotion" to the language, increasingly a vocation, rather than a folly. So in the midst of her writing career she moved to Rome for a "trial by fire, a sort of baptism" into a new language and world.

Lahiri describes the mind-set that took her into such unfamiliar territory: "I renounce expertise to challenge myself. I trade certainty for uncertainty." The writer Domenico Starnone writes to her that for a writer, "a new language is almost a new life, grammar and syntax re-cast you, you slip into another logic and another sensibility." Writing in a new and relatively unfamiliar language, she describes the journey of an author seeking to find a new voice, which is like "crossing a small lake. It really is small, and yet the other shore seems too far away, beyond my abilities."

She draws inspiration from Fernando Pessoa, who invented four different versions of himself: four separate, distinct writers, which enabled him to "go beyond the confines of himself." She also draws upon Ovid's classic work *Metamorphosis*—feeling "transformed, almost re-born." "One could say that the mechanism of metamorphosis is the only element of life that never changes."

PREPARING YOUR MIND
TO COMPLETE A FULL LIFE

By 9 p.m. Saturday, the line of cars snaked more than half a mile along the two-lane blacktop, and church organizers gave in. Drivers were ushered into the church parking lot by Jill Stuckey, a board member of this National Historical Site, who seemed to have evolved beyond the need for sleep. "Thank you for coming," she told the drivers as she passed out seat numbers. "Thank you for putting up with us. We wish we could come up with a better way. Maybe we will by next week."

The occasion for this commotion was that promptly at 10:00 a.m. on Sunday morning, ninety-year-old former president Jimmy Carter would speak at the local Sunday school. That in itself was not re-markable. The former president has taught all-ages Sunday school in his quiet, backwater hometown of Plains, Georgia, for decades, typically speaking to maybe a hundred people in front of a wooden cross that he built himself. Tourists in the congregation could go from there to a one-block downtown dominated by the Carter pea-nut warehouse and his old campaign office. Or they could visit the boyhood farm that still produces fresh food for the former president and his wife Rosalynn.

What made this weekend special was that Carter had announced just a few days before that the melanoma cancer he had previously revealed had now spread to his liver and brain. In a press conference, memorable for its candor and wit, he had publicly confronted his impending mortality. People now felt they had to come and see him in person, and it needed to be now. "I said to my wife, if you want to do it, we need to go," said Justin Vann, aged thirty-three, who works for a food packaging company in Lyman, South Carolina, and drove five hours to get in the pews.

As it happens, I first came to the United States in the midst of the 1980 presidential election between Jimmy Carter, the incum-bent Democratic president, and the Republican challenger, Ron-ald Reagan. The election was played out against the backdrop of a weak economy, a wider feeling that America was not doing well in the global marketplace—which Carter himself had described as a "malaise"—and a pervasive sense that the United States was in thrall to Middle Eastern oil interests. But the most important context for the election was the yearlong Iran hostage crisis, which seemed to serve as an almost daily national torture.

When Jimmy Carter was decisively defeated in November 1980, he was viewed as a failure—a one-term president, rejected in one of the biggest landslide defeats ever handed to an incumbent. I vividly recall the day in January 1981 when Ronald Reagan was sworn in as president, while almost simultaneously the fifty-two Iranian hostages were released to return home—all of this playing out on live television. In some respects it was the ultimate humiliation for Carter—although he characteristically referred to it as "one of the happiest moments of my life."

The view of Carter as an unsuccessful president remained conventional wisdom for years. Even Bill Clinton told reporters during his presidential campaign in 1992 that "Jimmy Carter and I are as different as daylight and dark." And thirty-five years after Carter left office, in the early stages of the 2016 primary campaign, two Republican contenders almost made fun of Carter—although they were quickly upbraided for their insensitivity.

Carter is still largely viewed as an unsuccessful president. But he is not viewed as an unsuccessful person—far from it. Apart from the self-evident observation that it is hard to think of somebody who became the most powerful person in the world as a failure—there is a much broader sense of what Carter achieved throughout his life, perhaps especially in the more than thirty-five years since he left political office at the age of fifty-five. Like Bill Clinton and Al Gore—although in very different ways—Carter has already come to be appreciated, even celebrated, as much for what he has done since he left the White House as for what he did while he was there or before. In Carter's case that period includes the award of the 2002 Nobel Peace Prize for his humanitarian work with the Carter Center.

Carter addresses this directly in a book that few get to write or even contemplate, given the subtitle *Reflections at Ninety*. The main title of the book is *A Full Life*—and it addresses how this final phase of his life has been almost as important as those that went before: "Teaching, writing and helping The Carter Center evolve during more recent times seem to constitute the high points in my life." More generally, he seeks to put the component parts of his "full life" in context: "I spent four of my ninety years in the White House, and they were, of course the pinnacle of my political life. Those years, though, do not dominate my chain of memories, and there was never an orderly or planned path to get there during my early life. At each step of my career, I made somewhat peremptory decisions about the next one."

He points out that these stages of life included eleven years in the Navy as a nuclear submarine engineer, and seventeen years as (to use his words) "a farmer involved in local community affairs"—before his serious entry into politics. Despite this seemingly limited political platform, he was elected governor of Georgia at the age of forty-seven and president of the United States at the age of fifty-two. When he was defeated in 1980, he became one of the youngest-ever "postpresidents."

At one point in his writing he seems almost to suggest that the governorship and presidency were just a preparation for the re-mainder of his life—and he points especially to the way in which they broadened his perspective: "Being governor and president were life-changing experiences. Rosalynn and I had to expand our in-volvement in the lives of many people, and we developed knowledge and personal relationships that provided a foundation for the many gratifying and enjoyable projects of The Carter Center during the next 35 years."

While compiling his presidential memoirs, he found that he en-joyed writing and that his books sold well—fortunately for him, be-cause they have been his principal income ever since. He describes one of the benefits of becoming a prolific author later in life: "Writ-ing and promoting the sale of these books has given me an oppor-tunity to study a wide range of subjects in great detail, to analyze what I have learned, and to present my views to the general public in America and many foreign countries."

At the age of seventy-five, he even wrote a book entitled *The Vir-tues of Aging,* "considering how enjoyable and gratifying my expe-riences had been since my 'retirement' from politics." Some of his friends joked that it would be the shortest book ever written—but he observed that "describing how much unprecedented freedom we have to undertake new projects after we no longer have to meet a regular work schedule, the book has been quite popular." In a later book, *Sharing Good Times,* he "described the many things we [he and Rosalynn] have taken up together for the first time at a relatively advanced age, including downhill skiing, mountain climbing, bird watching, and fly-fishing in many countries."

He concludes *A Full Life* with these words: "It seems, at least in retrospect, that all the phases of my life have been challenging, but successful and enjoyable. [Nowadays] we have an expanding and harmonious family, a rich life in our church and the Plains community, and a diversity of projects at The Carter Center that is adventurous and exciting. The life we have now is the best of all."

And that life continues. In March 2016 Jimmy Carter announced that, as a result of a successful treatment program, he was now cancer-free.

––––––

EARLIER I SUGGESTED that we now have six life phases, rather than the traditional four. Those six are childhood, adolescence, odyssey, adulthood, *active retirement,* and old age. It is evident that the fifth phase—which some people also call "pseudoretirement" is an increasingly important aspect of shaping a broad life. A series of studies obviate the notion that retirement is a period of surrender or serenity. Instead, they portray it as a period of sustained development, a period during which new and broader options can open, especially if you're on the lookout for them. And it is a further stage of life for which you need a prepared mind.

There is lots of evidence that people get happier as they get older—"they've unconsciously learned the power of positive perception." The neurologist Oliver Sacks writes of his father, who lived to ninety-four, that the eighties had been one of the most enjoyable decades of his life. "He felt, as I begin to feel, not a shrinking but an enlargement of mental life and perspective. One has had a long experience of life, not only one's own life, but others' too. One has seen triumphs and tragedies, booms and busts, revolutions and wars, great achievements and ambiguities." You can prepare your mind for a period when you are "freed from the fractious urgencies of earlier days, free to explore whatever I wish, and to bind the thoughts and feelings of a lifetime together."

As David Brooks observes, the evidence suggests that "people get better at the art of living" as the years go by. He adds that by their sixties many people have "found their zone." It's not so much that people get wiser as they get older—but they certainly don't get less wise. The tests that try to assess wisdom (a combination of social, emotional, and informational knowledge) suggest a kind of plateau. But it's the durability of that plateau that is the most significant. People achieve a level of competence, which holds steady until at least the age of seventy-five. So more and more people are going into the "active retirement" era with a mind prepared for new and broader opportunities, which they will have the capacity to maintain for many years.

Take Ron Daniel, who is now approaching a sixty-year association with McKinsey, which he led as worldwide managing partner from 1976 to 1988. Daniel's active retirement has now been going on for more than two and a half decades and shows no sign of ending. When he stood down as managing partner in 1988, he started to rebuild his client portfolio and engagement activity at the firm. But no sooner was he into that phase than he had the opportunity—totally out of the blue—to become the treasurer of Harvard University and a fellow of the Harvard Corporation (the university's principal governing body). He spent more than half his time working on the governance and administration of Harvard University for the next fifteen years.

The same is true of Ronald Cohen, who was prepared to build a whole new career in his active retirement. His primary career had been as a pioneer in the development of the British venture capital industry. In 1972 he cofounded Apax Partners, which by the 1990s had become Britain's largest venture capital firm and one of the three truly global firms of its kind, providing start-up finance for more than five hundred companies. Cohen earned the title of "father of the industry."

When he was fifty-five years old (that age again), Cohen started to wind down his involvement in Apax and to engage more directly in causes about which he felt strongly, notably the nascent field of social investing and entrepreneurship. He started getting more involved in public policy and nonprofit activities, notably in his role as chair of the government's Social Investment Taskforce, with a remit to "set out how entrepreneurial practices could be applied to obtain higher social and financial returns from social investment." And in 2002, he began to participate directly in social investing when he co-founded Bridges Ventures, "an innovative sustainable growth investor that delivers both financial returns and social and environmental benefits."

One outcome of his work was the recommendation that a substantial amount of unclaimed funds in dormant UK bank accounts could be used to help finance charitable and voluntary projects by providing seed capital and loan guarantees. That led to the early development of the "social impact bond"—a financial instrument that serves as an "outcomes-based contract" in which public service commissioners commit to pay for significant improvements in social outcomes for a defined population. For instance, an early use of the bond was to reduce reoffending among male prisoners after the completion of short sentences.

When David Cameron was elected as UK prime minister in 2010, he provided strong political support for this idea, championing the establishment of Big Society Capital under Cohen's chairmanship. Described as Britain's first social investment bank, its role is to ensure that socially oriented organizations have greater access to affordable capital, using an estimated £600 million left dormant in bank accounts for over fifteen years.

Cohen has become an evangelist for an arena that he helped to build after the age of sixty. He now says, "If I had been leaving university in 2010, this would be the area I would be going into." He notes that private equity arose because professional private equity firms came into existence and began to get institutional investors to invest in venture funds. He and others want to do the same thing for social entrepreneurship. They want to connect the capital markets to the social sector. He adds, "We want to preserve a decent society. We're going to see an entrepreneurial wave in the social sector now. We're going to see people who have been highly trained to manage organizations that are growing fast, applying their skills to dealing with social issues."

PREPARING YOUR MIND
FOR THE COMPLETELY UNEXPECTED

What happens when your life is transformed by something completely unexpected—something that immeasurably broadens your life but that challenges you in ways you never expected to be challenged? Can you prepare your mind for that? And once it's happened to you once, will you be better prepared the next time?

That's what happened to Michael Ignatieff, the Canadian academic, author, and broadcaster, whose adventure into politics I briefly mentioned in an earlier chapter. Ignatieff opens his remarkable political memoir *Fire and Ashes* with these words: "One night in October 2004, three men we had never met before—and whom we would later call 'the men in black'—arrived in Cambridge, Massachusetts to take my wife and me out to dinner." He goes on, "After a drink or two, [they] came to the point: Would I consider returning to Canada and running for the Liberal Party? They were proposing a run from outside, and their ambition, they said plainly, was to make me prime minister one day." On the day that he was approached, Ignatieff was fifty-seven years old.

It was, as Ignatieff freely observes, "an astonishing proposition"—not least because he had not lived in Canada for more than thirty years. He had spent much of that time—from 1978 to 2000—in the UK, where I used to watch and listen to him as a television and radio broadcaster, and read him as an op-ed columnist. He was very much at the intellectual end of the media spectrum—a fellow in politics at Kings College, Cambridge, and an author of books aimed at the high end of the market. Then in 2000 he took up a professorial post at the

Kennedy School at Harvard—where he was first approached by "the men in black."

Ignatieff decided to follow the course they suggested, and it led first to success and then to abject failure. He was elected to the Canadian Parliament in 2006. Almost immediately he was put forward to run for the leadership of the Liberal Party. Although on this occasion he lost to Stephane Dion, he served as the deputy leader and then took over when Dion resigned late in 2008. He led the Liberal Party for the next two years and into the 2011 federal election against the incumbent Conservative government of Stephen Harper.

The 2011 election was an unmitigated disaster for the Liberal Party and for Ignatieff personally. The party won only thirty-four seats, placing a distant third behind the Conservatives and the New Democratic Party, and thus lost its position as the official opposition. Ignatieff himself lost his own seat and promptly resigned as leader. He retired from politics less than seven years after he was first approached and returned to the academic life that he had previously left behind.

The obvious questions are, What would persuade someone to accept an opportunity like that, and what lessons has he learned from his success and failure? Was his mind prepared, and would it be better prepared next time? Ignatieff asks the same questions in his own words as he seeks to explain "how it becomes possible for an otherwise sensible person to turn his life upside down for the sake of a dream, or to put it less charitably, why a person like me succumbed, so helplessly, to hubris."

For my purposes, the first question is the more important: Why accept such an opportunity, especially when there is limited time to prepare your mind? A partial reason lay in his professional study of political philosophers, and notably of Machiavelli, who observed that "the goddess Fortuna rules politics"—that Fortuna is a fickle woman who must be courted, wooed, and won, adding that "she more often submits to those who act boldly than to those who proceed in a calculating fashion." (Forgive the sexist language; Machiavelli was writing in the sixteenth century, after all.)

Ignatieff decided—perhaps on the spur of the moment—to act boldly in response to Fortuna. Despite an ultimately bruising, even humiliating, experience, he seems not to regret it: "I entered politics with a lot of baggage and I paid full freight for it, but it's better to have paid up than to have lived a defensive life. A defensive life is not a life fully lived. If you take prudence as your watchword, your courage will desert you when the time comes to show your mettle. You can be sure that politics will demand more of you than prudence." And he links this thought to his well-studied belief in political chance: "Since Fortuna largely determines political careers, you have no reason to rail at fate if she turns against you. Don't make the mistake of supposing you control your fate. That's called hubris."

Given his belief in Fortuna, he had no qualms about giving politics a shot, despite his amateur status. He recognized that most politicians these days start their careers in their twenties as staffers and then move into elective office in their late thirties; so they spend their entire life in the bubble of the political world. But despite this trend and his own experience, he argues that "politics isn't a profession . . . , since a profession implies standards and techniques that can be taught. There are no techniques in politics; it is not a science, but a charismatic art, dependent on skills of persuasion, oratory and bloody-minded perseverance, all of which can be learned in life."

He adds one further observation about the nature of politics: "It's also not a profession in the sense of a steady career. Your life in politics can be upended in an instant, so you need to make sure you had a life before and can be prepared to resume a new life afterwards. Knowing that you can stand to lose is the best guarantee that you can stay honest." In other words, if you're in politics, you always need to have a mind prepared for the possibility of losing your job. Coaches of sports teams have the same requirement—and so increasingly do corporate CEOs.

All of that said, Ignatieff is the first to acknowledge that political success does not come easily—that political skills are not readily learned. As I observed in an earlier chapter, it is one of the severest tests of contextual intelligence in part because political knowledge is different from conventional knowledge—it is "knowing an issue in your guts, not just in your head, and knowing which cause may become your battle cry." He had to unlearn being clever, being rhetorical, being fluent, and start appreciating how much depends upon making a connection, any connection, with the people listening to you.

Failure to conquer this first requirement of a new entrant to any walk of life—and especially politics—prevents you from gaining standing, the authority to make your case and ensure a hearing. Ignatieff never really felt that he secured standing—not least because he was understandably chastised as a carpetbagger, an elitist with no fixed connections, out for himself and not for Canadians.

In the course of seven years in the political world, two leadership elections and one general election as leader, he learned one other thing that—despite everything that happened—made sense of his decision to take such a bold path down the road less traveled: "I loved every minute of it. The best thing about being a politician is that you live the common life of your country: at the lobster festivals, county fairs, demolition derbies, corn roasts, rodeos, backyard barbecues, and holy days at the synagogues, temples, mosques and churches." And he concludes eloquently, "What you learn from this is that the common life runs deeper than politics, runs below the fault lines of partisan acrimony and taps into our deep need as human beings to be together, to do things with a common purpose, to achieve more by being together than we could possibly achieve alone."

———————

A PREPARED MIND is not a onetime thing. It's a personal and professional journey. Few of us retain the exact same interests and objectives throughout our lives—our mind evolves. The question is, Will it evolve to broaden our options, to encourage a wider range of interests and opportunities? And since we have some control over this, how can we ensure that the choices we make enable us to build a broader and more remarkable life and career?

PART 3

HOW TO BUILD A REMARKABLE LIFE
AND CAREER

9

HOW TO BROADEN YOUR CAREER

Do I contradict myself? Very well then I contradict myself. I am large, I contain multitudes.

—Walt Whitman, "Song of Myself," 1855

THE THESIS OF THIS BOOK is that you can overcome your external constraints and internal doubts to build a broader, more interesting, more impactful, more enjoyable, and fundamentally better life and career. In the preceding chapters, I laid out the six dimensions of the Mosaic Principle that can help you in that pursuit. In this chapter, I describe how you might apply them coherently to build a remarkable career at work, and in the following chapter I explore how you might apply them to build a remarkable life. The combination, I hope, might help you to merge your various interests and aspirations into the cohesive tapestry of a full life—indeed into the compelling mosaic of a remarkable life and career.

I vividly recall that when I told David Bradley about some of the people who would appear in this book, he responded, "Oh, those people have had remarkable careers. That's what you're really talking about—remarkable careers." He was right—I am talking about remarkable careers and what it takes to have one. So the central questions I would pose to you are: How will you build your remarkable career? How will you shape your professional life? Will you shape it in the direction of breadth or depth?

I have argued that you are most likely to shape your professional life successfully, to have a remarkable career, if you are able to develop and apply the six dimensions of the Mosaic Principle:

1. *Apply your moral compass*—so that you can build your career with a coherent purpose and secure morality, and trade off one source of motivation against another when you need to.
2. *Define an intellectual thread*—so that your pursuit of professional breadth is not random or quixotic but is built upon robust foundations and a T-Shaped Approach to professional development.
3. *Develop transferrable skills*—so that you are able to solve problems, lead teams, and drive change by applying the best combination of skills from each context in which you have operated.
4. *Invest in contextual intelligence*—so that you are sensitive, responsive, and adaptable to each unique context and set of operating conditions—professionally aware of important differences in objectives, motivations, cultures, and language.
5. *Establish extended networks*—so that you can leverage authentic and substantive relationships across different walks of life to solve problems, build teams, and support your own career aspirations.
6. *Develop a prepared mind*—so that you are ready to accept opportunity when it presents itself, to "zigzag" through life with an entrepreneurial mind-set and occasionally to take the road less traveled.

Taken together these six dimensions provide ways of coping with professional complexity, and a road map that should enable you to chart and navigate the path to a broad and fulfilling professional career.

Each dimension is within your reach. Some build upon innate aspects of your personal character—for instance, a search for meaning and ethical assurance (moral compass), making an authentic connection with a new environment or group of people (contextual intelligence), and curiosity and excitement about new experiences (prepared mind). Others reflect aspects of your personal capacity, teachable and learnable capabilities that you can seek to develop further—learning more about an issue you really care about (intellectual thread), applying skills and insights from one arena to another (transferrable skills), and building diverse relationships that you can draw upon when you need them (extended networks).

These six dimensions also enable you to develop a checklist of issues and questions that you can ask of yourself and of others in a more or less structured process of self-discovery. Here is an initial checklist of the key questions you might ask in pursuit of each dimension:

1. *Moral compass:* What are the meaning and purpose of my career? What are my most important professional and personal aspirations? Where are the actual or potential conflicts between my aspirations? How can I reconcile them—and if I can't reconcile them, what order of priority and importance should I place them in? What motives have I been neglecting for too long, and what can I do about that? Am I doing anything that directly or indirectly conflicts with my moral compass—either in reality or perception?

2. *Intellectual thread:* What issue(s) am I most inherently interested in; what do I find myself instinctively drawn to; what issue or challenge do I want to understand better and have the most impact on? What capability or expertise do I want to be best known for—to be the "go-to person" for? What are the horizontal and vertical bars in my T-Shaped Approach to professional development? Where are the environments in which I can both enhance and apply my intellectual thread?

3. *Transferrable skills:* What have I already proved I am good at, and in what context? In what other walks of life would these skills be relevant and applicable? What kinds of organizations might benefit the most from my skills and capabilities? And how can I extend the skills I have and build a bigger tool kit with broader application?

4. *Contextual intelligence:* What do I understand and not understand about a new context? How can I learn more about the nuances of this context and adapt more effectively? How can I develop and exercise my contextual intelligence in order to ensure that I have a heightened awareness of how I come across and how others perceive me?

5. *Extended networks:* Across which walks of life am I most and least connected? What events can I attend, and which relationships can I strengthen, in order to broaden and diversify my networks? How can I authentically contribute to those people in my networks, and how can I best derive value as well?

6. *Prepared mind:* What kind of opportunities do I want to prepare myself for—professionally, personally, financially? What steps do I need to take to feel better prepared? What is the ideal path for somebody with my prior experiences and knowledge? Am I just following a conventional path; and can I forge something new and distinctive instead? What opportunities in different walks of life will differentiate me from others and help me build the broadest and most successful professional career?

WHERE ARE YOUR BREADTH SWEET SPOT AND FRONTIER?

You already configure your approach to your career somewhere on a spectrum between extreme breadth and extreme depth—we all do. If you are closer to the extreme breadth end of the spectrum, there is an evident risk of becoming a "jack-of-all-trades, master of none." If you are closer to extreme depth, the risk is of becoming a "one-trick pony."

At any time in your career, you have the option to move one way or the other along that spectrum—to adjust the mix between being deep in some areas and broad in others. And while you may conceivably pick any point along the spectrum, you would be well-advised to focus on finding your own specific *breadth sweet spot*—the ideal point that reflects your intrinsic capacity and character for breadth. This is where you can be most effective at addressing complex and multidimensional problems and feel most at ease with your range of professional activities and interests.

Experience suggests that you are most likely to feel comfortable when you can think of yourself as "jack-of-all-trades, master of *some*." That may well happen by mastering one field—even to the extent of the 10,000 hour rule—and then moving on to another. You might think of that as a kind of *serial depth*, which aggregates over time into *accumulated breadth*.

Serial depth is *accretive*—that is to say, experiences build upon each other to enable enhanced pattern recognition. The whole of what you know about and can do is greater than the sum of the parts. Each area that you have mastered will stay with you—not to the same extent but rather like a language you once spoke well. You may not be as current or as fluent as you were when you were speaking it every day, but you will feel confident that after a quick refresher you could pick it up again.

This is illustrated by the work of two researchers, Wai Fong Boh and Andrew Ouderkirk, who examined the breadth and depth of expertise among a sample of research scientists. To control for different institutional contexts, all of the subjects came from 3M, a company known for its consistent ability to develop new and unique commercially viable products. They classified their subjects as "generalists," "specialists," or "polymaths"—with the latter being individuals who, after a decade or so of specialization, begin to explore other areas while maintaining the specialized skills and knowledge that they have already established.

The study found that the subjects they described as polymaths—the scientists with "serial depth"—were able to apply their specialist knowledge to a variety of problems across various subspecialties in a way that the pure specialists could not. "Polymathic inventors find that they not only learn about new technological domains, but they also gain greater understanding of their own core technologies. The disciplined practice of repeatedly applying and integrating the same technologies with new ones results in experience, which makes it easier for the polymathic inventors to make new applications, even though the process may not be a simple one."

The researchers showed that pure specialists could analyze problems in greater detail; persevere to make breakthroughs in the area of their core knowledge; and make trade-offs as to which inventions could be manufactured more easily, assuming similar performance. In contrast, generalists could identify new ways of looking at things, understand how technologies could apply to other areas, and not be overburdened by prior knowledge. But polymathic research scientists, more than their broader or deeper counterparts, could bring both "breadth and depth of expertise to help evaluate ideas and identify the most fruitful ideas to work with, and both dimensions of expertise help to identify novel ideas that have the potential to bring commercial value to the firm."

In a related study, academic Beatrice Van der Heijden also identified the ability of people with broad knowledge and core-area expertise to go beyond the status quo in order to push the boundaries of opportunity—the type of professionals she calls *flexperts*. Van der Heijden explains that "these are people who are both flexible and in possession of expertise. They are, for example, good at adjusting flexibly to technological changes and they demonstrate that they know how to respond quickly and alertly at times when there are opportunities in adjacent areas."

There is also a spectrum within the concept of depth. Think about how you build up depth of knowledge and expertise over time. You start out as a novice, then move to competent, then become authoritative, and finally become an acknowledged expert. At any point along that progression, you can stop and say, "That's enough for me. I know as much as I want or need to do. I don't want or need to go any deeper."

You may do so because you conclude that you have reached the point of *diminishing returns* to depth. You may have reached the point of competency in an area—or perhaps established yourself as authoritative—as a businessperson, a public servant, a scientist, a marketer, a fund-raiser. At that point, you may resist the temptation to move further in the direction of deeper expertise, since you fear— with some justification—that you will start to narrow your options and undermine your own capacity and character.

Adam Grant observes that "as we gain knowledge about a domain, we become prisoners of our stereotypes"; we become more entrenched in a specific way of seeing the world around us, less adaptable to changing rules and conditions. He cites Rice University professor Erik Dane, who has shown that expert bridge players find it more difficult to adapt when the rules are changed and that the most expert accountants are less adept than their junior colleagues in applying a new tax law. In contrast, says Grant, "it is when people have moderate expertise in a particular domain that they're most open to radically creative ideas."

Throughout my career, and especially now, I have been fortunate to work alongside people who had previously trained and practiced in other professions—doctors, lawyers, academics, journalists. They have spent years acquiring quite specific and demanding professional accreditation over several years—they have completed their medical residencies or passed their bar exams or secured their PhDs in some very challenging specialty, served in the military, or trained as a reporter or editor. But at some point, they have concluded that that was not enough for them, not what they wanted to do for the rest of their life. They have even started to see their area of specialty as a "gilded cage" from which they wanted to escape—so that they could operate on a broader canvas and achieve more as a consequence.

However, there may also come a point when you have gone too far toward the breadth end of the spectrum—when you know a little about a lot, but feel overextended and unable to convert your knowledge into practical application. You might think of this as your *breadth frontier*—the point when you need to adjust to acquire greater focus and depth of knowledge and insight. One of my colleagues once observed that his "distinctive spike has turned into a lofty plateau." He was implying that he was no longer the go-to person on any particular issue. In a marketplace of ideas that could mean the phone stops ringing, which is not what you want.

Ethan Bernstein has used a simple mathematical formula to chart his own career along the breadth spectrum. He calls it his "4+4+4 approach"—by which he means that he aims to spend about four years in any one given area to go sufficiently deep, and then moves on to another to ensure he is sufficiently broad. When he is deciding whether to stay or go and where to go next, he makes the decision based upon whether he is still learning. Bernstein's *serial depth* approach has led him from business and law degrees (which he actually did concurrently) to corporate law to management consulting to government service and now to Harvard Business School where he is a professor. No news yet on where he will go next.

Bernstein used to joke that "the only thing I got out of my JD was meeting my wife," whom he met while studying for the New York Bar in Albany. But that perception changed when he "got a call from Washington" one morning. The call was from Elizabeth Warren, now a high-profile Democratic senator from Massachusetts but then a Harvard Law School professor who had been charged by President Obama with setting up the US Consumer Financial Protection Bureau (CFPB). Warren had actually been one of Bernstein's professors at law school, and when she called, she said, "What I need is an all-purpose player—somebody who can be good at all sorts of things. I thought of you."

Bernstein said yes, partly because he admired Warren and partly because "this was the most important piece of legislative work in modern financial history, an opportunity that would give me the highest level of responsibility and learning." In his time at the CFPB, he gave it his all: "I applied everything I knew in pursuit of the

CFPB's mission. I helped conduct market analyses, make policy and design regulations, develop strategy, and grow the agency from 70 to 1,200 people in just two years. I did all this although I had never worked in government or studied political science. I never planned for this to happen—but all of a sudden my uncommon background was highly relevant."

Bernstein now studies, writes, and teaches on the issue of transparency versus privacy—how they affect workplace culture and results—a subject on which he is becoming the go-to academic. He observes that most people who are known for something are that way because they are deep, not because they are broad. But in reality, you can be both. For many, not knowing what they want to do next is a reason to stick with the status quo, to keep doing what they're currently doing. Bernstein thinks the opposite is true: "When you don't know what you want, go broad. The broader you are, the higher the probability you'll discover what you want to be known for. And don't overthink it—just be yourself. The edges of authenticity are broad."

Executive change consultants M. J. Ryan and Dawna Markova believe that each new opportunity should be "in the stretch zone where activities feel a bit awkward and unfamiliar. It's in that stretch zone where true change occurs." But they add, try not to spend too much time in the "stress zone, where a challenge is so far beyond current experience to be overwhelming."

Over time (and as you get better) the activities you undertake will shift zones—from stress to stretch, and then stretch to comfort. Remember the borders between these zones are sloped and curved—hence the concept of a "learning curve." You have a degree of control over the degree of difficulty you undertake and the degree of intensity with which you do so. From time to time, you can even dwell for a while in the comfort zone—but not for too long. The chances are that that's not where you'll find your breadth sweet spot.

1 0

HOW TO BROADEN YOUR LIFE

> Largeness is a lifelong matter. You grow because you are not content not to. You are like a beaver that chews constantly because if it doesn't, its teeth grow long and weak. You grow because you are a grower; you're large because you can't stand to be small.
>
> —Wallace Stegner, *Crossing to Safety*

WHEN OUR LONDON FRIEND and former neighbor David Kitchin became a High Court judge in 2005, my wife and I viewed it as a rite of passage not just for David but for ourselves. Oh my goodness, we thought, we're now at the age when our friends are becoming senior judges—we must be getting really old. Of course, this was very unfair to David, who was—and remains—youthful and sprightly, far removed from the crusty image attached to the senior ranks of the judiciary. That has remained the case even since he was promoted to the Court of Appeals in 2011, with the title Lord Justice Kitchin.

David and I have had a long-running dialogue about books, so when I saw him a while ago I asked him what he was reading. He paused for a moment, and then said, "Obituaries." He added, "I read the *Times* obituaries every day; and whenever I can, I read anthologies of obituaries. It's not just that I'm getting older, and have a more elevated sense of mortality—although I do appreciate that my time is not unlimited. It's just that I love to read life stories—and I learn something every time." When I asked, "What do you learn?" he answered, "How to live a full life."

I share David's fascination with lives well lived—especially of those who have built a broad and well-rounded life. It is one of the ironies of our existence that the qualities and achievements of such people become most evident at the moment of their death—or when there is some intimation of approaching mortality. Perhaps that sense is even richer in the immediacy of their passing than in subsequent more reflective biography or history. Because it is at that moment that the emotional impact of their lives—and of our loss—is most profoundly felt.

Occasionally, I read an obituary that has an especially profound impact on me—intellectually or emotionally, or both. For instance, in the time that I have been researching and writing this book, I have been especially moved by four obituaries, each of a person who built a broad and remarkable life—albeit in very different circumstances and over varying lengths of time, at least two of them ending way too early.

The first was of the neurologist and author Dr. Oliver Sacks, who died on August 30, 2015. His life and impact were of such note that the opening lines of a lengthy obituary were published on the front page of the *New York Times*. In one of the opening sentences, it says of him, "Dr. Sacks, who died on Sunday, at 82, was a polymath and an ardent humanist, and whether he was writing about his patients, or his love of chemistry or the power of music, he leapfrogged among disciplines, shedding light on the wonderful interconnectedness of life—the connections between science and art, physiology and psychology, the beauty and economy of the natural world and the magic of the human imagination."

"Polymath," "ardent humanist," "interconnectedness of life"— there are the words that define the essence of a broad life, fully lived. The obituary notes that he lived his life in a way that epitomized the ideal doctor, with "keen powers of observation and a devotion to detail, deep reservoirs of sympathy, and an intuitive understanding of the fathomless mysteries of the human brain, and the intricate connections between the body and the mind."

As the obituary makes clear, he lived a life as eclectic and adventurous as his intellectual pursuits, taking him from medical school in England to a stint as a forest firefighter in British Columbia to medical residencies and fellowship work in San Francisco and Los Angeles. He held a weight-lifting record in California, and on weekends sometimes drove hundreds of miles on his motorcycle, from California to Las Vegas or the Grand Canyon. By his own description, he was a man with an "extreme immoderation in all my passions" and "violent enthusiasms"—which encompassed all the marvels of the natural world as well as swimming, chemistry, photography, and perhaps most of all, writing.

In his writing, he was able to communicate the romance of science and the creative and creaturely blessings of being alive. So while his own broad and eclectic life as a polymath is a shining illustration of what this book is all about, it is his written exploration of the lives lived by his subjects that chronicles its challenges and complexities. Because in those writings—books like *Awakenings* and *An Anthropologist on Mars*—he explores how people with fewer natural gifts, and often severe challenges to overcome, were able to shape their lives. The *New York Times* obituary describes how "his case studies became literary narratives as dramatic, richly detailed and compelling as those by Freud and Luria—stories that underscored not the marginality of his patients' experiences, but their part in the shared human endeavor and the flux and contingencies of life."

In a short book published shortly after his death, and evocatively entitled *Gratitude,* Sacks says almost apologetically—at least to himself—"I am sorry I have wasted (and still waste) so much time; I am sorry to be as agonizingly shy at eighty as I was at twenty; I am sorry that I speak no other languages but my mother tongue and that I have not traveled or experienced other cultures as widely as I should have done." But as he prepares to "complete" his life—since he knows that he is terminally ill—he says, "My predominant feeling is one of gratitude. I have loved and been loved; I have been given much and I have given something in return; I have read and traveled and thought and written; I have had an intercourse with the world, the special intercourse of writers and readers."

The second obituary was that of a much younger man, Dave Goldberg, whose death at the age of forty-seven of an undiagnosed heart condition on May 1, 2015, evoked a powerful reaction, well beyond his own Silicon Valley community. This was in part because of his professional influence as a serial entrepreneur and venture capitalist—who most recently had built his Survey Monkey business into a provider of web surveys on every topic imaginable, be it customer service or politics. But it was at least as much because of the example he set as a husband, a father, a friend, and a mentor to many.

As his obituary observes, "Mr. Goldberg was always quick with a wisecrack, and he kept a sense of humor about being the least famous half of one of Silicon Valley's pre-eminent power couples." His wife, Sheryl Sandberg, the COO of Facebook, often said she would not have been as successful in her career without his substantial assistance at home. In her book *Lean In,* she also writes, "There is far more to life than climbing a career ladder, including raising children, seeking personal fulfillment, contributing to society, and improving the lives of others." Thirty days after Goldberg's death (the end of *sheloshim* in the Jewish faith), Sandberg wrote her own kind of obituary, an essay posted on Facebook in which she reflected upon her husband's life and her struggles in getting over her grief. The post was "liked" by more than 800,000 people, shared by 300,000, and received more than 60,000 comments.

I didn't know Dave Goldberg, although we were only one degree removed through mutual friends. But I was deeply affected by the tributes from people I did know, like Adam Grant, who writes of Goldberg that he was "a loving father and husband, the heart and soul of Silicon Valley, a lifelong advocate for women, best friend to many, a compassionate leader, and a gracious connector." He adds, "I don't believe this [Goldberg's death] happened for a reason, but it has given us all a reason to be more present parents, more loving spouses, more supportive friends, and more caring leaders." He lived a broad and full life, which sadly became most apparent only at the moment of his passing.

The third obituary was for James B. Lee, a vice chair of the banking giant JPMorgan Chase, who died of a heart attack at the age of sixty-two after working out at his home in Darien, Connecticut, on June 17, 2015. Universally known as Jimmy, he was a behind-the-scenes consigliere to the world's top corporate chieftains, hatching mergers and public offerings for companies as diverse as General Motors, Facebook, and Alibaba. He had a forty-year career in investment banking, all with JPMorgan Chase or its predecessor companies.

I didn't know Jimmy Lee either—although again there was only one degree of separation. He was a frequent collaborator with my current colleagues at Brunswick. But even before his death, I was aware that he exemplified many of the ideas in this book. His obituary describes him as a "throwback, part of a different generation of bankers on Wall Street who were trusted advisers to corporate America based on deep relationships and insights, even as much of investment banking had become commoditized."

And in his eulogy at a packed funeral, JPMorgan Chase CEO Jamie Dimon addressed the breadth and fullness of his life: "People may not know that you were a Renaissance man. In college you majored in Econ, but you also majored in Art History. You loved music. In fact, you helped form a band at JPMorgan Chase, the Bank Notes, in which you played lead guitar. You loved God and country. You considered yourself a great fisherman . . . and an even better golfer. You were an incomparable force of nature—because your intellectual talent was accompanied with a huge heart, unyielding passion, and a love of life and humanity."

One of Jimmy Lee's most tangible legacies was an unpublished list of what he called "work habits that have served me well during my career." After his death, I was given a copy of this list by my Brunswick partner and colleague Steve Lipin, who had worked closely with Jimmy Lee and was consequently especially moved by his premature death. You will recognize quite a few of Lee's recommended work habits from this book:

- Don't rely on the knowledge of a specialist when you talk to a client. You must be viewed as an expert and be prepared for every conversation.
- Build your network. Find people that have the skills or characteristics you want to learn, and ask for their help in acquiring those skills.
- Ask questions. Whatever the question, chances are you aren't the first and won't be the last to ask it.
- Have several mentors—since there are countless talented people who can mentor you and help you acquire the skills you need.
- Take ownership of your own career. Otherwise, someone else will and you might not like the direction they take it in.

The fourth obituary was for somebody I did know—Asa Briggs, who died in March 2016 at the age of ninety-four. I knew Briggs in the late 1970s when he was the head of my college at Oxford University. Like most people I thought of him as one of Britain's leading social historians and educationists—the author of numerous celebrated works of nineteenth-century social history and a voluminous history of the BBC, as well as an educational pioneer as vice-chancellor of the University of Sussex before he returned to Oxford.

But when I read his obituary, it became apparent there was much about Briggs that I hadn't previously known—especially about his earlier life. For instance, I learned that Briggs was one of the "Oxbridge brains" recruited in secrecy to work at Bletchley Park, the Buckinghamshire country house devoted to cracking German wartime codes; and that while working in Bletchley's Hut 6, Briggs, the youngest warrant officer in the British army, worked alongside Alan Turing, the mathematical genius and computer pioneer.

His obituary in the *Guardian* continues, "Turing was among the first of the great and good with whom Briggs spent his long life rubbing shoulders. His friends and contacts reflected the broad span of his interests, from Winston Churchill, whose *History of the English-Speaking Peoples* Briggs proofread as a young academic, to Chairman

Mao's loyal lieutenant Zhou Enlai and J. Robert Oppenheimer, father of the atom bomb."

One of the few things that Oliver Sacks, Dave Goldberg, Jimmy Lee, and Asa Briggs had in common was that they all died in 2015 or early 2016. Otherwise, they occupied very different walks of life and died at different stages of life—in their eighties, forties, sixties, and nineties respectively. But they each exhibited a willingness and ability to live their lives to the fullest—and to inspire others by doing so. They each took seriously the opportunity we each of us have—to shape a broad life story with multiple chapters.

WHAT IS YOUR LIFE STORY?

Much of this book has focused on the options and choices you face at work. But that is not the full extent of your life—it is only a part of it. As the obituaries of Sacks, Goldberg, Lee, and Briggs illustrate, what you do outside the conventionally defined workplace can be at least as important in building a remarkable life—sometimes more so. And you face similar, if not precisely the same, options and choices in the parts of your life that are not related to work. You can choose breadth or depth in any aspect of your life. And in so doing, you can serve to develop a holistic narrative for your life.

Northwestern University has an institution called the Foley Center for the Study of Lives. Led by Professor Dan McAdams, it is an interdisciplinary research project committed to studying psychological and social development in the adult years. The core element of the research is what the center calls *life stories*—"research into the structure, function, and development of life stories across the adult life course." They have developed what they call the "life-story model of adult identity."

According to this model, people living in modern societies begin to organize their lives in narrative terms in late adolescence and young adulthood. They create within themselves evolving life stories that serve to reconstruct the past and anticipate the future in ways that provide their lives with some degree of unity and purpose. Another social psychologist has called this "ego identity"—a personal narrative that situates a person in a particular psychosocial niche in the modern world. Like other literary constructions, life stories may be analyzed in terms of plots, settings, scenes, characters, and themes.

The Foley Center's research has started to focus on frequently observed patterns in these life stories. For instance, a common theme across many life stories is what they call *generativity*—"an adult's concern for and commitment to promoting the well-being of youth and future generations through involvement in parenting, teaching, mentoring, and other creative contributions that aim to leave a positive legacy of the self for the future."

Another common theme is the *redemptive self*—a frequently observed sequence in which a negative life-narrative scene is followed by a positive outcome. The good ultimately redeems or salvages the bad that precedes it. David Brooks refers to this redemptive narrative structure when he observes that "a happy life has its recurring set of rhythms: difficulty to harmony, difficulty to harmony."

He also says that people who have traveled what he calls the "road to character . . . had to go down to go up. They had to descend into the valley of humility to climb to the heights of character." And he adds that the road to character often involves moments of moral crisis, confrontation, and recovery. The struggle against weakness has a *U* shape. You are living your life and then you get knocked off course—either by love, or failure, illness, loss of employment, or twist of fate. The shape is advance-retreat-advance. You are ultimately saved by grace, however you define that. As Kierkegaard puts it, "Only the one who descends into the underworld rescues the beloved."

The way in which so many of us think of our life stories in terms of recovery and redemption is captured in the narrative theory of Joseph Campbell. His book *The Hero with a Thousand Faces* has influenced generations of writers and artists since it was first published in 1949—from George Lucas with *Star Wars* to J. K. Rowling with *Harry Potter*. Campbell observes that important myths from around the world that have survived for thousands of years all share the same fundamental structure, which he calls the *monomyth*. He discovers that every culture tells similar stories about virtuous characters. These stories are variations of a basic plot that he calls "the hero's journey."

The hero's journey, the mythological adventure of the hero, follows a standard path or formula: separation-initiation-return. Campbell describes the instantly recognizable sequence: "A hero ventures forth from the world of common day into a region of supernatural wonder: fabulous forces are there encountered and a decisive victory is won: the hero comes back from this mysterious adventure with the power to bestow boons on his fellow man." The most common "boon" is the discovery of important self-knowledge, which the hero can choose to pass on or keep to himself. Campbell argues that the universal repetition of this plotline reveals general aspects of the human psyche.

You can learn a lot about yourself if you consider your own life story—retrospectively and prospectively—as a hero's journey. Although it is less "fantastic" than the myths that Campbell described, it is nevertheless likely that your story will be full of challenges and opportunities to demonstrate your greatness across a broad or narrow canvas.

People often use redemption imagery to depict a third common feature of life stories, the importance of *significant life transitions* or *turning points*. The concept of a turning point is both literary and psychological, and it has enjoyed strong currency in Western cultural life for hundreds of years. But researchers are now employing qualitative and narrative methods to examine the turning points that people describe in their lives—focusing particularly on the most frequent transitions, which are career changes, and the most powerful, such as religious conversions.

So let me ask you now, How would you tell your own life story? How would you tell it in a paragraph, in a page, in an essay, in a book? And, of course, implicit in the question is how would you write your own prospective obituary? It would almost certainly contain elements of generativity, of redemption, of transitions and turning. points. It would contain plots, settings, scenes, characters, and themes. It would also contain what the Foley Center calls "traits, goals and stories"—the substructure of your life and its purpose. But what specific weight would you give to these features and in what sequence?

How, above all, can you tell (or foretell) a life story of breadth and diversity, of far-reaching and wide-ranging professional attainment and personal fulfillment? The solution to this challenge is probably not to have a definitive life plan that you follow as if it provided a preordained road map—seeking to "connect the dots" prospectively rather than retrospectively. But it is to live consciously—to take a conscious and purposeful approach to building your life toward what Aristotle called the "highest good," which is happiness.

Sarah Bakewell suggests just such a conscious and purposeful approach to building a life story in her acclaimed book *How to Live*. She takes her inspiration from the sixteenth-century essayist Michel Eyquem de Montaigne—a nobleman, government official, traveler, philosopher, counselor, and winegrower who lived in the Perigord region of southwestern France from 1533 to 1592. At the age of thirty-eight, he took charge of the family estate, retired from public life, and began writing the essays for which he is treasured—107 essays, amounting to more than a thousand pages. He didn't write to record his own deeds and achievements, as was the custom at the time; rather, he wrote "exploratory, free-floating pieces" to which he gave simple, often intriguing titles—"Of Friendship," "Of Cannibals," "Of the Custom of Wearing Clothes," "How we cry and laugh for the same thing," "Of Cruelty," "How our mind hinders itself," "Of Diversion," "Of Experience."

But although these essays are modestly titled and written, they have profoundly affected many people over the centuries. Writing an article on the subject for the *Times* in 1991, the journalist Bernard Levin said, "I defy any reader of Montaigne not to put down the book at some point and say with incredulity: 'How did he know all that about me?'" Gustave Flaubert wrote in a similar vein, "Don't read him as children do, for amusement, nor as the ambitious do, to be instructed. No, read him in order to live."

Sarah Bakewell herself observes of Montaigne that "he wanted to know how to live a good life—not just a correct and honorable life, but also a fully human, satisfying, flourishing life." So from his essays, she constructs twenty attempts to answer the most fundamental question of all, how to live—with chapter headings such as "Pay Attention," "Read a Lot, Forget Most of What You Read," "Be Slow-Witted," "Survive Love and Loss," "Wake from the Sleep of Habit," "See the World," "Let Life Be Its Own Answer."

In a similar vein, the contemporary historian Theodore Zeldin has created a foundation called the Oxford Muse to foster "research into the art of living." He does this primarily by encouraging people to write their personal histories—brief self-portraits that describe their everyday lives and the things they have learned. He assembles these essays into a *Portrait Gallery*—"expressions of the many sides of the personality and experience of living people, their dreams and unanswered questions." As Zeldin observes, the great adventure of this or any other time is "to discover who inhabits the world, one individual at a time."

So the Oxford Muse website is full of personal essays with titles like "Why an Educated Russian Works as a Cleaner in Oxford," Why Being a Hairdresser Satisfies the Need for Perfection," "How Writing a Self-Portrait Shows You Are Not Who You Thought You Were," "What a Person Adds When Writing About Himself to What He Says in Conversation." Zeldin's hope is that this process of self-revelation brings "excitement and a divine spark" into people's lives, that it creates more imaginative awareness of the diversity of human potential and "new kinds of networks that bring wider ethical, aesthetic and intellectual benefits, serving the public good, as well as enhancing individual lives."

David Brooks also initiated an approach to cataloging life stories through the platform of his regular op-ed column in the *New York Times*. In 2011 he asked people over the age of seventy to write a life report, including an evaluation of what they had done well in their lives so far, what they had not done so well, and what they had learned along the way—and he asked them to grade their professional and personal lives so far. Drawing upon the analogy of the essays that some colleges ask their alumni to write for their twenty-fifth and fiftieth reunions, he suggested that these life reports might be helpful to young people who are trying to understand how life develops, how professional careers and personal lives evolve, and how modern adulthood is characterized by common mistakes and common blessings.

The reports that Brooks received—like the Oxford Muse essays—provide a portrait gallery of observations about how we build our lives and tell our life stories. Brooks himself observes that most people give themselves higher grades for their professional lives (averaging A–) than for their personal lives (averaging B+). Most are satisfied with how they contributed at work; those who started their own businesses seem especially happy, even more so if they have handed them down to their children.

The essays suggest that the most important key to professional success—and especially to happiness—is active management of your career and life. Those who have divided their life into chapters and leaned toward risk have the strongest sense of purpose and fulfilment. He says:

> The unhappiest of my correspondents saw time as an unbroken flow, with themselves as a cork bobbing on top of it. . . . The happier ones divided time into (somewhat artificial phases). They wrote things like: There were six crucial decisions in my life. Then they organized their lives around those pivot points. By seeing time as something divisible into chunks, they could more easily stop and self-appraise. They had more control over their fate.

Although Brooks asked people to reflect upon their lives, he notes a risk in excessive self-examination. Those who were prone to obsession about each passing emotion typically did not lead the happiest or most fulfilling lives. "Many of the most impressive people . . . were strategic self-deceivers. When something bad was done to them, they forgot it, forgave it or were grateful for it. When it comes to self-narratives, honesty may not be the best policy." In the same vein, he describes "resilience" as a central theme of the essays. "I don't think we remind young people enough that life is hard. Bad things happen." But while there are many tales of frustration and disappointment—especially of opportunities missed or deep personal failings—"many of the writers have integrated the ups and downs into an enveloping sense of *gratitude,*" the same word that Oliver Sacks used as the title of his final book.

The Foley Center, Michel de Montaigne, Sarah Bakewell, the Oxford Muse, David Brooks's "Life Reports"—each has sought to help us tell and understand our life stories. In the process, they have also helped us think about what it will take to live a better, fuller, broader, more remarkable life.

As we build our lives and tell our life stories—each of us should be able to answer the most basic, but often the most confounding, of questions: Where am I coming from? Where am I now? Where am I going? We should be able to answer these questions, so that we can live consciously. We should be wary of the cautionary observation, "The person who aims at nothing is sure to hit it," or the advice given by the legendary sage of New York Yankees baseball, Yogi Berra, who with characteristic obliqueness advised, "When you come to a fork in the road it, take it."

From late adolescence onward it is never too soon and never too late to develop a conscious life story. It is a valuable and perhaps necessary exercise as you seek to shape your life. It enables and requires you to reconstruct in your mind what you have done so far in your life and, more importantly, what you have still to do. It also helps to clarify the choices you have made and have still to make, the degree to which these choices are within your control, and perhaps most acutely of all, how much time you have.

HOW MUCH TIME DO YOU HAVE FOR A BROAD LIFE?

When it comes to building a broad life, there is one constraint that seems to get in the way for all of us—that is shortage of time. In the narrow sense, we all believe that we are time starved. When he was secretary of state, Henry Kissinger said to his staff, "There can't be a crisis next week. My schedule is already full." And then there is time in the absolute sense of how much time we have in our whole lives. When Bobby Layne, the great quarterback for the Detroit Lions, was inducted into the Pro Football Hall of Fame in Canton, Ohio, it was said of him: "Layne never lost a game . . . time just ran out on him."

In 1910, Arnold Bennett—a distinguished, if somewhat austere, British novelist, journalist, and civil servant—published a short book with the intriguing title *How to Live on 24 Hours a Day*. In the book he observes that "the supply of time is a daily miracle. Time is the inexplicable raw material of everything. With it, all is possible; without it, nothing." He adds that "no one can take it from you. It is unstealable. And no one receives either more or less than you receive."

Out of your twenty-four hours a day, Bennett observes, "You have to spin health, pleasure, money, content, respect, and the evolution of your immortal soul. Its right and most effective use is a matter of the highest urgency and of the most thrilling actuality." And he pointedly asks, "Which of us really lives on twenty-four hours a day? And when I say 'lives,' I do not mean 'exists' or 'muddles through.' Which of us is free from that uneasy feeling that the 'great spending departments' of his daily life are not managed as they ought to be?" What is required, he argues, is a "minute practical examination of daily time-expenditure."

Bennett's conclusion is clear. He believes that you can make much better use of the hours not spent working or sleeping. He bemoans the sorry state of his readers "who are haunted, more or less painfully, by the feeling that the years slip by, and slip by, and slip by, and that they have not been able to get their lives into proper working order." He asserts that the average person "is constantly haunted by a suppressed dissatisfaction which springs from a fixed idea that we ought to do something in addition to those things to which we are loyally and morally obliged to do." And to nudge you to tackle this condition with urgency, he exhorts, "Oh man, what hast thou done with thy youth? What are thou doing with thine age?"

To illustrate his thesis, he describes a typically unproductive evening that starts when you leave work: "You are pale and tired. At any rate, your wife says you are pale, and you give her to understand that you are tired." It ends when "at last you go to bed, exhausted by the day's work. Six hours, probably more, have gone since you left the office—gone like a dream, gone like magic, unaccountably gone." Does this sound familiar?

And then, there are weekends—how do we use those? Writing forty years after Bennett, but still a long time ago, Viktor Frankl diagnosed a previously undocumented psychological condition that he called *Sunday neurosis*. He defined this as "a form of anxiety resulting from awareness in some people of the emptiness of their lives once the working week is over. Some complain of a void and a vague discontent. This arises from an existential vacuum, or feeling of meaninglessness, which is a common phenomenon and is characterized by a subjective state of boredom, apathy, and emptiness. One feels cynical, lacks direction, and questions the point of most of life's activities."

In my experience and observation, the risk of developing this condition becomes more prevalent and threatening in the middle years of life and beyond. In the early adult years—especially after the "odyssey" period, you tend to devote every waking hour to succeeding in your career and to building or sustaining a vigorous social life. Later on, you devote most of your "spare time" to raising your kids—initially on playgrounds and then on sports fields. But there comes a time—perhaps when your kids are teenagers, and neither need nor want so much of your attention—that you find yourself thinking, "I seem to have a lot more time on my hands; what am I doing with it?"

Carl Jung's work also addresses the risk that we might not take full advantage of the time available to us. He writes of how, as we approach the middle of life, we might have succeeded in our social objectives—had children, made some money, perhaps even gained status and recognition in our chosen field. The risk, however, is that we "overlook the essential fact that the social goal is attained at the cost of diminution of the personality. Many—far too many—aspects of life which should have been experienced lie in the lumber-room among dusty memories."

But, Jung wants us to know, it is almost never too late—because sometimes these seemingly dusty memories are actually "glowing coals under grey ashes." And he shares the view that the later years can be those when we rediscover the creative and cultural dimension of our personality that we have previously suppressed.

> A human being would certainly not grow to be 70 or 80 years old if this longevity had no meaning for the species to which he belongs. The afternoon of human life must also have a significance of its own and cannot be merely a pitiful appendage of life's morning. The significance of the morning undoubtedly lies in the development of the individual, our entrenchment in the outer world, the propagation of our kind and the care of our children. But . . . whoever carries over into the afternoon the law of the morning must pay for so doing with damage to his soul. Moneymaking, social existence, family and posterity are nothing but plain nature—not culture. Culture lies beyond the purpose of nature. Could by any chance culture be the meaning and purpose of the second half of life?

My own parents clearly think so. Since they retired from the teaching profession more than twenty-five years ago, both have dedicated themselves to the development and expression of their cultural DNA. My mother—a former English teacher—has further intensified her prodigious reading while learning foreign languages, while my father has rediscovered a passion and no little talent for both piano playing and painting. As a consequence, their house near London—the house in which I grew up—now doubles as a modestly informal art gallery and music studio.

The approach that they have taken to their "afternoon years" would presumably be applauded by Arnold Bennett. In his book he outlines his prescription for the condition that he has diagnosed— although he stresses that "there is no easy way, no royal road." He argues that the most important remedy is to devote as much as possible of one's "spare time" to "some important and consecutive cultivation of the mind."

More generally, Arnold Bennett believes that we can make much more of the two-thirds of our life that is not devoted to work, traditionally defined: "If a man makes two-thirds of his existence subservient to one-third, for which admittedly he has no absolutely feverish zest, how can he hope to live fully and completely? He cannot." Bennett's preferred remedy is to broaden your life—not only by making big career decisions in favor of breadth but by broadening your approach to each day.

He even suggests that you stretch the day further to ensure that you have plenty of time for your other pursuits: "Briefly get up earlier in the morning. . . . [R]ise an hour and a half, or even two hours earlier. And with the extra time that you have now re-captured from unproductive slumber, pursue a productive and engrossing hobby or passion, since that will quicken the whole life of the week, add zest to it, and increase the interest you have in even the most banal occupations."

WHAT ABOUT THE 10,000 HOUR RULE?

So perhaps we have more time than we think to build a broad life. But we still have to contend with the 10,000 hour rule—Malcolm Gladwell's observation that it takes 10,000 hours to get really good at doing something meaningful. That is taken by most people as a convincing argument for deep specialization and against building a broad life. Gladwell also adds that "ten thousand hours is an *enormous* amount of time. It's almost impossible to reach that number all by yourself by the time you're a young adult."

That is mathematically true. But while we're talking about mathematics, let's consider the hours available to you in a whole life—not just before you become a young adult. If you're like most people, your working life will last at least forty years—that's around 9,000 working days, or 75,000 hours at work. You'll notice that 75,000 hours is more than seven times 10,000 hours. So even assuming that the 10,000 hour rule is right, you get more than seven shots at it in your career.

That's actually a conservative estimate of the time you have at your disposal in a modern professional career. Some combination of desire and economic necessity will push many of us (me included) to extend our professional careers to fifty years or more, which gives you well over 90,000 hours, and consequently more than nine shots at the 10,000 hour rule. And, of course, Jimmy Carter went much further than that by adding the thirty-five years after his presidency, during which I suspect he has worked pretty much every day, seven days a week. In his very full life, Carter has probably worked more than 130,000 hours and counting.

David Rubenstein, the co-CEO of the Carlyle Group, did a similar kind of mental arithmetic, and it changed his life. When he got to fifty-four (slightly younger than I am now) he realized that, on average, he had twenty-seven years left—that he might have already lived two-thirds of his life. He decided that he wanted to spend much less of his remaining time on accumulating further wealth and more on furthering the social causes he held dear, through his philanthropic activities. I think of this as an applied variation of the concept of QALYS—quality-adjusted life years—used by the health insurance industry to assess the cost-benefit ratio of a medical intervention. It is typically calculated as a function of "length of life adjusted by functionality or health." You can influence the quality adjustment in this calculation by the life choices you make, and by how they enhance or reduce your "functionality or health."

There is another way of thinking about the time you have to build a broad life. It is quite likely that over the course of your career, you will change jobs or roles every four years or so (as implied by Ethan Bernstein's 4+4+4 formula). This amounts to ten or more distinct career changes. That's probably another conservative estimate—because of the extended working lives that I mentioned earlier and because of the accelerated metabolic rate of many careers, in which talented people change roles faster than every four years, especially in high-intensity environments like political and business leadership. And you might add to this the likelihood that you will undertake five to ten part-time roles of various durations and time commitments.

This way of thinking applies whether you spend most of your career with the same institution (as I have done) or with multiple different institutions. Ron Daniel observes of his more than sixty years at McKinsey that "very few career lifers stay in the firm without having multiple careers of some kind within it that provide opportunities to meet new challenges, to develop new skills, to keep on learning and growing, and in effect to create stimulating changes in one's life. Often these mini-careers are presented to us. . . . [O]ften, however, these new opportunities are carved out and created by us as individuals."

As I reflect upon my own three decades at McKinsey, I can chronicle at least half a dozen material changes of role and direction within the firm. And then there were the various part-time roles I played outside the firm. And since I left McKinsey in 2012, I have done a bunch of new things. So I reckon that I have already gotten close to that figure of twenty career shifts—and I am certainly not finished yet. It's that series of moves and changes of direction that have enabled me to build a broad professional life despite—or perhaps because of—the fact that I stayed within a single institution for so long.

There are two sensible answers to the question, How much time do I have to build a broad life? The first is, not as much as I would like. Time is an unavoidable constraint on the development of your life story, which will have a beginning, middle, and (sadly) an end. So it certainly matters how you allocate your time, both on a daily basis and over the course of your life.

The second sensible answer is, more than I thought. You may decide to take some of Arnold Bennett's advice and use more of the twenty-four hours a day that are available to you. And taking the longer view, you may believe in the sanctity of the 10,000 hour rule, but still appreciate that you will have at least seven times 10,000 hours in your professional career—not to mention all the time that you have outside the conventional workplace, which may offer many more opportunities to broaden your life.

You will probably make at least twenty material professional and personal decisions over the course of your life. Individually and collectively, these choices will determine the nature and direction of your career. How will you make those choices? Will you make them in favor of breadth or depth—or some combination of the two? What approach will you take—if you are just getting started and all those choices lie ahead of you, if you are midway through your life and your options appear to be narrowing, or if you are nearing the end of your life and have only a few choices left to make?

HOW SHOULD YOU SPEND YOUR SPARE TIME?

Alan Rusbridger was the editor in chief of the *Guardian* newspaper when it was giving me such a hard time about the "revolving door" between McKinsey and No. 10 Downing Street. Fortunately, the paper soon had bigger stories to cover—like the WikiLeaks story and the UK tabloid newspaper phone-hacking scandal in 2010 and 2011. Then in 2013, the *Guardian* once again broke big news around the world when it was the first newspaper to reveal the Edward Snowden story of leaked classified information from the National Security Agency. Its campaigning zeal in reporting three of the most dramatic news stories of our era enabled the *Guardian* to secure a global reputation that it had never had before. So when Rusbridger stepped down from his post in 2014 after more than twenty years, his retirement was news well beyond the shores of the UK.

He then wrote and published a personal diary that showed the extent of his aspirations for breadth outside of the workplace. It showed his desire not to become prone to "Sunday neurosis"—the emptiness of your life once the workweek is over, described by both Arnold Bennett and Viktor Frankl.

The instrument (very literally) that he chose to broaden his life was the piano. In the midst of what turned out to be one of the busiest and most remarkable years of his professional life, he committed himself to learn and play to a public audience one of the most difficult of piano pieces, Chopin's Ballade No. 4 in G Minor. He did so in the knowledge that he is a competent but not exceptional amateur pianist, and that this is a piece of music that professional soloists view nervously because of its degree of difficulty.

He explains, "I felt this . . . instinct to wall off a small part of my life for creative expression, for 'culture.'" He shares the observation that this gets easier with the passage of time. His kids are teenagers "and would happily spend much of their daylight hours asleep," and at such moments—weekends and holidays—he rediscovers time that he had forgotten. He dusts off the watercolors and experiences again the feeling—lost since art lessons at age fourteen—of applying wet paint on paper. And he plays the piano.

Rusbridger was still at a stage in his career when free time was at a premium. His working week varied from sixty-five to eighty hours depending on the intensity of the news cycle. He lived a life of "low-level stress much of the time, with periodic eruptions of great tension. Above all, the sense of perpetual momentum that comes from the news itself. If you make your life the news business, the news will to some extent dictate your life."

Nonetheless, Rusbridger was able not just to learn the Chopin piece but to write the diary that he later published—and along the way to interview people who can shed light on the exercise to which he has committed himself. For instance, he interviewed Condoleezza Rice, who was a concert-level pianist before she became US secretary of state and has remained one since. He also notes that in the "serviceable-to-decent" category of political pianists are former US president Harry Truman, former German chancellor Helmut Schmidt, former Israeli prime minister Ehud Barak, and former UK foreign secretary William Hague.

In his published diary, Rusbridger addresses the most fundamental questions: Is there time? Is it too late? He responds, "Yes, there's time—no matter how frantically busy one's life. There's always enough time in a week to nibble out the odd twenty minutes here and there if one wants to make it a priority." He adds, "More than that, by making time, life improves: under the great pressure and stress of the year, I've discovered the value of having a small escape valve—something so absorbing, so different, so rebalancing."

And he is equally clear that it's not too late. When he started he had no idea how capable a fifty-six-year-old brain was of learning new tricks. But the brain plasticity that I mentioned earlier turns out to be more significant than he had expected. Strengthened by a new-found or rediscovered will and motivation to learn music, he finds it "heartening to know that, quite well into middle age, the brain is plastic enough to blast open hitherto unused neural pathways and adapt to new and complicated tasks. So, no, it's not too late."

Above all, Rusbridger wants people to see the bigger picture: the audience for his piano recital needs to understand "what on earth I'm doing standing up in public to play an impossible bit of Chopin.

The real point is not that I can play it to concert standard: it's been part of a much broader experiment in how to use your time, how to relish—and revel in—being an amateur." And on the night of the concert he adds, "If one person leaves the room tonight intent on re-learning an instrument, that wouldn't be a bad result."

We are entering an age when it is more important, and potentially more valuable, to think about how we spend our spare time—and what we do as an amateur. We certainly have the spare time, if we want to use it. In his book *Cognitive Surplus,* Clay Shirky estimates that 200 billion hours every year would be freed up if Americans used fewer mental hours passively consuming television. He then looks at what might instead be done with this time and illustrates how the development of *Wikipedia* as a shared volunteer enterprise has already productively absorbed so much time and energy. He observes that "every edit made to every article, and every argument about those edits, amounts to something like one hundred million hours of human thought."

Jonathan Haidt, a professor at the University of Virginia and author of *The Happiness Hypothesis,* propounds the equation H = S + C + V. That is, happiness (H) equals your genetic set (S) point band (the disposition you are born with), plus the conditions (C) of your life (gender, age, where you live, profession, relationships), plus the voluntary (V) activities you choose to engage in (that build on your strengths and give you satisfaction). Your set point is largely an inherited trait—but you can do things to skew toward the top of your band. And research suggests that the factor that will most influence your happiness equation is V—the voluntary activities you choose. Our professional careers may seem unavoidably narrow—at least for the moment—but our whole lives need not be. That is the significance of V, which is more or less within our control.

And in the digital age, this amateur or voluntary spirit need not simply be a matter of self-indulgence. As Shirky points out, the rise of amateurism in the digital world—amateur journalists, filmmakers, musicians who can make their work as widely available as a professional might—is enabling the rise of a "participatory culture" that seemed lost to us in the second half of the twentieth century.

Steven Johnson highlights the significance of this revived participatory culture when he says, "The digital economy, with its profusion of free content, was supposed to make it impossible to make money by making art. Instead creative careers are thriving—but in complicated and unexpected ways." The principal reason is that there are now more ways to buy creative work, thanks to the proliferation of content-delivery platforms—and thus more ways to be compensated for making that work.

To illustrate the point, Johnson tells the story of Robyn Schneider, who writes fiction for young adults and who also has a YouTube channel with 18,000 subscribers. Her inspiration is John Green, the author of the wildly successful novel *The Fault in Our Stars,* who built his extensive fan base on the video site. Throughout graduate school, Robyn says, "If I was bored for, like, two hours, I could make a video." Those videos now make maybe $3,000 a year. For several summers, she also wrote books under a pen name and sold them—making the equivalent of a paid summer internship. Then she took her own novels to market under her own name, and they sold for a lot of money (six figures). Though she had never taken the YouTube thing very seriously, she realized that her success was, in part, because of this audience. She had built a following, and now she could monetize it.

The biggest change in the digital age is the ease with which art can be made and distributed. The cost of consuming culture may have declined—although not as much as perhaps we anticipated—but the cost of producing it has dropped far more dramatically. This profound change lies at the boundaries of professionalism. It has never been easier to start making money from creative work, for your passion to undertake that critical leap from pure hobby to part-time income source. Johnson notes that "the new environment may well select for artists who are particularly adept at inventing new career paths, rather than single-mindedly focusing just on their craft"—for instance, the writer who builds an audience and following through YouTube videos.

The digital economy has moved more of our creative breadth out of the realm of the purely amateur into that of the semiprofessional.

Not that truly amateur breadth is a bad thing—art, dancing, music, theater. There is strong scientific evidence to support the notion that you can accrue real psychological benefits from broadening your life by the pursuit of such personal passions. This evidence shows that cross-disciplinary activity of this kind seems to enhance our cognitive and learning skills.

One recent study commissioned by the Dana Foundation and summarized by Dr. Michael Gazzaniga of the University of California, Santa Barbara, suggests that studying the performing arts actually improves one's ability to learn anything else. Collating several studies, the researchers found that the performing arts generate much higher levels of motivation and focus than do any other pursuits. These enhanced levels of motivation make people aware of their ability to focus and concentrate on improvement.

In his book *Originals,* Adam Grant cites a Michigan State University study that compares Nobel Prize–winning scientists from 1901 to 2005 with more "typical" or "ordinary" scientists of the same period. The study found that both groups had deep expertise in their respective scientific fields. But there was a notable difference in their relative engagement with the arts. It turns out that the Nobel Prize winners were much more likely to have a substantive involvement in the arts than did the less distinguished scientists—two times more likely to be involved in music, seven times more likely to be involved in the visual arts and crafts like painting or woodworking, twelve times more likely to be involved in writing—not just of scientific reports but of plays and novels, and twenty-two times more likely to be involved in the performing arts—for instance, as amateur actors, dancers, or magicians.

Another study shows similar results for entrepreneurs and inventors—that people who started businesses and participated in patent applications are more likely to have leisure-time hobbies that involve drawing, painting, architecture, sculpture, and literature. Grant concludes from this research that "interest in the arts among entrepreneurs, inventors, and eminent scientists obviously reflects their curiosity and aptitude. People who are open to new ways of looking at science and business also tend to be fascinated by the expression of ideas and emotions through images, sounds and words." And as he points out, this is not just a matter of what people do to relax and divert themselves from their main pursuits: "The arts also serve in turn as a powerful source of creative insight."

I think of this as the cultural equivalent of cross-training. Just as runners enhance their physical performance through swimming, cycling, and yoga, so we can strengthen our brains through applications that go well outside our normal range of activities. And by moving from comfort activities to stretch activities—well, that's the equivalent of interval training. Cross-training plus interval training is a terrific formula for success in any walk of life.

While there is no preset formula for building a broad life as an amateur or a semiprofessional, there are practical and tangible steps you can take, even in the margins of time. They might go in roughly this sequence:

- *Read and research:* As you identify areas in which to broaden your life, take the time to read news and literature that you don't typically read, watch films and documentaries you don't typically watch, and confer with friends about your newfound interests. Make a habit to learn something new each week—and keep a running list of questions to explore as you go deeper. That list will certainly come in handy as you move to the next step.
- *Network:* Reach out to people who are in the area that you're interested in—following the example of Brian Grazer's "curiosity conversations"—and ask them for thirty minutes of their time to share ideas and experiences. As you grow more knowledgeable and comfortable in the arena, seek out more public events—conferences and other gatherings— where you can listen and occasionally be heard.
- *Engage:* Get actively involved in the arena by volunteering, traveling, studying, and finding any other way to engage in purposeful cross-training. Find thoughtful ways of putting yourself in the shoes of true exponents—even if it is only for an evening, a weekend, or a week at a time.

- *Dive in:* If you have really found a new focus for your life, then you will want to make a commitment to it. You might have the flexibility to restructure your life—to take a leave of absence from your current role. You might prefer to "walk before you can run" through some kind of part-time program that enables you to experience new opportunities directly. But you may also just decide to take the plunge and change your life completely. Nothing can substitute for the quality of full immersion in a new sector, country, or issue.

- *Relax:* Finally, don't overstress about your new way of living your life. Stay fit, maintain your health, and do what you can do. At seventy-one, Michael Wilson is still at the peak of his game as a Canadian banking and nonprofit leader. How does he maintain his energy and commitment? "Exercise, a bowl of Wheaties every morning, and vitamin pills. When I was young, I realized that if you aren't reasonably fit for demanding roles like this, you'll get tired."

Arnold Bennett leaves us with one further and encouraging thought—the future is up to us: "The chief beauty about the constant supply of time is that you cannot waste it in advance. The next year, the next day, the next hour are lying ready for you, as perfect, as unspoilt, as if you had never wasted or misspent a single moment in all your career. Which fact is very gratifying and reassuring. You can turn over a new leaf every hour if you choose." But he ends with a cautionary note: "There is no object that is served in waiting till next week, or even till tomorrow. You may fancy that the water will be warmer next week. It won't. It will be colder."

EPILOGUE

SEEKING PROFESSIONAL SUCCESS AND PERSONAL FULFILMENT

> For our genius of a father did not limit himself to math. His brain
> was an octopus, the tentacles of which extended in all directions.
> —Sylvie Weil, *At Home with Andre and Simone Weil*

IT IS ALWAYS INSPIRING to meet exceptional people who are building remarkable lives and careers, especially when they are dedicated to addressing some of our society's most vexing problems. The worry is that people like this, some of whom we've met in this book, are becoming the exception rather than the rule. Today's society reveres deep specialists—even when their supposed expertise steers us in the wrong direction. We are steering our education system heavily in the direction of depth, just as our models of success in the professional world narrow their focus.

But deep specialism has severe drawbacks as a model for life—confining you as it does to a single sector, industry, function, discipline, and culture. And it is not a good model for the leaders of the future, who will need to solve complex, multidimensional problems in imaginative and creative ways. It is not a modern or contemporary model, nor is it attuned to the rapidly evolving and constantly changing opportunities and challenges of the digital era. Edward O. Wilson observes, "Humanity entered our present, hyperconnected technoscientific era only two decades ago—less than an eyeblink in the starry message of the cosmos. Now we are launched into a new cycle of exploration—infinitely richer, correspondingly more challenging, and not by coincidence increasingly humanitarian."

Nevertheless, building a remarkable life of breadth is not easy to do in today's world. It requires tough choices, some sacrifices, and a lot of discipline along the way. But if you pursue the aspiration of a broad life, you will have an enlarged perspective from which to analyze problems, a transferrable skill set to apply to those problems, a diverse network to learn from and to deploy, a contextual ability to empathize with the most divergent stakeholders, an elevated appetite to take professional and personal risks, and a moral compass to guide you through an enriched life.

You will build a remarkable life and career—and that won't just make our society a better place to live. It will make you a better person, and happier too.

IN THE PROLOGUE, I wrote that this book was for "children of all ages"—that whatever your current stage of life, you have important choices to make about how you build (or in some cases, rebuild) your life and career. At each stage you can make those choices in the direction of greater breadth or greater depth and thus determine the future direction of your life. That is true at the outset of your career, in the middle and at its peak, in active retirement, and even in old age. As I have reflected upon how the Mosaic Principle applies at each of these stages, I have drawn upon the experience and inspiration of people in my own professional and personal life—and I would encourage you to do the same, since we all have much to learn from the people around us.

For instance, I have drawn inspiration and direction from my own parents—liberal, broad-minded people who have built lives of breadth, and who still are doing so in their mideighties. As young, newly graduated teachers in the 1950s, they moved to New Zealand for five years—with the incidental benefit that I was born there, which has been my "fun fact" in icebreakers most of my life. After professional lives of distinction and meaning in education, they have devoted their active retirement to the release and application of their cultural and creative DNA.

At the other end of the spectrum, my children are now approaching the launch of their own independent lives and careers—starting with the *odyssey* phase of their early twenties. They share eclectic interests and intense personalities—and a contemporary mastery of all things digital that already enables them fully to engage in the participatory culture (as illustrated by my oldest son's Twitter feed). They have all their options open to them, they have already rejected narrow and early specialism, and they seem intent on building their lives according to the Mosaic Principle.

In between these generations lie my professional colleagues and personal friends—in the midst of their careers, making important choices for themselves and their families, and seeking to provide guidance and inspiration to those who come after them. At McKinsey, Albright Stonebridge, and now at Brunswick, I have been privileged to work with intrinsically talented people with eclectic personalities and interests, intent upon building broad lives and willing to make significant adjustments along the way. At Brunswick, in particular, I work alongside former journalists, editors, lawyers, management consultants, bankers, accountants, and NGO activists in a kind of "melting pot" of diverse experiences and disciplines.

And then there is my wife. Alyssa's career profile so far reads: banker, consultant, commercial entrepreneur, social entrepreneur, NGO activist, and now business school professor—oh, and wife and mother. She has built this life across two continents with four children born within six years of each other. She is the queen of the to-do list and exemplifies all the traits of a broad life outlined in this book—most especially perhaps her prodigiously extensive network, enabled in part by the fact that she never loses touch with anybody for long, maintaining a remarkable range of strong, weak, and dormant ties.

As for me, my life so far has been wonderfully diverse and enriching. As a lifelong adviser, I have remained largely in the background—trying to follow Alan Parker's theatrical maxim of "don't get between your clients and the footlights." When I have become "the story," as I briefly did in 2005, it was deeply uncomfortable and I was happy when the footlights were diverted elsewhere. Other than these "fifteen minutes of fame," my public notoriety has been limited. So when you google me, don't expect to find much of interest—except perhaps this excerpt from a recently published book:

> Nicholas Lovegrove's professional reputation was by then firmly es-
> tablished. British-born and educated, he was regarded as the most
> sought-after art consultant in the world—a man so powerful he
> could move markets with an offhand remark or a wrinkle of his ele-
> gant nose. Lovegrove no longer had to troll for clients; they came to
> him, usually on bended knee and with promises of vast commissions.

Would that any of this were true—but sadly it comes from a work of fiction, *Portrait of a Spy,* by Daniel Silva. My only comfort is that Daniel—who is a friend—did consciously "borrow" my name and some aspects of my personal profile! So at least in fiction, I am leading a remarkable life and career.

In real life, I am now fifty-seven years old—roughly the same age that Alan Rusbridger was when he learned to play the piano to concert level while editing a national newspaper; two years older than Jimmy Carter when he left the White House and embarked on his thirty-five-year postpresidency, which he described as the happiest and most fulfilling period of his life; and three years older than David Rubenstein when he calculated that (on average) he had already consumed two-thirds of his life and didn't want to just keep "accumulating wealth" in the last third.

Each of these people—and others—have convinced me that the key to this "afternoon" of life is to pursue a broad and eclectic set of interests and to live on twenty-four hours a day. Writing this book has been part of that enterprise—almost a form of therapy. Among many other benefits, it has enabled me to think of myself as a consultant, coach, managing partner, government adviser, nonprofit board member, political obsessive, sports fanatic, husband, father—and now author.

ACKNOWLEDGMENTS

I have been thinking about writing a book most of my adult life, and I have been thinking about writing this book for several years. That I finally made the leap from thinking to writing is thanks to a remarkably broad network of people who inspired, cajoled, and supported me throughout the process. I am grateful to them all.

I am especially grateful to my tremendous part-time research team of Matthew Thomas and Connor Lyons. Matthew was a young associate at McKinsey's Toronto Office when we first started working together in 2012 on the initial research into trisector athletes. Later he was joined by Connor, and together they helped with every aspect of the book's early formation—important interviews, literature reviews, early chapter drafts, and later refinements to the text. Matthew is now building a technology company called Paddle, aiming to scale nonlinear career development (www.mypaddle.com).

In 2013, Matthew coauthored with me the *Harvard Business Review* article "Triple-Strength Leadership." The publication of that article was enabled by two people—Rik Kirkland, McKinsey's director of publishing, who agreed to nurture the article, applying his distinctive experience as a former editor of *Fortune* magazine; and Andrea Ovans, the *Harvard Business Review* editor to whom I was fortunate enough to be assigned, who saw the potential power of the trisector concept.

The *Harvard Business Review* article led me to the two people who are most directly responsible for bringing this book to fruition—both of them masters of their respective crafts, who have left an indelible mark on me. Richard Pine is an extraordinary literary agent, who finds ideas and people that reshape the way we approach the world. That he would agree to add me to his stable of authors was an honor in itself. But he did much more than that—helping me to define the dichotomy between breadth and depth that runs throughout this book. I could not be more grateful to Richard and his team at Inkwell Management.

He also found John Mahaney, who turned out to be the perfect editor for my book—along with his colleagues at PublicAffairs, especially the editorial

302

director Clive Priddle. John has stuck with me through the three years that it has taken to complete the book—during some of which not much was happening! As one of the most distinguished editors of books about business and leadership, he saw what made this book different—that it was not just about professional success but also about personal aspiration and fulfilment. He crystallized the concept of the Mosaic Principle as a governing framework for a remarkable life and career. As the book has neared publication, I have been wonderfully supported by the PublicAffairs team, notably Sandra Beris, Katie Haigler, Melissa Raymond, and Carrie Watterson. I am also immensely grateful to the team at Profile Books in London, who have marshalled so energetically the preparation of the UK and international edition of *The Mosaic Principle*—especially Clare Grist-Taylor, Louisa Dunnigan, Penny Daniel and Hannah Ross.

As I mention in the book, the remarkable Wharton professor Adam Grant played an important cameo role—not just as a personal inspiration and source of more than a few ideas upon which I have tried to build. On the basis of one conversation in his office on the Wharton campus, he agreed to champion the book to his (and now my) agent, Richard Pine. And he has continued to provide moral support, even as his own books—*Give and Take* and more recently *Originals*—have generated such well-deserved excitement.

I am grateful for the dozens of people who make appearances—small and large—in the book. In particular, I would mention the following people whom I have profiled at length to illustrate one or more of the six dimensions: Don Baer, John Berry, Lael Brainard, Michael Boyd, Carol Browner, Aneesh Chopra, John Delaney, Jack Donahue, Paul Farmer, Bernie Ferrari, Julius Genachowski, Josh Gotbaum, Tony Hall, David Hayes, Ronald Heifetz, Robert Hormats, Jim Yong Kim, Stanley Litow, Jonathan McBride, David McCormick, Archie Norman, Jennifer Pryce, Steve Rattner, Roger Sant, and Patty Stonesifer.

I have also been inspired and educated by the research and writing of Dan Ariely, Susan Cain, Clayton Christensen, Malcolm Gladwell, Doris Kearns Goodwin, Brian Grazer, Stephen Greenblatt, Reid Hoffman, Michael Ignatieff, Walter Isaacson, Tracy Kidder, Fred Kofman, Nannerle O. Keohane, Michael Lewis, Margaret Lobenstine, Erin Meyer, Daniel Pink, Alan Rusbridger, Sheryl Sandberg, Dan Senor, Saul Singer, Gillian Tett, Peter Thiel, Edward O. Wilson, and Fareed Zakaria. Chief among my sources of literary inspiration has been David Brooks, who through his books and twice-weekly *New York Times* columns regularly teaches me—and many others—what and how to think.

The gestation period for this book included time spent at three different professional firms. It was conceived at McKinsey & Company, incubated at the Albright Stonebridge Group, and finally born at the Brunswick Group. I am grateful to the partners and staff of each firm for their ideas and support.

McKinsey has shaped every dimension of my professional life and personality—and that is reflected throughout this book. At its best McKinsey embodies as a firm the excitement and energy of the Mosaic Principle—especially its remarkable leader Dominic Barton, who for the past several years has crisscrossed the globe expounding on the importance of trisector leadership. He has consistently supported me both during my time at the firm and beyond—as have countless other current and former McKinsey partners, especially Byron Auguste, Ron Daniel, Ian Davis, John Dowdy, Diana Farrell, Fred Gluck, Larry Kanarek, Conor Kehoe, Vik Malhotra, Lenny Mendonca, Michael Patsalos-Fox, Scott Rutherford, and Kevin Sneader. I am especially grateful to Sean Brown, who looks after all McKinsey alumni, and to Pat Butler and Quentin Woodley provided important ideas and suggested sources—as well as friendship. Caroline Webb was writing her own groundbreaking book, *How to Have a Good Day,* at roughly the same time and provided inspiration and moral support. And Courtney Stockland was a wonderful assistant and friend during my five years in McKinsey's Washington Office.

I wrote the proposal and early chapters of the book during my two years at the Albright Stonebridge Group. There I was surrounded by people who have lived and are living broad and eclectic lives of remarkable substance and impact. That was certainly true of the founders—former secretary of state Madeleine Albright and the late Sandy Berger, as well as Tony Harrington, Carlos Gutierrez, and Carol Browner. It equally applied to my close friends—Michael Warren, Jim O'Brien, and Suzy George. And I have continued to be inspired and supported by Alan Fleischmann, whose eclectic and cosmopolitan life underpins the success of his own firm, Laurel Strategies.

I signed a contract to write this book a week before I signed another contract to join the Brunswick Group as its managing partner in the United States. At first, these two contractual commitments seemed incompatible, since my work at Brunswick was all-consuming. But gradually I came to realize that it was the perfect place to write a book about a multidimensional life and career, since that is the defining concept of the firm.

That this has been possible reflects the inspiration and support I have received from Brunswick's senior leaders—Sir Alan Parker, Louise Charlton, Andrew Fenwick, Susan Gilchrist, Rob Pinker, and Catherine Samy. Susan's husband, the renowned historian Andrew Roberts, provided a much-needed prod when he told my wife at a dinner that I absolutely had to write the book. In a similar vein, Lucy Parker and Jon Miller—Brunswick partners and the authors of *Everybody's Business*—provided moral and intellectual support throughout and helped me especially with the crafting of the prologue.

And then there are the people I work with every day in our offices across the United States—especially Steve Lipin, Harry Clark, Amanda Duckworth, Maria Figueroa Kupcu, Mike France, Laurie Hays, Julie Jensen, Sarah Lubman, Bob Moran, Ellen Moskowitz, Bill Pendergast, Nicole Reboe, Jayne Rosefield, David Sutphen, and Mark Palmer. I am privileged also to work with a wonderful team of Lauren Odell, Chipo Sachirarwe, Lauren Nadig, Lissette Marcelo, Dale Nissenbaum, and Josh Pasichow. And above all, I have an extraordinary assistant, Lyuba DiFalco, who has helped me through every stage of this process.

In addition to these three firms, my research has benefited from sojourns at two of the world's great universities—Oxford and Harvard. I drew ideas and intellectual succor from my time as a senior fellow with the Kennedy School at Harvard—specifically at the Center for Business and Government. That this happened was thanks primarily to two of my Kennedy School classmates of thirty-plus years ago—Jack Donahue and John Haigh, both now senior members of the faculty—as well as the benign patronage of Professor Richard Zeckhauser.

At roughly the same time, I had the profound good fortune to be drawn into the global community that swirls around Ngaire Woods. As the founding dean of the Blavatnik School of Government at Oxford, Ngaire is creating a contemporary academic institution that offers every prospect of improving the way we govern around the world. In the midst of doing that, she has miraculously found time to guide and inspire me at every stage of this book, and I have often had her in mind as I have sought to define the Mosaic Principle.

Ultimately, writing a book is a family affair. It has been a special pleasure to include my parents, Bill and Isobel Lovegrove, in the text of the book, not just for the sake of it but because they fit perfectly into any discussion of the Mosaic Principle. It is no coincidence that my father first wrote in defense of broad-based liberal education more than fifty years ago, and no surprise that my parents have chosen to live their own lives according to that principle—which has in turn engendered the same spirit in me and my brothers, Peter and Colin. They have supported me in everything I have done—as have my parents-in-law, Allan and Arlene Karger.

Now it is time to hand down this concept to our own children—Jamie, Greg, Susannah, and Michael. They have experienced the development of this book more directly than most, since much of it has been written on successive family "vacations" when the communal area of our rental accommodations has been converted into "Dad's writing room." That they went along with this concept reflected that as college and precollege students, they had plenty to keep them busy—and I hope that they were rather intrigued by the whole process. Of course, I hope and expect that they will lead their adult lives according to the Mosaic Principle, and I plan to check in from time to time to find out how it's going.

The person who makes this all happen—and who indeed runs our whole family—is my wife Alyssa. There is no earthly possibility that I would have completed the book without her—I have done so at least in part because she made it clear that it was a condition of our continuing marital happiness that I do so. To enable this to happen, I have written words on a page—and she has done everything else. Without Alyssa, nothing works—with her, it all makes sense. This book will appear almost exactly twenty-five years since I first met Alyssa, and like everything else that I have done since then, I have written this book out of my enduring love for her.

NOTES

22   **The benefits of liberal education:** Kay, "Benefits of a Liberal Education."
23   **Skills at the heart of the humanities:** Faust, "To Be 'a Speaker of Words and a Doer of Deeds.'"
28   **Team of rivals:** Goodwin, *Team of Rivals.*
28   **We face adaptive challenges:** Heifetz, *Leadership Without Easy Answers.*
29   **Chance favors only the prepared mind:** Pasteur, lecture at the University of Lille.
31   *Ambivert:* Cain, *Quiet,* 14.
33   **How the world became modern:** Greenblatt, *Swerve,* 164.
34   *Growth mind-set:* Dweck, *Mindset,* 10.
36   **Global financial crisis:** Cassidy, "No Credit," and "What Good Is Wall Street?" Also, Lizza, "Inside the Crisis." and Stewart, "Eight Days."

CHAPTER 2: THE PERILS OF DEPTH, THE GIFTS OF BREADTH

37   **When the music stops:** Blinder, *After the Music Stopped.*
38   **Why we were so duped by the specialist experts:** Kay, *Other People's Money,* 118.
38   **In his definitive analysis:** Galbraith, *Great Crash 1929,* 132–133.
38   **Valuations of future claims:** Kay, *Other People's Money,* 119.
39   **The most complex and opaque securities:** Blinder, *After the Music Stopped,* 75.
40   **Great Reckoning:** Lewis, *The Big Short,* xiii–xv. In this section, Lewis is referring to his earlier book *Liars' Poker.*
40   **This financial crisis was avoidable:** *Financial Crisis Inquiry Report.*
41   **Degree of oracular authority:** Blinder, *After the Music Stopped,* 81.
42   **Very poor predictors of the future:** Gardner, *Future Babble.*
42   **Analyze the accuracy of forecasts:** Tetlock and Gardner, *Superforecasting,* 16, 93, 170–171, 291–292.
44   **Our crisis:** Geithner, *Stress Test,* 513–514.
45   **On October 13, 2008:** McLean and Nocera, *All the Devils Are Here,* 359.
45   **Cultural translators:** Tett, *The Silo Effect,* 249.
46   **Forces of evil and infamy:** This section is based upon several personal interviews and discussions with Jeff Seabright during 2012, 2013, and 2014.
49   *Trisector athlete:* Lovegrove and Thomas, "Triple-Strength Leadership."
51   **The *Golden Triangle*:** Kent, "Opinion."
51   **Unlikely story of how big business can fix the world:** Miller and Parker, *Everybody's Business.*
52   **Led a recruiting campaign:** Ibid.
53   **Bezos wanted Amazon to be an "unstore":** Stone, *Everything Store,* 183.
54   **Most of the issues that vex humanity daily:** Wilson, *Consilience,* 11.
54   **The rainbow colors:** Nietzsche, *Human, All Too Human.*
55   *Supervenience:* Greene, "2011: What Scientific Concept Would Improve Everybody's Cognitive Toolkit."
55   **We already think of these four domains:** Wilson, *Consilience,* 9.
56   **The sad truth:** Meyer, *Culture Map,* 10.
57   **People who have international experience:** Maddux, Galinsky, and Tadmor, "Be a Better Manager." See also Unruh, "Join the Global Elite."

57 **Typically moved to new geographies:** Grant, *Originals*, 48–49; Godart et al., "Fashion with a Foreign Flair."

58 **Cultural relativity:** Meyer, *Culture Map*, 11.

59 ***Eleven Conversations:*** Miller and Parker, *Everybody's Business*, 339–395.

60 **Much like a sports team:** Ferrari, *Power Listening*.

60 **A 2016 study of:** Torres, "Generalists Get Better Jobs"; **wisdom of crowds:** Surowiecki, *Wisdom*.

60 **Those leaders who are able:** Zaleznik, "Managers and Leaders."

61 **Theodore Roosevelt:** Goodwin, *Bully Pulpit*.

62 **In the recent theatrical adaptation:** Mantel, *Wolf Hall*.

63 **A fine instructor:** McCulloch, *In the Lion's Court*.

63 **Among more recent leaders:** Goodwin, *Bully Pulpit*, 75, 315.

64 **The tale he tells is all about addition:** Smith, "Speaking in Tongues."

65 **Benjamin Franklin would have felt:** Isaacson, *Benjamin Franklin*, 3.

CHAPTER 3: DOING WHAT SEEMS RIGHT

69 **In the early days:** Kidder, *Mountains Beyond Mountains*, 101.

71 **Above all the other necessities:** Quoted in Brooks, *Social Animal*, 118.

71 **Man's behavior is exquisitely rational:** Quoted in Brooks, "When Cultures Shift," "The Secular Society."

72 **Our moral salvation:** Taylor, *A Secular Age*.

77 **Tony Blair himself would later bemoan:** Blair, *A Journey*.

77 **There has been a well-worn path:** Sorkin, "Roadblocks En Route from Wall Street to Washington."

79 **Look deeper:** Strohminger and Nichols, "Neurodegeneration and Identity."

80 **If the outer mind hungers:** Brooks, *Social Animal*, 2.

80 **Farmer himself has followed:** Farmer, "How Liberation Theology Can Inform Public Health."

81 **I cannot have my integrity put in question:** Personal interview with Michael Wilson, 2014.

83 **In his landmark work:** Frankl, *Man's Search for Meaning*.

84 **What is the ultimate goal:** Koffman, *Conscious Business*, 81–82.

85 **Perhaps more than any other business thinker:** Christensen, Allworth, and Dillon, *How Will You Measure Your Life?*, 3.

88 **First I need to earn an okay living:** Livingston, *Founders at Work*.

88 **Facebook aspires to build the services:** Letter from Mark Zuckerberg to potential investors as part of Facebook's filing for an initial public offering, San Francisco, January 2012.

89 **Bill Novelli has been:** Personal interview with Bill Novelli at Georgetown University McDonough School of Business, 2013.

89 **The cultural, technological, and meritocratic environment:** Brooks, *Road to Character*, 257.

91 **But thirteen years later:** www.teachfirst.org.uk.

91 **Through their shared platform:** www.teachforall.org.

93 **The research suggests:** UCLA's Cooperative Institutional Research Program (CIRP) Freshman Survey was introduced in 1966 by Dr. Alexander "Sandy" Astin during his time at the American Council on Education. He brought the

project to UCLA in 1973 and since then it has been administered by the Higher Education Research Institute. The survey has been administered to more than 15 million students at over 1,900 institutions. I became aware of it through a David Brooks column in the *New York Times*.

93 **Government is impermeable:** Personal conversation with Jack Donahue.

94 **When a young girl asks Mitt Romney:** Kranish and Helman, *Real Romney*, 3.

95 **I have always admired:** Ignatieff, *Fire and Ashes*, 3.

96 **I didn't go into government:** Geithner, *Stress Test*, 70.

98 **Argues strongly for singularity of purpose:** Thiel with Masters, *Zero to One*, 61–69, emphasis mine.

100 **Jennifer Pryce has been navigating:** Personal interview with Jennifer Pryce, Washington, DC, 2013.

102 **The Calvert Foundation is a unique asset:** www.calvertfoundation.org.

CHAPTER 4: ON BEING T-SHAPED

104 **In the spring of 2010:** Personal interview with David Hayes at the US Department of the Interior, Washington, DC, June 2012.

106 **The same was true:** Personal interviews with Carol Browner at Albright Stonebridge Group, Washington, DC, June 2013, September 2013.

109 **It was most vividly expressed:** Berlin, *Hedgehog and the Fox*.

110 **I've got no either envy of or obsession:** Interview with Isaiah Berlin by Michael Ignatieff, 1991, quoted in 2013 Princeton University Press edition of *The Hedgehog and the Fox*.

111 **Berlin loved categorizing individuals:** Magee, "Isaiah as I Knew Him," 53.

111 **Ambiverts:** Cain, *Quiet*, 19.

111 **Otherish givers:** Grant, *Give and Take*, 157.

113 **Another benefit of mixing depth and breadth:** Grant, *Originals*.

114 **That is exactly what has happened:** Personal interviews with Roger Sant, Washington, DC, June 2013, February 2014.

115 **So the company goes:** Grose, *Power to the People*.

117 **Time to prepare:** Paulson, *On the Brink*.

117 **"System 1" thinking:** Kahneman, *Thinking, Fast and Slow*.

118 **McCormick grew up:** Personal interviews with David McCormick, Washington, DC, June 2007, and by phone, February 2013.

119 **It was a relatively smooth transition:** Personal interview with Lael Brainard at the US Department of Treasury, Washington, DC, June 2012.

122 **The freeze-up hit hundreds of companies:** Erdman, "Banks Asked to Commit Billions to ABCP Rescue."

123 **Canada has done more:** Zakaria, "Canadian Solution."

124 **The sad experience:** Comstock, "What Really Happened."

124 **The change of style:** Fleming and Schafer, "Davos Shows Mark Carney's Style."

125 **You can't connect the dots:** Jobs, commencement address.

125 **Intuitive approach to work and life:** Lobenstine, *Renaissance Soul*, 86–102.

126 **He was outgoing:** Kolata, "Power in Numbers"; Fallows, "When Will Genomics Cure Cancer."

128 **Declares its commitment:** www.broadinstitute.org.

128 **The most successful scientist:** Wilson, *Social Conquest of Earth*.

129 **Portfolio-of-options approach:** Lobenstine, *Renaissance Soul,* 86–102.
130 **It's easier to be seen as an expert:** Kolata, "Power in Numbers."
130 **Let the young soul survey:** Nietzsche, *Human, All Too Human.*

CHAPTER 5: THE FOUNDATION
THAT IS COMMON TO THEM ALL

131 **That's what happened to Steve Rattner:** Personal interview with Steve Rattner, New York, September 2012; Rattner, *Overhaul.*
135 **That is what happened to Tony Hall:** Conversation with Lord Tony Hall, London, July 2013, and numerous conversations with Tony Hall in the 1990s.
137 **Tony Hall must now be:** Ford, "Lunch with the FT."
138 **System 1 thinking:** Kahneman, *Thinking, Fast and Slow.*
139 **Not to teach that which is peculiar:** Committee of the Corporation and the Academic Faculty, *Reports on the Course of Instruction at Yale College* (New Haven, CT, 1828). Quoted in Zakaria, *In Defense of Liberal Education.*
140 **Many of the best leaders:** Collins, *Good to Great,* 12.
140 **Surveyed a century's worth of research:** Grant, *Give and Take.*
140 **A subsequent study:** Kaplan, Klebanov, and Sorensen, *Which CEO Characteristics and Abilities Matter?*
142 **After Nate Fick left the Marine Corps:** Fick, *One Bullet Away;* Fick, Center for New American Security. Also, Fang, "A Reluctant Warrior."
144 **In a 2014 paper:** Grant, "Where Great Leaders Earn Their Stripes."
145 **A landmark study:** Benmelech and Frydman, *Military CEOs.*
145 **Landmark book about business leadership:** Chandler, *Visible Hand.*
146 **If we wanted to find:** Davidson, "On Money."
146 **Over the past 50 years:** Faust, "To Be 'a Speaker of Words and a Doer of Deeds.'"
147 **The gift of the many-colored voice:** Smith, "Speaking in Tongues."
147 **Pivotal role that the Israeli military has played:** Senor and Singer, *Start-up Nation,* 71–73.
149 **A lot like LinkedIn:** Davidson, "On Money."
149 **The evidence is growing:** Grant, "Where Great Leaders Earn Their Stripes."
150 **A large and growing group:** O'Keefe, "Battle-Tested."
150 **Josh Gotbaum grew up mostly in New York:** Personal interview with Josh Gotbaum, Pension Benefits Guaranty Corporation, Washington, DC, July 2012.
153 **Paul Brinkley:** Gimbel, "In Iraq, One Man's Mission Impossible"; Dowdy, "Stabilizing Iraq"; conversation with Barney Gimbel, New York, December 2015.
157 **Aneesh Chopra and Todd Park have shared:** Personal interview with Aneesh Chopra, White House, Washington, DC, September 2012.
157 **Also the son of immigrant parents:** Personal interview with Todd Park, White House, Washington, DC, March 2013.
158 **The technologies behind today's entertainment:** Shear, "Obama, at South by Southwest, Calls for Law Enforcement Access in Encryption Fight."
159 **The now-energized Todd Park:** Brill, *America's Bitter Pill,* 401–403; Brill, "Code Red."
160 **The first tech president:** Shear, "Obama, at South by Southwest, Calls for Law Enforcement Access in Encryption Fight."
160 **Construct his career:** Kranish and Helman, *Real Romney,* 224–259.

160 **Pursue data aggressively:** Ibid.
161 **The knowledge of influencing men:** Weber, "Politics as a Vocation."
162 **One reason why private-sector leaders:** Conversation with Hank Paulson at Kellogg School of Management, Northwestern University, January 26, 2011.
162 **He consulted with his trusty lieutenants:** Keohane, *Thinking About Leadership,* 39–40.
163 **Who are not averse to causing a ruckus:** Kramer, "Great Intimidators."
163 **Politics is a much more internally complex:** Philp, *Political Conduct.*
163 **The irony is:** Kranish and Helman, *Real Romney,* 99–129.
164 **You know there is an element of truth:** Personal interview with Roger Sant.
164 **Global banking giant:** Green. *Serving God? Serving Mammon?*
164 **A subsequent book:** Green. *Good Value. Reflections on Money, Morality, and an Uncertain World,* 20.
165 **Discouraging words:** Moreton, "Archbishop of Canterbury: You have no future in the Church".
165 **Marked him out for promotion:** Brown,"Justin Welby: the hard-nosed realist holding together the Church of England".
165 **A clear sense of something changing:** Moore, "Archbishop Welby: I was embarrassed. It was like getting the measles".
165 **A very dark time:** Ord, "Profile: Anglican Bishop of Durham".
166 **More intangible skills:** Fraser, "The Sunday Interview: Bishop of Durham".
166 **Combine the cunning:** McCrum, "Justin Welby: from mammon to man of God".
166 **An executive type:** Brown, "Justin Welby".
166 **Hard-nosed realism:** Brown, "Justin Welby".
166 **Don't worry:** McCrum, "Justin Welby".
166 **His original theology dissertation:** Welby, Justin. *Can Companies Sin?*
167 **A society which has built:** Moore, "Archbishop Welby".
167 **The longer I go on:** Evans & Percy. Managing the Church?
167 **Take Irfhan Rawji:** Personal interview with Irfhan Rawji, Toronto, September 2013.

CHAPTER 6: LISTEN, LEARN, ADAPT

171 **The speaker who has so captured our attention:** Personal recollection of Ronald Heifetz lecture to McKinsey London off-site in 1996; Heifetz, *Leadership Without Easy Answers;* Heifetz, "Work of a Modern Leader"; Heifetz and Linsky, "Survival Guide for Leaders"; Heifetz and Lurie, "Work of Leadership."
174 **Estimates suggest:** Andrei, "Heaviest Living Organism in the World."
175 **The men who took commanding roles:** Rakove, *Revolutionaries.*
175 **What an individual actually does:** Spencer, *Man Versus the State.*
176 **Seeks to isolate the most important lessons:** Mayo and Nohria, *In Their Time,* xv–xxx.
176 **A slightly different and fuller definition:** Khanna, "Contextual Intelligence."
177 **Many leaders fail to meet:** Heifetz and Linsky, "Survival Guide for Leaders."
178 **We are successful when:** Machiavelli, *Prince.*
178 **The art of life:** Kakuzo, *Book of Tea.*
178 **Every businessperson knows a story:** Goleman, "What Makes a Leader?"
179 **For the first six years:** Personal interviews with Jonathan McBride, September 2015, January 2016.

179   **You have to start:** Personal interviews with Roger Sant.
180   **What is the beating heart:** Personal interviews with Jeff Seabright.
180   **People typically focus too much:** Watkins, *First 90 Days;* Watkins, Daly, and Reavis, *First 90 Days in Government.*
181   **Understand the structural and temporary elements:** Personal interviews with Diana Farrell, September 2012.
182   **One of the best people I know:** Personal interviews with Bernie Ferrari, June 2014, January 2016; Ferrari, *Power Listening,* 30–31.
184   **Surveyed the social interactions:** Chartrand and Bargh, "Chameleon Effect."
185   **So, as you can see:** Personal recollections of Royal Shakespeare Company Board meetings.
185   **Michael Boyd:** Crompton, *The Modest Man.*
186   **It is almost impossible to exaggerate:** Salter, "Michael Boyd, Royal Shakespeare Company"; Dickson, "Life in Theatre."
187   **In time, every post tends:** Peter and Hull, *Peter Principle,* 9–16.
187   **Swiss mime-clowns:** Dickson, "Life in Theatre."
189   **Though we didn't have bosses:** Personal recollections of conversations with Archie Norman in the 1980s and 1990s.
189   **When Kissinger was national security adviser:** Personal conversation with David R. Young, founder and president of Oxford Analytica. From 1969 to 1971 he was administrative assistant and then from 1971 to 1973, special assistant to Dr. Henry Kissinger in the White House and a member of the National Security Council staff.
191   **Hard and soft approaches:** Nohria and Beer, "Cracking the Code of Change."
193   **It was like a different world:** Wheeler, "If Anyone Understands."
193   **Public issues involving private enterprise:** Personal interview with Richard Cavanaugh, Kennedy School of Government, Harvard, September 2012.
194   **It was in the early days:** Cavanaugh, "Why the Government's Business Isn't Business-like."
195   **A similar kind of early experience:** Personal interview with Don Baer, Washington, DC, June 2013.
196   **I dealt with climate change issues:** Personal interviews with David McCormick.

CHAPTER 7: STRUCTURED SERENDIPITY

199   **America's gilded capital:** Leibovich, *This Town.*
199   **Are almost embarrassed:** Conversations with Congressman John Delaney and April Delaney, November 2014.
200   **Delaney had always been involved:** Douglas, "John Delaney's Business Record Key."
202   **If the outer mind:** Brooks, *Social Animal,* 2.
203   **But some people take:** Grazer and Fishman, *Curious Mind.*
204   **Great creators:** Sheryl Sandberg, foreword to Grant, *Originals,* x.
204   **Fascination about ourselves:** Wilson, *The Meaning of Human Existence,* 42–43.
205   **Power of professional and personal networks:** Hoffman and Casnocha, *Start-up of You,* 158–160, 161.
206   **Network literacy:** Ibid., 191.
206   **Israeli entrepreneurs benefit:** Senor and Singer, *Start-up Nation,* 100.
207   **Social explorers:** Pentland, Pan, and Altschuler, *Decoding Social Influence.*

208   **Eroding effectiveness of the civic institutions:** Putnam, *Bowling Alone.*

209   **"Force multiplier" effect:** Donahue and Zeckhauser, *Collaborative Governance,* 4, 122.

209   **Most complex forms:** Wilson, *Consilience,* 11, 183.

210   **Leadership in a complex institution:** Keohane, *Thinking About Leadership,* 198.

211   **At that time:** Gans, *Urban Villagers.*

212   **Many leaders recruit:** Keohane, *Thinking About Leadership,* 92.

212   **Skills mismatch:** Personal interview with Stanley Litow, New York, September 2012; www.ptech.org.

213   **They had a looming problem:** Tett, *Silo Effect,* 164–191.

215   **The only job I actually applied for:** Personal interview with John Berry, Office of Personnel Management, Washington, DC, June 2013.

215   **Most common metaphor:** Sandberg, *Lean In,* 53.

215   **How the diversity and quality of network relationships:** Granovetter, *Getting a Job.*

216   **Small organizations typically operate:** Granovetter, "Strength of Weak Ties," "Strength of Weak Ties: Revisited."

217   **The tendency of individuals:** McPherson, Smith-Lovin, and Cook, "Birds of a Feather."

217   **People tend to choose spouses:** Miller, *Mating Mind.*

218   **"Closed circle" bias:** Rivera, *Pedigree.*

219   **Wharton now has:** Wharton Social Impact Initiative, socialimpact.wharton .upenn.edu; Beeck Center for Social Impact and Innovation, www.impact .georgetown.edu.

219   **When I went into government:** *McKinsey Conversations.*

220   **Before it was just a cause:** Personal interviews with Roger Sant.

220   **Many of the most successful cross-sector leaders:** Personal interview with Richard Cavanaugh.

221   **The people on your board:** Coleman, *Ask.*

222   **If there's one thing:** Conversation with Pat Butler, September 2012. He also introduced me to the work of Edward O. Wilson and the concept of consilience, which I have drawn upon in parts of this book.

222   **Nearly 17 percent:** Granovetter, "Strength of Weak Ties," "Strength of Weak Ties: Revisited."

223   **Brunswick is looking for:** Conversation with Harry Clark, January 2014.

223   **Otherish giver:** Grant, *Give and Take,* 157.

224   **Adults accumulate thousands:** Levin, Walter, and Levin, "Dormant Ties."

CHAPTER 8: CARPE DIEM

227   **Sitting in his mahogany-lined office:** Personal interview with Robert Hormats, US Department of State, Washington, DC, October 2012.

228   **In the fields of observation:** Pasteur, lecture at the University of Lille.

230   **Fortuna is the arbiter:** Machiavelli, *Prince.*

230   **If I had to distill one lesson:** Ariely, *Predictably Irrational.*

230   **The human mind:** Brooks, *Social Animal,* 218.

231   **Business strategies employed:** Hoffman and Casnocha, *Start-up of You,* 41.

232   **Decision rule:** Personal interview with Josh Gotbaum.

232 **Different kind of prepared mind:** Personal interview with Patty Stonesifer, Smithsonian Institution, Washington, DC, September 2010; Bryant, "Corner Office."

233 **Connecting the dots:** Isaacson, *Steve Jobs;* Jobs, commencement address.

234 **If you think adventure is dangerous:** Paulo Coelho, Twitter, November 14, 2011.

237 **Seth Siegel, now in his early sixties:** Siegel, *My Career Choice.*

239 **The United States produces:** Barone, *Hard America, Soft America.*

239 **We can recognize at least six:** Brooks, *Social Animal,* 190.

240 **Who would have thought:** Personal interview with Julius Greenblatt, White House, Washington, DC, March 2014.

240 **Anti-Defamation League:** www.adl.org.

241 **Also served in the Clinton administration:** Personal interview with Julius Genachowski, US Federal Communications Commission, Washington, DC, June 2012.

242 ***Wired* magazine named the "new FCC":** *Wired,* "Top 7 Disruptions of the Year."

242 **Proposals to reallocate airwaves:** National Broadband Plan, *Connecting America.*

243 **How does a physician and college professor:** Cunningham, "Trying to Change the World Bank."

244 **What Jim had, above all:** Kidder, *Mountains Beyond Mountains,* 169.

247 **David Bradley was also in his midforties:** Conversations with David Bradley, Atlantic Media Company, Washington, DC, March 2012, June 2012, July 2013; Jaffe, "Citizen Bradley."

249 **She tells the story of this transition:** Lahiri, *In Other Words,* "Teach Yourself Italian."

249 **By 9 p.m. Saturday:** Weigel, "With an Outpouring of Good Wishes for Carter."

251 **Teaching, writing and helping:** Carter, *Full Life,* 1–2.

253 **A series of studies obviate:** Brooks, *Social Animal,* 190.

253 **He felt, as I begin to feel:** Sacks, *Gratitude,* 10.

254 **People get better at the art of living:** David Brooks on the *Charlie Rose* show, Bloomberg Television, March 29, 2016.

254 **Who is now approaching a sixty-year association:** Daniel, *Daniel on McKinsey.*

254 **The same is true:** Personal interview with Sir Ronald Cohen, London, May 2013.

256 **That's what happened to Michael Ignatieff:** Ignatieff, *Fire and Ashes,* 2, 5, 30, 35, 127, 186.

CHAPTER 9: HOW TO BROADEN YOUR CAREER

263 **Oh, those people have had remarkable careers:** Conversation with David Bradley, Washington, DC, 2012.

267 **Examined the breadth and depth of expertise:** Wai and Ouderkirk, *Balancing Breadth and Depth of Expertise for Innovation.*

268 **In a related study:** Heijden, "Prerequisites to Guarantee Life-Long Employability."

269 **As we gain knowledge about a domain:** Grant, *Originals,* 41.

270 **Simple mathematical formula:** Personal interview with Ethan Bernstein, Cambridge, MA, October 2014.

271   **In the stretch zone:** Ryan and Markova, Professional Thinking Partners website, www.ptinc.org.

CHAPTER 10: HOW TO BROADEN YOUR LIFE

272   **Obituaries:** Conversation with Lord Justice [David] Kitchin, April 2014.
273   **Neurologist and author Dr. Oliver Sacks:** Kakutani, "Appraisal-Doctor."
274   **I am sorry I have wasted:** Sacks, *Gratitude*, 7.
275   **Accidental death at the age of forty-seven:** Goel and Hardy, "Dave Goldberg."
275   **There is far more to life:** Sandberg, *Lean In*, 18.
275   **Sandberg wrote her own kind of obituary:** Sandberg, Facebook posts.
275   **A loving father and husband:** Grant, "Remembering Dave Goldberg."
276   **The third obituary:** Sorkin, "Jimmy Lee, Investment Banking Force."
276   **People may not know:** Dimon, "Funeral Eulogy for James B. Lee."
276   **A copy of this list:** Lee, *Rules of Working Life*.
277   **Turing was among the first:** Jones, Asa Briggs obituary.
278   **Interdisciplinary research project:** Foley Center for the Study of Lives, Northwestern University, School of Education and Social Policy, www.sesp .northwestern.edu.
279   **A happy life:** Brooks, *Social Animal*, 208.
279   **Only the one who descends:** Kierkegaard, *Fear and Trembling*, 30.
279   **The way in which so many of us think:** Campbell, *Hero with a Thousand Faces*, 210–211.
281   **Conscious and purposeful approach:** Bakewell, *How to Live*.
281   **I defy any reader of Montaigne:** Quoted in ibid.
282   **Contemporary historian Theodore Zeldin:** The Oxford Muse.
282   **Cataloging life stories:** Brooks, "The Life Report."
283   **The thousands of life reports:** Brooks, "The Life Reports."
284   **When Bobby Layne, the great quarterback:** "Famed quarterback Bobby Layne Dies," *Pittsburgh Post-Gazette*, December 2, 1986.
285   **In 1910:** Bennett, *How to Live on Twenty Four Hours a Day*.
286   ***Sunday neurosis:*** Frankl, *Man's Search for Meaning*, 107.
286   **Overlook the essential fact:** Jung, *Stages of Life*.
288   **Ten thousand hours is an *enormous* amount of time:** Gladwell, *Outliers*, 38–69, emphasis in the original.
289   **When he got to fifty-four:** *McKinsey Conversations*.
289   **Very few career lifers:** Daniel, *Daniel on McKinsey*.
291   **Personal diary:** Rusbridger, *Play It Again*.
293   **200 billion hours:** Shirky, *Cognitive Surplus*.
293   **H = S + C + V:** Haidt, *Happiness Hypothesis*.
294   **The digital economy:** Johnson, "New Making It."
295   **Studying the performing arts:** Gazzaniga, *Learning, Arts and the Brain*.
295   **Nobel Prize–winning scientists:** Grant, *Originals*, 46.
297   **Exercise, a bowl of Wheaties:** Personal interview with Michael Wilson, Toronto.

EPILOGUE

298   **Humanity entered our present:** Wilson, *The Meaning of Human Existence*, 54.
301   **Nicholas Lovegrove's professional reputation:** Silva, *Portrait of a Spy*, 52.

REFERENCES

BOOKS

Ariely, Dan. *Predictably Irrational: The Hidden Forces That Shape Our Decisions.* New York: Harper, 2009.

Barnard, Chester. *The Functions of the Executive.* Cambridge, MA: Harvard University Press, 1938.

Barone, Michael. *Hard America, Soft America: Competition vs. Coddling and the Battle for the Nation's Future.* New York: Crown Forum, 2004.

Bennett, Arnold. *How to Live on Twenty Four Hours a Day,* 1910.

Berlin, Isaiah. *The Hedgehog and the Fox.* Weidenfeld and Nicolson, 1953.

Blair, Tony. *A Journey: My Political Life.* New York: Alfred A. Knopf, 2010.

Blinder, Alan S. *After the Music Stopped: The Financial Crisis, the Response, and the Work Ahead.* New York: Penguin Books, 2013.

Brill, Steven. *America's Bitter Pill: Money, Politics, Backroom Deals, and the Fight to Fix Our Broken Healthcare System.* New York: Random House, 2015.

Brooks, David. *The Road to Character.* New York: Random House, 2015.

———. *The Social Animal: The Hidden Sources of Love, Character and Achievement.* New York: Random House, 2011.

Burstein, David D. *Fast Future: How the Millennial Generation Is Shaping Our World.* Boston: Beacon Press, 2013

Cain, Susan. *Quiet: The Power of Introverts in a World That Can't Stop Talking.* New York: Crown, 2012.

Campbell, Joseph. *The Hero with a Thousand Faces.* Pantheon Books / Bollingen Foundation, 1949.

Carter, Jimmy. *A Full Life: Reflections at Ninety.* New York: Simon & Schuster, 2015.

Chandler, Alfred D. *The Visible Hand: The Managerial Revolution in American Business.* Cambridge, MA: Belknap Press, 1977.

Christensen, Clayton M., James Allworth, and Karen Dillon. *How Will You Measure Your Life?* New York: Harper Business, 2012.

Coelho, Paulo. *The Alchemist.* New York: HarperCollins, 1993.

Coleman, Priscilla H. *Ask . . . How to Get What You Want and Need at Work.* Insights, 2002.

Collins, Jim. *Good to Great: Why Some Companies Make the Leap . . . and Others Don't.* New York: HarperCollins, 2001.

Daniel, D. Ronald. *Daniel on McKinsey.* New York: McKinsey, 2013.

Donahue, John D., and Richard J. Zeckhauser. *Collaborative Governance: Private Roles for Public Goals in Turbulent Times.* Princeton, NJ: Princeton University Press, 2011.

Dunbabin, Katherine M. D. *Mosaics of the Greek and Roman World.* Cambridge: Cambridge University Press, 1999.

Dweck, Carol S. *Mindset: The New Psychology of Success.* New York: Random House, 2007.

Eichenwald, Kurt. *Conspiracy of Fools: A True Story.* New York: Broadway, 2005.

Evans, G.R. & Percy, Martin. *Managing the Church? Order and Organization in a Secular Age.* London: Bloomsbury T&T Clark, 2000.

Farmer, Paul. *Haiti After the Earthquake.* New York: Public Affairs / Perseus Books Group, 2011.

———. *In the Company of the Poor: Conversations with Dr. Paul Farmer and Fr. Gustavo Gutierrez.*

Ferrari, Bernard T. *Power Listening: Mastering the Most Critical Business Skill of All.* New York: Portfolio/Penguin, 2012.

Fick, Nathaniel. *One Bullet Away: The Making of a Marine Officer.* New York: Houghton Mifflin, 2005.

Financial Crisis Inquiry Report: Final Report of the National Commission on the Causes of the Financial and Economic Crisis in the United States. United States Government Printing Office, Washington, DC, January 2011.

Frankl, Viktor E. *Man's Search for Meaning.* Boston: Beacon Press, 2006. Originally published in 1959.

Fuller, Buckminster. *Operating Manual for Spaceship Earth,* 1963.

Galbraith, John Kenneth. *The Great Crash 1929.* 50th anniversary ed. New York: Houghton Mifflin, 1988.

Gans, Herbert J. *The Urban Villagers: Group and Class in the Life of Italian-Americans.* New York: Free Press of Glencoe, 1962.

Gardner, Dan. *Future Babble: Why Expert Predictions Are Next to Worthless, and You Can Do Better.* New York: Dutton, 2011.

Gawande, Atul. *The Checklist Manifesto: How to Get Things Right.* New York: Metropolitan Books, 2009.

Geithner, Timothy F. *Stress Test: Reflections on the Financial Crisis.* New York: Crown, 2014.

Gladwell, Malcolm. *Outliers: The Story of Success.* New York: Little, Brown / Hachette Book Group, 2008.

Goodwin, Doris Kearns. *The Bully Pulpit: Theodore Roosevelt, William Howard Taft and the Golden Age of Journalism.* New York: Simon & Schuster, 2013.

———. *Team of Rivals: The Political Genius of Abraham Lincoln.* New York: Simon & Schuster, 2005.

Granovetter, Mark. *Getting a Job: A Study of Contacts and Careers.* Cambridge, MA: Harvard University Press, 1974.

Grant, Adam. *Give and Take: A Revolutionary Approach to Success.* New York: Viking / Penguin Group, 2013.

———. *Originals: How Non-conformists Move the World.* New York: Viking, Penguin, Random House, 2016.

Grazer, Brian, and Charles Fishman. *The Curious Mind: The Secret to a Bigger Life.* New York: Simon & Schuster, 2015.

Green, Stephen. *Good Value. Reflections on Money, Morality, and an Uncertain World.* London: Penguin, 2009.

———. *Serving God? Serving Mammon?* London: Marshall Pickering, 1996.

Greenblatt, Stephen. *The Swerve: How the World Became Modern*. New York: W. W. Norton, 2011.

Greene, Joshua. *Moral Tribes: Emotion, Reason, and the Gap Between Us and Them*. New York: Penguin, 2013.

Grose, Peter. *Power to the People: The Inside Story of AES and the Globalization of Electricity*. With an introduction by Roger Sant. Washington, DC: Sant Associates, 2007.

Haidt, Jonathan. *The Happiness Hypothesis: Finding Modern Truth in Ancient Wisdom*. New York: Basic Books, 2005.

Heifetz, Ronald A. *Leadership Without Easy Answers*. Cambridge, MA: Belknap Press of Harvard University Press, 1994.

Hoffman, Reid, and Ben Casnocha. *The Start-up of You: Adapt to the Future, Invest in Yourself, and Transform Your Career*. New York: Crown Business, 2012.

Ignatieff, Michael. *Fire and Ashes: Success and Failure in Politics*. Boston: Harvard University Press, 2013.

Isaacson, Walter. *Benjamin Franklin: An American Life*. New York: Simon & Schuster, 2003.

———. *Steve Jobs*. New York: Simon & Schuster, 2011.

Johnson, Steven. *Where Good Ideas Come From: The Natural History of Innovation*. New York: Riverhead Books, 2010.

Jung, Carl. *The Stages of Life*, 1930.

Kahneman, Daniel. *Thinking, Fast and Slow*. New York: Farrar, Straus and Giroux, 2011.

Kakuzo, Okakura. *The Book of Tea*. New York: Putnam's, 1906.

Kay, John. *Other People's Money: The Real Business of Finance*. London: Profile Books; New York: Public Affairs / Perseus Books, 2015.

Keohane, Nannerl O. *Thinking About Leadership*. Princeton, NJ: Princeton University Press, 2010.

Kidder, Tracy. *Mountains Beyond Mountains: The Quest of Dr. Paul Farmer, a Man Who Would Cure the World*. New York: Random House, 2003.

Koffman, Fred. *Conscious Business: How to Build Value Through Values*. Boulder, CO: Sounds True, 2006.

Kranish, Michael, and Scott Helman. *The Real Romney*. New York: Harper, 2012.

Lahiri, Jhumpa. *In Other Words*. Translated from the Italian by Ann Goldstein. New York: Bloomsbury, 2015.

Leibovich, Mark. *This Town: Two Parties and a Funeral—plus, Plenty of Valet Parking!—in America's Gilded Capital*. New York: Blue Rider Press, 2013.

Lewis, Michael. *The Big Short*. New York: W. W. Norton, 2010.

———. *Liar's Poker*. New York: W. W. Norton, 1989.

Levitin, Daniel J. *The Organized Mind: Thinking Straight in the Age of Information Overload*. New York: Plume / Penguin Random House, 2014.

Livingston, Jessica. *Founders at Work: Stories of Startups' Early Days*. New York: Apress, 2007. Cited at www.brainpickings.org/2014/10/21/craig-newmark-moral-compass.

Lobenstine, Margaret. *The Renaissance Soul: How to Make Your Passions Your Life—A Creative and Practical Guide*. New York: Harmony Books, 2006.

Machiavelli, Niccolo. *The Prince*, 1532.

Mayo, Anthony J., and Nitin Nohria. *In Their Time: The Greatest Business Leaders of the Twentieth Century*. Boston: Harvard Business Review Press, 2005.

McCulloch, Diarmaid. *In the Lion's Court: Power, Ambition and Sudden Death in the Reign of Henry VIII*. London: SMP, 2002.

McLean, Bethany, and Peter Elkind. *Smartest Guys in the Room: The Amazing Rise and Scandalous Fall of Enron,* 2003.

McLean, Bethany, and Joe Nocera. *All the Devils Are Here: The Hidden History of the Financial Crisis.* New York: Portfolio/Penguin, 2010.

Meyer, Erin. *The Culture Map: Breaking Through the Invisible Boundaries of Global Business.* New York: Public Affairs / Perseus Books Group, 2014.

Miller, Geoffrey. *The Mating Mind: How Sexual Choice Shaped the Evolution of Human Nature.* New York: Doubleday, 2000.

Miller, Jon, and Lucy Parker. *Everybody's Business: The Unlikely Story of How Big Business Can Fix the World.* London: Biteback, 2013.

Nietzsche, Friedrich. *Human, All Too Human: A Book for Free Spirits.* New York: Bison Books, 1996.

Paulson, Henry M., Jr. *On the Brink: Inside the Race to Stop the Collapse of the Global Financial System.* New York: Business Plus / Hachette Book Group, 2010.

Peter, Laurence J., and Raymond Hull. *The Peter Principle: Why Things Always Go Wrong.* New York: HarperCollins, 1969.

Philp, Mark. *Political Conduct.* Cambridge, MA: Harvard University Press, 2007.

Putnam, Robert D. *Bowling Alone.* New York: Simon & Schuster, 2000.

Rakove, Jack. *Revolutionaries: A New History of the Invention of America.* New York: Houghton Mifflin, 2010.

Rattner, Steven. *Overhaul: An Insider's Account of the Obama Administration's Emergency Rescue of the Auto Industry.* New York: Houghton Mifflin Harcourt, 2010.

Rivera, Laura. *Pedigree: How Elite Students Get Elite Jobs.* Princeton, NJ: Princeton University Press, 2015.

Rusbridger, Alan. *Play It Again: An Amateur Against the Impossible.* London: Jonathan Cape, 2013.

Sacks, Oliver. *Gratitude.* New York: Alfred A. Knopf / Random House, 2015.

———. *On the Move: A Life.* New York: Alfred A. Knopf / Random House, 2015.

Sandberg, Sheryl. *Lean In: Women, Work, and the Will to Lead.* New York: Alfred A. Knopf / Random House, 2013.

Senor, Dan, and Saul Singer. *Start-up Nation: The Story of Israel's Economic Miracle.* New York: Twelve, Grand Central, 2009.

Shirky, Clay. *Cognitive Surplus: How Technology Makes Consumers into Collaborators.* New York: Penguin, 2010.

Silva, Daniel. *Portrait of a Spy.* New York: Harper, 2011.

Smith, George David, John T. Seaman, and Morgan Witzel. *A History of the Firm.* New York: McKinsey, 2011.

Spencer, Herbert. *The Man Versus the State,* 1884.

Stegner, Wallace. *Crossing to Safety.* New York: Random House, 1987.

Stone, Brad. *The Everything Store: Jeff Bezos and the Age of Amazon.* Little, Brown / Hachette Books Group, 2013.

Surowiecki, James. *The Wisdom of Crowds.* New York: Doubleday, 2004.

Taylor, Charles. *A Secular Age.* Cambridge, MA: Belknap Press of Harvard University Press, 2007.

Taylor, Frederick Winslow. *Principles of Scientific Management.* New York: Harper and Brothers, 1911.

Tetlock, Philip E., and Dan Gardner. *Superforecasting: The Art and Science of Prediction.* New York: Crown, 2015.

Tett, Gillian. *The Silo Effect.* New York: Simon & Schuster, 2015; London: Little, Brown, 2015.

Thiel, Peter, with Blake Masters. *Zero to One: Notes on Startups, Or How to Build the Future.* New York: Crown Business, 2014.

Watkins, Michael. *The First 90 Days: Critical Success Strategies for New Leaders at All Levels.* Boston: Harvard Business Review Press, 2003.

Watkins, Michael, Peter H. Daly, and Cate Reavis. *The First 90 Days in Government: Critical Success Strategies for New Public Managers at All Levels.* Boston: Harvard Business Review Press, 2006.

Webb, Caroline. *How to Have a Good Day: Harness the Power of Behavioral Science to Transform Your Working Life.* New York: Crown Business, 2016.

Welby, Justin. *Can Companies Sin? "Whether", "How" and "Who" in Company Account-ability.* Dissertation at Durham University, 1992.

Weil, Sylvie. *At Home with Andre and Simone Weil.* Chicago: Northwestern University Press, 2010.

Wharton, Edith. *A Backward Glance,* 1934.

Wilson, Edward O. *Consilience: The Unity of Knowledge.* New York: Knopf, 1998.

———. *The Meaning of Human Existence.* New York: Liveright, 2014.

———. *The Social Conquest of Earth.* New York: Liveright, 2012.

Zakaria, Fareed. *In Defense of Liberal Education.* New York: W. W. Norton, 2015.

ARTICLES AND OTHER SOURCES

Addison, Joseph. *Spectator,* 1854.

Andrei, Mihae. "The Heaviest Living Organism in the World." *ZME Science.* http://www.zmescience.com. February 9, 2015.

Baer, M. "The Strength-of-Weak-Ties Perspective on Creativity: A Comprehensive Examination and Extension." *Journal of Applied Psychology* 95 (2010): 592–601.

Benmelech, Efraim, and Carola Frydman. *Military CEOs.* Washington, DC: National Bureau of Economic Research, November 2009.

Brill, Steven. "Code Red—Inside the Nightmare Launch of Healthcare.gov and the Team That Figured Out How to Fix It." *Time,* March 10, 2014. (Vol. 183, No. 9, pp. 27–36)

Brooks, David. "The Big University." *New York Times,* October 6, 2015.

———. "The Life Report." *New York Times,* October 27, 2011.

———. "The Life Reports." *New York Times,* November 24, 2011; November 28, 2011.

———. "The Secular Society." *New York Times,* July 8, 2013.

———. "When Cultures Shift." *New York Times,* April 17, 2015.

Brown, Andrew. "Justin Welby: the hard-nosed realist holding together the Church of England". *Guardian,* April 18, 2014.

Bryant, Adam. "Corner Office—Zigzag Your Way to the Top: Interview with Patty Sto-nesifer." *New York Times,* September 13, 2015.

Cassidy, John. "No Credit: Tim Geithner's Financial Plan Is Working—and Making Him Very Unpopular." *New Yorker,* March 15, 2010. (Vol. 86, No. 4, p. 26–30)

———. "What Good Is Wall Street? Much of What Investment Bankers Do Is Socially Worthless." *New Yorker,* November 29, 2010. (Vol. 86, No. 38, p. 49)

Cavanaugh, Richard. "Why the Government's Business Isn't Business-like." *Wall Street Journal,* July 27, 1981.

Chartrand, Tanya L., and John A. Bargh. "The Chameleon Effect: The Perception-Behavior Link and Social Interaction." *Journal of Personality and Social Psychology* 76, no. 6 (1999): 893–910.

Comstock, Courtney. "What Really Happened When Jamie Dimon Went Toe-to-Toe with the Head of the Bank of Canada." *Business Insider*, October 3, 2011.

Crompton, Sarah. "Michael Boyd: The Modest Man Who Saved the RSC." *Daily Telegraph*, September 14, 2012.

Cunningham, Lillian. "Trying to Change the World Bank." *Washington Post*, April 10, 2014.

Davidson, Adam. "On Money: Rebuilding the Middle Class the Army Way." *New York Times Magazine*, December 15, 2015 (p. 16).

Dear, John. "Gutierrez and Farmer's 'In the Company of the Poor.'" *National Catholic Reporter*, November 5, 2013.

Dickson, Arthur. "A Life in Theatre: Michael Boyd." *Guardian*, November 16, 2012.

Dimon, Jamie. "Funeral Eulogy for James B. Lee." June 17, 2015, St. Patrick's Cathedral, New York.

Douglas, Danielle. "John Delaney's Business Record Key to His Congressional Campaign—and His Opponent's Criticism." *Washington Post*, March 23, 2012.

Dowdy, John. "Stabilizing Iraq: A Conversation with Paul Brinkley." *McKinsey on Government*, Spring 2010.

Erdman, Boyd. "Banks Asked to Commit Billions to ABCP Rescue." *Toronto Globe & Mail*, December 14, 2007.

Fallows, James. "When Will Genomics Cure Cancer: A Conversation with Biogeneticist Eric S. Lander About How Genetic Advances Are Transforming Medical Treatment." *Atlantic*, January/February 2014. (Vol. 313, Issue 1, pp. 28–30)

Fang, Bay. "A Reluctant Warrior in Iraq." *U.S. News & World Report*, January 1, 2006.

Farmer, Paul. "How Liberation Theology Can Inform Public Health." *Sojourners*, January 2014. http://sojo.net/magazine/2014/01/sacred-medicine.

Faust, Drew. "To Be 'a Speaker of Words and a Doer of Deeds': Literature and Leadership." Speech delivered at United States Military Academy, West Point, New York, March 24, 2016.

Fick, Nathaniel. Center for New American Security. http://cnas.org/FickNathaniel.

Fleming, Sam, and Daniel Schafer. "Davos Shows Mark Carney's Style as BOE Governor." *Financial Times*, January 24, 2014.

Foley Center for the Study of Lives. Northwestern University, School of Education and Social Policy website. https://www.sesp.northwestern.edu/foley/.

Ford, Jonathan. "Lunch with the FT: Tony Hall." *Financial Times*, March 20, 2015.

Fraser, Giles: "The Sunday Interview: Justin Welby, Bishop of Durham". *Guardian*, July 20, 2012.

Gazzaniga, Michael. *Learning, Arts and the Brain: A Conversation with Michael S. Gazzaniga*. Dana Foundation, May 22, 2008.

Gimbel, Barney. "In Iraq, One Man's Mission Impossible." *Fortune*, September 4, 2007.

Gladwell, Malcolm. "Open Secrets—Enron, Intelligence, and the Perils of Too Much Information." *New Yorker*, January 8, 2007.

———. "The Talent Myth—Are Smart People Overrated?" *New Yorker*, July 22, 2002.

Godart, Frederic C., William M. Maddox, Andrew V. Shipilov, and Adam D. Galinsky. "Fashion with a Foreign Flair: Professional Experiences Abroad Facilitate the Creative Innovations of Organizations." *Academy of Management Journal* 58 (2015): 195–220.

Goel, Vindu, and Quentin Hardy. "Dave Goldberg, Half of a Silicon Valley Power Couple, Dies at 47." *New York Times*, May 2, 2015.

Goleman, Daniel. "What Makes a Leader?" *Harvard Business Review,* November-December, 1998. (Vol. 76, No. 6, pp. 93–102)

Granovetter, Mark. "The Strength of Weak Ties." *American Journal of Sociology,* May 1973. (Vol. 76, No. 6, pp. 1360–1380)

———. "The Strength of Weak Ties: A Network Theory Revisited." *Sociological Theory,* 1983.

Grant, Adam. "Remembering Dave Goldberg, the Ultimate Mensch." *LinkedIn Pulse,* May 10, 2015.

———. "Where Great Leaders Earn Their Stripes." *Adam Grant's Blog,* February 22, 2014. www.adammgrant.tumblr.com.

Greene, Joshua. "2011: What Scientific Concept Would Improve Everybody's Cognitive Toolkit—Supervenience." www.edge.org.

Heifetz, Ronald A. "The Work of a Modern Leader: An Interview with Ron Heifetz." *Harvard Management Update,* 1997.

Heifetz, Ronald A., and Marty Linsky. "A Survival Guide for Leaders." *Harvard Business Review,* June 2002.

Heifetz, Ronald A., and Donald L. Lurie. "The Work of Leadership." *Harvard Business Review,* December 2001.

Heijden, Beatrice Van der. "Prerequisites to Guarantee Life-Long Employability." *Personnel Review* 31, no. 1 (2002): 44–61.

Jaffe, Harry. "Citizen Bradley: He Has a Drop-Dead Office Overlooking the Potomac Yet Hides Away at McDonald's; He Wanted to Be a Senator but Got Rich Instead; Now Is He Going to Be the Next Big Media Mogul?" *Washingtonian Magazine,* October 1, 2000.

Jobs, Steve. Commencement address. Delivered at Stanford University, June 12, 2005. http://news.stanford.edu/news/2005/june15/jobs-061505.html.

Johnson, Steven. "The New Making It: The Digital Economy, with Its Profusion of Free Content, Was Supposed to Make It Impossible to Make Money by Making Art; Instead, Creative Careers Are Thriving—but in Complicated and Unexpected Ways." *New York Times Magazine,* August 23, 2015, 30–37.

Jones, Nigel. Asa Briggs obituary. *Guardian,* March 15, 2016.

Kakutani, Michiko. "An Appraisal-Doctor Who Found Magic in the Disorders of the Human Mind." *New York Times,* August 31, 2015.

Kaplan, Steven M., Mark M. Klebanov, and Morten Sorensen. *Which CEO Characteristics and Abilities Matter?* National Bureau of Economic Research. NBER Working Paper Series, Working Paper 14195, July 2008.

Kay, John. "The Benefits of a Liberal Education Do Not Go Out of Date: The Belief That Study Should Be Focused on Job-Specific Knowledge Is Misconceived." *Financial Times,* August 25, 2015.

Kent, Muhtar. "Opinion—the Golden Triangle—Spearheading Change the Smart Way." November 7, 2012. www.coca-colacompany.com/stories.

Khanna, Tarun. "Contextual Intelligence." *Harvard Business Review,* September 2014. (Vol. 92, No. 9, pp. 58–68)

Kierkegaard, Søren. *Fear and Trembling.* Rept. ed. New York: Penguin Classics, 1986.

Kolata, Gina. "Power in Numbers: Profiles in Science." *New York Times,* January 2, 2012.

Kramer, Roderick M. "The Great Intimidators." *Harvard Business Review,* February 2006.

Lahiri, Jhumpa. "Teach Yourself Italian." *New Yorker,* December 7, 2015.

Lee, James B. *JBL's "Top 30" Work-Habit Workout.* JPMorgan Chase, 2015.

Levin, Daniel, Jorge Walter, and Daniel Z. Levin. "Dormant Ties: The Value of Reconnecting." *Organization Science,* July–August 2011.

Lewin, Tamar. "As Interest Fades in the Humanities, Colleges Worry." *New York Times,* October 30, 2013.

Lizza, Ryan. "Inside the Crisis: Larry Summers and the White House Economic Team." *New Yorker,* October 12, 2009.

Lovegrove, Nick, and Matthew Thomas. "Triple-Strength Leadership." *Harvard Business Review* 91, no. 9 (September 2013): 46–56.

Lovegrove, William R. "General Studies and the Sixth Form." Dissertation presented as part of the examination for the Associateship Diploma in Secondary Education at the Cambridge Institute of Education, May 1963.

Maddux, William W., Adam D. Galinsky, and Carmit T. Tadmor. "Be a Better Manager: Live Abroad." *Harvard Business Review,* September 2010. (Vol. 88, No. 9, pp. 24–34)

Magee, Bryan. "Isaiah as I Knew Him," in *The Book of Isaiah: Personal Impressions of Isaiah Berlin,* edited by Henry Hardy, 53. London: Woodbridge, 2009.

Mansharamani, Vikram. "All Hail the Generalist." *HBR Blog Network,* June 4, 2012. www.hbr.org.

———. "Keep Experts on Tap, Not on Top." *HBR Blog Network,* July 23, 2013. www.hbr.org.

Mantel, Hilary. *Wolf Hall.* Script for the Royal Shakespeare Company theater production in Stratford-upon-Avon, London, and New York, 2013–2015.

McCrum, Robert. "Justin Welby: from mammon to man of God". *Guardian,* January 26, 2013.

McKinsey Conversations with Global Leaders: David Rubenstein of the Carlyle Group. McKinsey, May 2010.

McPherson, Miller, Lynn Smith-Lovin, and James M. Cook. "Birds of a Feather: Homophily in Social Networks." *Annual Review of Sociology,* August 2001. (Vol. 27, No. 1, pp. 415–444)

Moore Charles. "Archbishop Welby: 'I was embarrassed. It was like getting the measles". *Daily Telegraph,* July 12, 2013.

Moreton, Cole. "Archbishop of Canterbury: You have no future in the Church". *Sunday Telegraph,* November 11, 2012).

National Broadband Plan. *Connecting America.* Federal Communications Commission, March 17, 2010. www.broadband.gov.

Nohria, Nitin, and Michael Beer. "Cracking the Code of Change." *Harvard Business Review,* May–June 2000. (Vol, 78, No. 3, pp. 133–141)

O'Keefe, Brian. "Battle-Tested: From Soldier to Business Leader." *Fortune,* March 22, 2010.

Ord, Mick. "Profile: Anglican Bishop of Durham". *BBC News,* November 8, 2012.

The Oxford Muse. www.oxfordmuse.com.

Pasteur, Louis. Lecture at the University of Lille, December 7, 1854. http://www.pasteurbrewing.com.

Pentland, Alex Sandy, Wei Pan, and Yaniv Altschuler. *Decoding Social Influence and the Wisdom of the Crowd in Financial Trading Network.* MIT Media Lab, September 2012.

Peterson, A. D. C. "Last Chance in the Sixth Form." *Spectator,* June 18, 1963.

Powers, William C., Jr., Raymond S. Troubh, and Herbert S. Winokur Jr. *Report of Investigation by the Special Investigative Committee of the Board of Directors of Enron Corp.*, February 1, 2002.

Ryan, M. J., and Dawna Markova. Professional Thinking Partners website. www.ptpinc.org.

Salter, Jessica. "Michael Boyd, Royal Shakespeare Company." *Daily Telegraph,* March 26, 2010.

Sandberg, Sheryl. Facebook posts, May 5, 2016; June 3, 2016.

Shear, Michael D. "Obama, at South by Southwest, Calls for Law Enforcement Access in Encryption Fight." *New York Times,* March 12, 2016.

Siegel, Seth M. "My Career Choice: All of the Above." *New York Times,* December 19, 2015.

Smith, Zadie. "Speaking in Tongues." *New York Review of Books,* February 26, 2009.

Sorkin, Andrew Ross. "Jimmy Lee, Investment Banking Force, Dies at 62." *New York Times,* June 17, 2015.

———. "Roadblocks en Route from Wall Street to Washington." Dealbook. *New York Times,* February 9, 2016.

Stewart, James B. "Eight Days—the Battle to Save the American Financial System." *New Yorker,* September 21, 2009. (Vol. 79)

Strohminger, Nina, and Shaun Nichols. "Neurodegeneration and Identity." *Psychological Science,* September 14, 2015. (Vol. 26, No. 9, pp. 1469–1479) Quoted by Maria Popova on her website www.brainpickings.org.

Tett, Gillian. "Go Mingle, Have Fun." *Financial Times,* August 22/23, 2015.

Torres, Nicola. "Generalists Get Better Job Offers Than Specialists." *Harvard Business Review,* June 2016. (Vol. 94, No. 6, pp. 32–33) [Cites research by Jennifer Merlucci, Columbia Business School.]

Twigger, Robert. "Master of Many Trades: Our Age Reveres the Narrow Specialist but Humans Are Natural Polymaths, at Our Best When We Turn Our Minds to Many Things." *Aeon Magazine,* November 4, 2013. http://www.aeonmagazine.com/world-views.

Unruh, Gregory C., and Angel Cabrera. "Join the Global Elite—Managers with a Cross-Cultural Perspective Are in High Demand." *Harvard Business Review,* May 2013.

Wai Fong Boh and Andrew Ouderkirk. *Balancing Breadth and Depth of Expertise for Innovation: A 3M Story.* Science Direct, Research Policy, March 2014.

Weber, Max. "Politics as a Vocation." Second lecture of a series of lectures given to the Free Students' Union of Bavaria, January 28, 1919.

Weigel, David. "With an Outpouring of Good Wishes for Carter, Pilgrims Pour into Plains, Ga." *Washington Post,* August 31, 2015.

Wheeler, Brian. "If Anyone Understands the Perils of Modernizing the Conservative Party It Is Archie Norman." *BBC News,* July 14, 2006.

Wired. "The Top 7 Disruptions of the Year," December 28, 2009.

Zakaria, Fareed. "The Canadian Solution." *Newsweek,* February 6, 2009.

Zaleznik, Abraham. "Managers and Leaders: Are They Different?" *Harvard Business Review,* January 2004.

INDEX